My
FAVORITE PLACE
on Earth

My FAVORITE PLACE on Earth

Celebrated people share their travel discoveries

Jerry Camarillo Dunn, Jr.

NATIONAL GEOGRAPHIC

Washington, D.C.

Founded in 1888, the National Geographic Society is one of the largest nonprofit scientific and educational organizations in the world. It reaches more than 285 million people worldwide each month through its official journal, *National Geographic,* and its four other magazines; the National Geographic Channel; television documentaries; radio programs; films; books; videos and DVDs; maps; and interactive media. National Geographic has funded more than 8,000 scientific research projects and supports an education program combating geographic illiteracy.

For more information, please call 1-800-NGS LINE (647-5463) or write to the following address:

National Geographic Society
1145 17th Street N.W.
Washington, DC 20036-4688 U.S.A.

Visit us online at www.nationalgeographic.com

For information about special discounts for bulk purchases, please contact
National Geographic Books Special Sales: ngspecsales@ngs.org

For rights or permissions inquiries, please contact National Geographic Books Subsidiary Rights: ngbookrights@ngs.org

Printed in Hong Kong

Cover Design: Sam Serebin; Interior Design: Cameron Zotter

Contents

Contents

To Merry, Locke, Graham, and Jessica

Wherever you are is my favorite place on Earth…

INTRODUCTION

*W*hat is your favorite place on Earth?

It's a question that may take you on a slow, winding journey through a lifetime of memories. Or the answer may pop into your head instantly, like a picture flashing on your digital camera.

I posed this question to 75 celebrated men and women. (You just joined them.) Their choices are fascinating and quirky: A lost city in Sri Lanka. The Emily Brontë landscape of England. The Pasadena Rose Parade. A private island in the Caribbean. A wild dog research camp in Botswana. The Moscow Country Club. A surfing paradise in Fiji. The Left Bank in Paris. A softball field in New York's Central Park. A winding road on Maui. You're about to discover some remarkable places, seen through the eyes of remarkable people.

For me it was a welcome change to look at the world through other people's eyes. I've been a travel writer for 30 years, and I've heard my own opinions plenty. On my office wall I've tacked up a cartoon of an automobile that's starting a trip across a dull, featureless desert. A road sign reads:

YOUR OWN

TEDIOUS THOUGHTS

NEXT 200 MILES

I learned the benefit of seeing places from another person's perspective years ago on assignment in Kenya. One day I went walking into the bush with a local guide named Galogalo. Fifteen minutes out of camp, we were alone on a grassy plain that stretched for a hundred miles in every direction. Zebras grazed, a giraffe loped past—it was a peaceable kingdom.

Then Galogalo pointed down at the dust. There was a paw print the size of a dinner plate. *"Simba!"* he hissed. "Lion!" The ground nearby was strewn with fresh bones: a splintered leg, a zebra's white skull. Suddenly I realized that I stood there— 6 feet 7 inches tall, in a red T-shirt—like a neon sign at a diner, saying *EATS!*

My ears picked up a low rumble…like a growl. And for the first time I noticed that Galogalo didn't carry a weapon—well, except for a bow cut from a tree branch and two arrows whose triangle points had been snipped from a tin can. It looked like a Boy Scout project.

A few nervous minutes passed, but the owner of the growl did not leap into our path. And that night, safely back in camp, I learned that I hadn't been in danger at all. People told me that across East Africa, Galogalo was legendary as a hunter and tracker. He could actually *smell* a leopard hiding in a tree—from a quarter of a mile away. I had been nervous in the wild because I couldn't read the landscape the way Galogalo did.

After a few weeks in Africa, though, my senses began to work better. Watching birds flit above an elephant herd, or walking along a river that was log-jammed with hippos, I could almost decode their signals. It was like reading secret messages from another world—the world where Galogalo lived every day. I felt the surprise and satisfaction of seeing a place through another person's eyes.

This is the experience I set out to create in *My Favorite Place on Earth*. You'll travel to destinations around the world with fascinating people and understand each place the way they do, learning why each person loves that special spot.

How do you choose a favorite place? It might be a world wonder—say, the Eiffel Tower—or a personal spot, such as the lake where you spent summers as a kid. It might be a crossroads where your life took a surprising turn. It might be a solo escape from the jangling world, or a place you went with the people you love. There are as many answers, and reasons for them, as there are human beings.

Before going further, though, we should ask what a "place" is, and how it fits into the greater world. Eminent geographer Yi-Fu Tuan answered these questions in elemental terms: "Place is security, space is freedom," he said. "We are attached to the one and long for the other."

This pull of opposites is ancient. We love home but can't resist the call of the unknown. What lies out there is uncertain, risky—but also filled with the promise of discovery and freedom. This is why in 1969 astronaut Buzz Aldrin left his home planet and flew half a million miles to the Moon and back—an epic hero's journey, and one as mythic as that of Odysseus.

Buzz Aldrin is not the only person in this book whose "trip of a lifetime" led to a favorite place. The same thing happened to Jane Goodall when she moved to Tanzania at age 26 to observe chimpanzees.

Favorite places can also be escapes, of course, getaways from the wear and tear of daily life. Actor Morgan Freeman told me he loves to sail solo in the blue Caribbean, from one tiny anchorage to another. And entrepreneur Richard Branson solved the "getaway" problem the easy way: He bought his own private island.

Several people in this book decided that their favorite place was their own house. (This seems perfectly legitimate. After all, Vincent van Gogh sometimes chose to paint pictures of his bedroom, and that turned out pretty well.) One home has an adjoining lighthouse (Jamie Wyeth). In another house a dummy figure of the owner speaks to arriving guests through a hidden microphone (Clive Cussler). Another house boasts its own skateboard park (Tony Hawk).

In choosing a favorite spot, some people looked backward to a formative period in their lives. Chef Alice Waters of Chez Panisse recalled her parents' World War II Victory Garden. Bursting with ripe strawberries and yellow corn, it would shape her philosophy of cooking with only the freshest ingredients.

Artistic people often see the world through their own lenses—the way fashion designer Calvin Klein saw the colorfully garbed Maasai in Tanzania. "Their height! Their faces! Their sense of style!" he exclaimed with delight. For him, the Maasai strutted across the savanna on a fashion runway.

Of course, it's often people that give a place its identity—perhaps even a single person from history or legend. When Deepak Chopra visited Jerusalem, he walked on the Via Dolorosa, the road that led Jesus Christ to the cross.

In Peru, ocean explorer Jean-Michel Cousteau forged a lifelong bond with a chief of the Achuar people. "Chief Kukus had nearly as much impact on me as my own father," Cousteau told me. For him, one person made a place matter.

Of course, a place can have its own personality and temperament. Filmmaker George Lucas spoke about Utah's Monument Valley, where he once made a student film. "I spent two months sitting in the desert, pretty much by myself," he told me, "watching the sun rise and the sun set, and the clouds go by, and the shadows on the mesas. And I fell in love with it."

I think we fall in love with places in the same way we do with people. It may happen at first sight, or develop slowly with time and familiarity. But in some mysterious way we recognize a spirit that is simpatico. We feel inexplicably complete and happy. A place, like a person, is a great gift.

In this book, I hope you enjoy seeing some remarkable people's favorite spots through their eyes. But even more, I hope you'll be inspired to lean back in your chair, close your eyes—and think about *your* favorite place on Earth.

Discoveries I

KAREEM ABDUL-JABBAR

TRINIDAD

*T*here is one place where I feel truly at home—the West Indies island of Trinidad. From here my grandparents set out in 1912 to come to the United States.

The culture on this lush green isle is a blend of African, East Indian, Chinese, and Native American, with a sprinkling of Lebanese and British, Spanish and French. Everybody has left a little bit in the genetic pool. You see people who look African and have Chinese names. And the cuisine represents the same blend, all mixed up and wonderful. In Trinidad I've tried foods based on Italian pasta, West African stews, Indian curry, and many other dishes.

Everyone there seemed to know who I was—they watched Lakers basketball games on TV—and when they found out that my family was from Trinidad, they took me all over the island. Because it lies only eight miles off the coast of

Port of Spain, Trinidad, reflects the island's mixture of new and old.

Venezuela, it has all sorts of colorful South American flowers and birds. But the highlight of the trip was a reunion with four generations of my family, ranging from my grandmother's first cousin through my own son.

I even got a chance to go to the little town where my grandfather was born. At the turn of the 20th century it took him and my grandmother a year and a half to make it to the United States, traveling to Panama and eventually hopping a banana boat to Mobile, Alabama, on their way to New York.

Seeing the place where it all began, I realized how much my grandfather had done to look out for all of us who came after him in America. I was profoundly moved, and making that connection, a bond of family and the heart, was the greatest treasure I've collected on my travels.

COMPASS POINTS

Where: Trinidad is the southernmost island in the Caribbean.
Backdrop: Trinidad is the largest island in the Republic of Trinidad and Tobago. The national bird is the scarlet ibis. The limbo dance originated in Trinidad.
Visitor Information: www.gotrinidadandtobago.com

Famous for his virtually unblockable, ambidextrous "sky hook" shot, the 7'2" **Kareem Abdul-Jabbar** *holds the National Basketball Association's career scoring record with 38,387 points. He was on the cover of* Sports Illustrated *29 times. Today he is a special assistant coach for the Los Angeles Lakers, as well as the author of best-selling history books that include* Brothers in Arms *and* On the Shoulders of Giants: My Journey Through the Harlem Renaissance.

BUZZ ALDRIN

TRANQUILITY BASE, THE MOON

The *Apollo 11* mission took me from the shores of Florida to the surface of the Moon—a quarter of a million miles, one way. On that trip I learned that space travel has some things in common with trips here on Earth. First, there's the moment when you tell your family that you're leaving. I told my wife at a Laundromat in Houston. I guess that was an unusual place to tell her I was going to the Moon, but then again, is there a *normal* place to break that kind of news?

When travelers depart, their family and friends often give them a send-off, whether it's saying a quiet goodbye at the airport or tossing paper streamers as a cruise ship sails. Around our launch site, the headlights of hundreds of thousands of cars shone in the darkness, lighting our way.

My fellow travelers, Neil Armstrong and Mike Collins, boarded the command module first. I stood alone on a platform part way up the 35-story-tall Saturn V rocket, holding my portable suit ventilator like a commuter carrying a briefcase. As far as I could see, people lined the beaches and highways. I couldn't hear anything inside my helmet, but as the sun came up I saw the surf rolling silently onto the beach below. It was the kind of personal moment you always want to remember.

The booster that propelled us into space had the power of an atomic bomb. For us there was only a slight increase in the background noise, not unlike what one notices when taking off in a commercial airliner. In less than a minute we were traveling faster than the speed of sound. After the third stage roared to life, we reached 25,000 miles per hour—literally "faster than a speeding bullet," as they used to say about Superman.

Although we were flying in the zero gravity of space far above Earth, we had some of the same mundane thoughts as airline passengers do: Can we get some sleep? How will the food be? We dozed on couches with netting attached, so we wouldn't float around and bump our heads. The food wasn't bad, things like freeze-dried shrimp cocktails and little hot dogs. Everything has to have enough pastiness not to separate. Peas served in space have to be mixed with cream sauce, or you'd have a cabin filled with drifting peas.

Buzz Aldrin on the lunar surface

After we touched down on the Moon, Neil said simply, "Houston: Tranquility Base. The Eagle has landed." We opened the hatch, and Neil backed out of the tiny opening. (Jokingly, I said I'd be careful not to lock the hatch on my way out.) Then I joined him on the Moon's surface. In the tradition of tourists everywhere, he had his camera ready to photograph my arrival.

The moon's gravity is only a sixth of that on Earth. My terrestrial weight, with the big backpack and heavy suit, was 360 pounds: on the Moon I weighed only 60 pounds. I had fun hopping like a kangaroo, and I discovered that reduced gravity means greater freedom of movement. On Earth, if you lose your balance you have to recover very fast, but not so on the Moon. When you leave the surface, even at a walking gait, you don't come right back down again. You just sort of push off and put your feet underneath you. It's like moving in slow motion.

As I planted the flag on the Moon, an unusual thought occurred to me: Six hundred million people were watching us on television. Often, travelers who go on trips to faraway places are "out of sight, out of mind." But human beings had never traveled farther away than we were, or had more people thinking about them.

I described the Moon as "magnificent desolation." Although the two words seem opposite, they both applied. The Moon was desolate, void of color, motion, and sound. But our being there, to us, made it magnificent.

Everything looked very crisp and clear, because there's no air on the Moon. The surface ranged from dusty gray to light tan and was unchanging except for one startling sight: our lunar module sitting there with its black, silver, and yellow-orange thermal coating shining brightly in the otherwise colorless landscape. We could also see Earth, a beckoning oasis shining far away in the sky.

When we were cleared for takeoff at the end of our visit to the Moon, I said: "Roger, Houston! We're number one on the runway." The return trip to Earth and the water landing went smoothly. Aboard the recovery ship, I took a shower — the best shower of my life. It was great to be home on our own planet.

Travelers like to bring back souvenirs, but NASA didn't give the astronauts any Moon rocks. I do have snapshots of myself on the Moon, though, and I carry them with me all the time.

COMPASS POINTS

Where: Tranquility Base is situated in the southwest part of the Sea of Tranquility.
Backdrop: It is believed that about 4.5 billion years ago an object at least as big as Mars hit Earth, and the debris from both bodies formed the Moon. In 1998 water ice was found at both poles by the Lunar Prospector; the water was deposited on the Moon during comet impacts.
Visitor Information: Space Adventures Ltd. *(www.spaceadventures.com)* sends private citizens into space. On suborbital flights, travelers experience weightlessness and see the horizon of Earth below (cost: $102,000). For $25 million they can orbit Earth for a week aboard the International Space Station. Buzz Aldrin serves on the advisory board.

Buzz Aldrin has spent 290 hours in space, including eight hours of extra-vehicular activity (space walks), for which he set a record during the 1966 Gemini 12 orbital flight. A graduate of West Point with a Doctorate in Astronautics from MIT, he founded ShareSpace, a nonprofit foundation devoted to affordable space tourism. Aldrin's mother's maiden name was Moon. His given name is Edwin Eugene Aldrin, Jr. The nickname Buzz came from his sister's mispronunciation of "brother" as "buzzer," and in 1988 he legally changed his first name to Buzz. Only a dozen people have walked on the Moon, making Dr. Aldrin a rarity; therefore, for this book he was allowed to choose a location on or off the planet.

WALLY "FAMOUS" AMOS

HANA, MAUI, HAWAII

The Hawaiian island of Maui is like a giant tranquilizer. Every time I'm there, all the tension and stress just leaves my body. I feel totally relaxed—and I've lived in Hawaii for 30 years!

Hana magnifies this feeling even more. When I go there, I melt. Before the last trip, I'd been working hard for two years at my new cookie store on Oahu. My wife, Christine, and I really needed a getaway—and Hana is a retreat in the widest sense of the word. There's nothing to do there—and that's just what we wanted. I knew we would return home renewed.

We drove there on the famous Hana Highway, one of the most spectacular rides you could possibly take. Around every turn there are waterfalls, bamboo jungles, tropical flowers, guava trees, and beautiful vistas of the ocean. With each curve you go, "Oh wow! Look at that!" It's just magical.

After a couple of hours, we reached Hana. We hadn't been there in well over 20 years, but it seemed as if time had stood still. Peace and quiet. No big developments. It's as if nowhere else exists in the world. I don't know another place where you get that feeling of nothingness. You're just absolutely content.

We spent our days lounging by the pool at the Hotel Hana-Maui. At night, rain pattered on the roof—it was so peaceful—and every morning we'd hear the birds singing.

A place like Hana can have a profound effect on you. It's like the moment I first saw the Grand Canyon. At the time I was a personal manager in Hollywood, and for so long I'd been striving to be important and make a lot of money. I was always busy being busy. But all of a sudden, there I was, on the South Rim of the Grand Canyon, and I had never in my life seen anything so magnificent. As the sun was setting, the light was beautiful and the canyon began to change with each passing minute. I said to myself: *My God, I'm running around Hollywood trying to be important. And all the Grand Canyon does is just sit here! It's majestic without trying.* It was an epiphany, a life-changing moment for me. I took that with me, and I'll have it with me forever. I realized that life is not about how busy I am, or how important I think I am. Life's answers come in stillness, in quiet.

The Hana Highway winds past lush waterfalls.

My Favorite Place on Earth

Hana has the same effect on me. It's a place where you have no worries, no cares. You peel away all those layers of busyness and activity, and you go back to your core. The people who live there are affected by this feeling, too. They aren't in a hurry to do things. They're courteous and friendly. They're very giving. They share their *aloha*. The essence of aloha is love. It doesn't really mean "hello" and "goodbye," although that's how it's most commonly used. Aloha is the sharing of yourself with another, without any expectations. In Hana, you feel that.

People call it "Heavenly Hana"—and if there is Heaven on Earth, then it could very well be this spot.

COMPASS POINTS

Where: Hana is located at the east end of Maui and is one of Hawaii's most isolated towns.
Backdrop: The Hana Highway runs 52 miles from Kahului to the town of Hana (about 2½ hours one-way in good weather), and another 14 miles to Kipahulu. The road has more than 600 curves and 59 bridges, 46 of them single-lane. Many of the fruit and flower stands along the way operate on the honor system. George Harrison had a house in Hana, and Oprah Winfrey has bought much prime land there. Aviation pioneer Charles Lindbergh spent the last years of his life at Kipahulu and is buried in the country churchyard. When residents drive out of Hana, they refer to it as going to "the other side."
Visitor Information: www.visitmaui.com

*The spirited creator of Famous Amos cookies, **Wally Amos** was the first African American agent at William Morris, booking the Supremes, Simon and Garfunkel, and other top performers. To unwind on weekends, he baked chocolate chip cookies, eventually deciding that he could sell them by becoming an entertainment personality himself. After building and then selling the Famous Amos company, he opened Uncle Wally's Muffin Company and the Chip & Cookie retail store on Oahu. He has received the President's Award for Entrepreneurial Excellence and the Horatio Alger Award. Devoted to the cause of literacy, Amos was national spokesperson for Literacy Volunteers of America and founded Read It LOUD America! (www.readitloud.org) to promote reading to children. On Saturdays, he reads to kids at his Hawaii store.*

SERGIO ARAGONÉS

MEXICO CITY, MEXICO

Whenever I have a chance to go to Mexico City, my heart starts beating faster. I grew up there, so it's not just a place—it's a place full of memories. Every corner I turn, I remember something that happened there.

On one trip, I went back to Estudios Churubusco, where my father had an office. He was a movie producer, and as a boy I used to go to the studio after school. I'd leave my books, and whatever movie they were making, I'd race to the prop department and get myself outfitted. The western town was my favorite. I'd put on western guns, get a big hat—and I was a cowboy!

I'd go out onto the set and throw open the cantina doors, and there was nothing on the other side—just fields, with some wooden supports holding up the façade of the building. In front was a railing for the cowboy actors to tie up their horses. When there wasn't a movie being shot, I loved to go there and challenge invisible bad guys. And I loved to get shot. I'd come banging out through the cantina doors, flip over the railing with my legs in the air, and land in the dusty street. Then I'd go back and get shot again, over and over, because I was a kid.

I think that that helped a lot later in my cartooning, in thinking up ideas. Your imagination really goes wild on a movie set.

Speaking of movies, after school, my friends and I used to go to a theater that showed three movies in a row. This was in the early fifties, and the tickets were very cheap—a peso apiece. We'd go up to the balcony, and there was never anybody there because it was daytime. Each of us would sit on a step and do our homework by the little light at the end of each row of seats, while we watched the movie. When I got home, my parents would say, "You went to the movies! What about your homework?" And I'd say, "It's done!"

Years later, I traveled to Mexico City with the staff of *Mad* magazine. The publisher, Bill Gaines, would organize a free trip every year for the magazine's regular contributors—the cartoonists, writers, and editors listed on the masthead as "The Usual Gang of Idiots." We went all over the place: Paris, Kenya, Hong Kong, Monte Carlo, Tahiti, Morocco, Venice.

Because I grew up in Mexico City, Bill asked me to organize this trip, so I went down beforehand to make arrangements. I planned things that tourists usually don't do, like a "do-it-yourself" bullfight. I found an old hacienda that has a beautiful bullring. Around it is a restaurant where everybody sits. If you want to be bullfighter, you go into the arena and a professional matador teaches you some basics. Meanwhile, your group sits at the tables, eats royally, and laughs their heads off at your stupidity for fighting a bull. The animals were real fighting bulls — a totally different breed from regular bulls — but they were only six months old and not very big. If one butted you, you'd just say, "Ouch!"

Some of the bravest *Mad* guys decided that they wanted to be bullfighters. So I had to do it, too. The professional bullfighter taught us some tricks, like how to put the cape in front of the bull's eyes to direct its charge away from you. He told us that the closer you pass the cape to yourself, the braver you are!

They let the bull out, we made a few passes, and the people at the tables laughed a lot. Then we were asked, who's the bravest guy in the group? We pointed at Jack Davis, a tall guy from Georgia who's game for anything. "You must wait for the bull on your knees," they told him, "and hold the cape in front of you. These are very dangerous bulls…but you are brave!"

Passenger boats at Mexico City's Xochimilco floating gardens

The bull was waiting behind a door with a slit in it, and you could see its eyes. Then *boom! boom!*—the bull started banging against the door. Jack knelt there, waiting. The door opened—and out strolled a mule. It made a circle around Jack and went back out the door—it was trained to do that—while the rest of us laughed hysterically.

The professional bullfighter taught us some tricks, like how to put the cape in front of the bull's eyes to direct its charge away from you.

On this trip we also saw some regular tourist spots, like Xochimilco, the famous floating gardens. Xochimilco is what's left of an ancient lake. People grow flowers on man-made islands called *chinampas* and travel on the canals in small boats.

Xochimilco is filled with memories for me because I used to go there every day before school to row. There were four of us and a coxswain. In the early morning, there was a low, thick fog that sat over the water. As we were rowing, the only thing we could see was heads!

Today, little boats take tourists around the floating gardens. Each boat has a flower arrangement on its canopy, and the flowers spell out things like "*Margarita,*" "*Viva México,*" or "*Amor*"—lovely little things. The *Mad* crew was always playing jokes on our publisher, Bill Gaines. So ahead of time I'd arranged for the sign on our boat to say something very rude and funny about Bill. When the guys saw it, they laughed their heads off. But the funny part was all the tourists—they almost fell in the water trying to get snapshots.

Later, we all went to my mother's house. She cooked a paella for us in the garden, which was decorated with canopies and lanterns.

So, I love Mexico City, but my pleasure in visiting has nothing to do with the wonderful history or great museums. It's my memories—and the fact that, spiritually, it's home.

COMPASS POINTS

Where: Mexico City, located on the central plateau of Mexico at 7,349 feet, is the nation's capital. **Backdrop:** With 19.4 million residents, greater Mexico City is the world's largest metropolitan area after Tokyo. It has 160 museums and the fourth highest number of theaters in the world (exceeded only by New York, London, and Toronto). In preparing for the 1968 Olympic Games, one of Xochimilco's canals was converted for the canoe competitions; later Xochimilco was declared a UNESCO World Heritage site. When the *Mad* staff once took a trip to Haiti, publisher Gaines had the whole group driven directly to the house of the magazine's one and only Haitian subscriber, where he formally presented the baffled man with a renewal card.

Visitor Information: www.visitmexico.com

Sergio Aragonés is said to be the world's fastest cartoonist and is certainly the most honored, having won every major award in the field, including the Reuben from the National Cartoonists Society. Born in Spain and raised in Mexico City, he came to the United States in 1962 and was soon contributing drawings to Mad. Since 1963, his work has appeared in every issue but one ("The post office screwed up"). His "Mad Marginals" are tiny wordless gags that appear in the magazine's white spaces, and he also draws a monthly feature about a timely topic, called "A Mad Look at...." Aragonés has also acted on television's Laugh-In, illustrated advertisements, and done animation for television shows. His Groo the Wanderer is one of the longest-running "creator-owned" comic book properties, outlasting many of the companies that published it.

DAVE BARRY

U.S. VIRGIN ISLANDS

*I*n these times of international tension, real news professionals disregard their personal safety and head for the world's trouble spots. Thus it was that recently I traveled to the U.S. Virgin Islands, where I faced the very real danger that, as a journalist in the field, many of my expenses would be tax-deductible.

The Virgin Islands are located in the Caribbean, which gets its name from the Indian words *Cari*, meaning "body of water," and *bbean*, meaning "that makes you really glad your computer has a spell checker." The Virgin Islands were discovered in 1493 by Christopher Columbus, who wisely elected to remain on the ship during the discovery process so as to avoid being turned into Purina Shark Chow by the people who already lived there.

Before sailing briskly away, Columbus named the islands "The Virgins" because he thought they looked like reclining women, which tells you how long *he* had been on a non-coeducational ship.

Although the islands were originally claimed by Spain, over the years they belonged to Holland, France, England, Denmark, Poland, Wales, Nigeria, and the New York Yankees farm organization, before they were finally purchased by the U.S. government for $25 million, which is coincidentally the exact amount that I spent down there on drinks with names like "Drambuie Kablooey."

This is pretty much how everybody passes the time in the Virgin Islands. You lie in the sun, listening to the soothing sounds of the wind and the surf and the precancerous lesions forming on your skin. The only remotely alarming thing I saw during my visit occurred at a small outdoor bar at a place called Sapphire Beach, where a wedding reception was going on, and the bride's bouquet was partially eaten (I am not making this up) by an iguana.

There are iguanas everywhere, roughly the size of squirrels, except that instead of being cute and furry, they look like cranky midget dinosaurs. They stand around all day, glaring and thinking, "If this were 25 million years ago, I would eat the whole *bride*."

There is also plenty of marine life in the Virgin Islands, although due to poor planning it is located underwater. To see it, you put on rental snorkel equipment and paddle around over a coral reef, which looks like rock but is actually billions of

People pass time as they please in the Caribbean.

tiny critters called "polyps" forming a living organism that eats, grows, and, when it feels frisky, messes around with another reef to produce a new little reeflet.

The underwater scenery is spectacular, and as I floated above it in the warm, clear water, I could not help but wonder: How many zillion other tourists have rented this particular snorkel mask? What was their level of nasal hygiene?

And so I paddled back to the beach, where my son, clearly thinking inheritance, talked me into windsurfing. This involves standing on a surfboard with a sail attached to it, and then, by shifting your weight and pointing the sail in a certain direction relative to the wind, falling into the water like a sack of gravel. I estimate that I got up on the surfboard, and immediately fell back off, 50 times, in the process traveling forward a total of 11 feet.

I was the source of much entertainment for the people on the beach. Even the reef was emitting billions of tiny but hearty polyp chuckles—which incidentally would be a good name for a rock band.

After I staggered back to the beach, a real windsurfer appeared, looking like a Greek god but with a better body. As he zipped effortlessly across the waves, muscles rippling, and my wife watching him, I scoffed, "I bet that guy couldn't handle the pressure of producing a weekly newspaper column! Right, honey? Right? Hello?"

So I decided to engage in a manly activity that I happen to be quite good at: building a sand castle. Not for *me*, of course—for my daughter. The problem is that she, being 2, soon became bored and wandered off, leaving me to work alone with my little blue pail and yellow shovel. I don't want to boast, but I made a very manly castle. I'm sure that Mr. Pectorals, out puffing around on his little board, was intimidated, although he pretended not to notice. But my wife was clearly impressed, because later on she accompanied me to our room for an intimate—and sometimes, frankly, wild—evening of trying to get the sand out of our daughter's hair.

And that, in a nutshell, is the situation in the U.S. Virgin Islands. In my journalistic opinion, it's perfectly safe to travel there, as long as you take certain commonsense precautions, such as iguana-proofing your bouquet. Also, if you mess up my castle, you're dead.

COMPASS POINTS

Where: The U.S. Virgin Islands are in the Caribbean Sea, about 50 miles east of Puerto Rico, among the Leeward Islands of the Lesser Antilles. The four main islands are St. Thomas, St. John, St. Croix, and Water Island.

Backdrop: The United States bought the islands from Denmark in 1917, and although residents are U.S. citizens, they cannot vote in presidential elections. This is the only part of the U.S. where cars drive on the left side of the road. Locals call St. Thomas "Rock City" and St. John "Love City."

Visitor Information: www.usvitourism.vi

For 25 years, **Dave Barry** *wrote a humor column for the* Miami Herald *that was syndicated in more than 500 newspapers. He won the Pulitzer Prize for Commentary in 1988. He has written 30 books, including* Dave Barry's History of the Millennium (So Far). *On national television, he once proved that it is possible to set fire to a pair of men's underpants with a Barbie doll. Dave Barry supports Fellowship House (www.fellowshiphouse.org) in South Miami, Florida.*

T. CORAGHESSAN BOYLE

SEQUOIA NATIONAL FOREST, CALIFORNIA

I grew up in Peekskill, New York, and had never been west of the Hudson River until I was 21. So the Wild West held a great fascination.

I moved to Los Angeles in 1978 when the University of Southern California offered me a job, but the city looked a little alien to me. I first lived in Tujunga, the white-trash capital of the world, but I liked it because I could hike up in the San Gabriel Mountains. But when winter came, and the holidays, it just didn't look right to me, those palm trees.

Luckily, I had a friend whose father had been one of the pioneers of a little development up at 7,200 feet in the Sierras, in the Sequoia National Forest. She brought me up there, and I've gone every year since.

I own some property there, but have never built on it. I think my lot will forever be the Boyle Squirrel Preserve. Instead, I rent a cabin, and I go up as often as I can when I'm not teaching or touring with my books. Touring gets me down after a while, but up in the mountains I'm able to escape the hassles. When I finish work for the day, I just go out into the woods.

I like to begin and end books up there, because there are very few distractions. It's incredibly boring—which I love. There's only one commercial establishment, a bar-restaurant that's open when the owners feel like opening it. And I can walk out my cabin door and be in the national forest.

I'm one of the few people who actually *walks* in the woods. Everybody else drives their three-wheel vehicles in the summer and their snowmobiles in the winter. Of course, I'm extremely tolerant of that sort of behavior: All of them should be executed.

But I almost never see anyone in the woods. After a Fourth of July party, I spent the entire afternoon sitting by my favorite creek where there's a little waterfall, just moving from the sun to the shade, reading a book, and disporting myself in the water.

I've had many encounters with wildlife—bears, deer, mountain lions. My fourth lifetime mountain lion sighting happened as I was coming up from the Kern River Valley. The lion was crossing the road, and I just saw its tail disappearing into the bushes. I pulled over, not expecting to see it again, but there it was, down a slope about 50 feet away. It didn't know I was there, because the wind was blowing toward

Rays of sun stream into the forest between the giant sequoias.

me, and I was able to watch it for a good 30 seconds, which was very exciting. It was a small-headed beast, probably a male on its 25-mile nightly trek, looking for food.

A few years back, when I was writing *Drop City,* I was out in the woods at another of my favorite creeks, a place where I had often seen lion scat and tracks. I came up to a waterfall and cracked a twig—and heard a twig crack behind me. And there was a mountain lion, very close but running from me—which is the way you want it to be. Really, all I wanted to do was mate with her, but I guess you have to ask Fish and Game about that.

Often mountain lions are like big kitties; they're curious and just want to see what you're doing. But they're known to stalk people, and that can be dangerous. The way you know a mountain lion is that a 150-pound animal with the strength of ten men—an animal that could jump three stories straight up onto a roof—has you by the back of the neck and is rubbing your face in the sand. That's how you know it's there.

Another time, I was fishing for golden trout — I just like to see them, then I let them go — and was crouching by the stream when I heard the tiniest sound. Behind me was a manzanita bush, and when I pushed it back, I saw the footprint of a lion, slowly filling with water. It was thrilling — the lion had been within a couple of feet of me, watching me without my knowing it. I got very excited and later called my wife on the phone to tell her about it. Her response was, "Will you please stop harassing that poor animal?"

Often mountain lions are like big kitties; they're curious and just want to see what you're doing.

Then there are the bears. One house I rented was right on a creek. I would go to bed at 11 o'clock, always leaving the windows open, and every night at 11:05 a bear would come by on his rounds to get food. I could hear the bear tromping around and crunching. It would wake me up briefly, I'd think *Ah, it's the bear,* and I'd go back to sleep.

This is rural California, which is still sort of like the Wild West. People wear cowboy hats — some of them, anyway. Christmas up in the Sierras is not the Christmas we had as children in New York, where it's Bing Crosby and all that. You've got your choice of Mexican Christmas with mariachi music, or cowboy Christmas with country-western. It's that kind of place, and that's all right.

My close friend Pete Brewer, who died not long ago, was sort of the major-domo of the mountain. He bought and invigorated the lodge, which is a communal gathering place. It's tough on the liver to be up there, of course, but he was great. I rented his house for 12 years. He would move out and go live in the lodge. He'd just take his underwear out of the drawer, and I'd put mine in.

One house I rented recently has a great library, so I reread *Walden,* one of my favorite books. Thoreau is such an incredible crank! As I get older, I love him more and more.

I like to be alone out there in the woods. It takes me out of myself in the same way as when you're a child and you don't yet know the names of everything — of every tree and animal. And you don't know about all the canker and rot and misery that life entails, or about death. You look around you and don't necessarily know that this tree is infested with pine bark beetle and will be dead soon, and the forests will be dead soon, and the water is gone. You don't necessarily see that when you're a child. And when you're in a place that is wild and still magnificent, you don't see it, either.

T. Coraghessan Boyle

To be stripped down to that lack of consciousness is a great thing. You're just a creature in nature. Your mind is free. And you're just amazed by the natural splendor all around you.

COMPASS POINTS

Where: The Sequoia National Forest is in the southern Sierra Nevada range in central California.

Backdrop: The Sequoia National Forest contains Giant Sequoia National Monument, which includes about half of the surviving giant sequoia groves. By volume, these are the world's largest trees; record-setters have grown to 311 feet high and 57 feet in diameter. One giant sequoia is 3,500 years old. A large tree may have 11,000 cones at one time and disseminate 400,000 seeds a year. Mountain lions are solitary creatures that ambush their prey, ranging from deer and domestic cattle to rodents and even insects. The lions hiss, growl, and purr like domestic cats, but their chirps, whistles, and screams are unique.

Visitor Information: www.fs.fed.us/r5/sequoia

T. Coraghessan (T. C.) Boyle is a novelist and short story writer whose books include Water Music, The Road to Wellville, The Tortilla Curtain, Drop City, The Inner Circle, Tooth and Claw, *and* Talk Talk. *He won the PEN/Faulkner Award for his novel* World's End; *other awards include the Commonwealth Gold Medal for Literature, the National Academy of Arts and Letters Award for Prose Excellence, and six O. Henry Awards for short fiction. He is a Distinguished Professor of English at the University of Southern California, where he founded the undergraduate creative writing program. His work has been translated into more than two dozen languages, and his stories have appeared in the* New Yorker, Harper's, Esquire, *and the* Atlantic Monthly.

RAY BRADBURY

PARIS, FRANCE

Every time I go to Paris, I buy a copy of *Tender Is the Night*, by F. Scott Fitzgerald, put it under my arm, and walk across the city from the Eiffel Tower to Notre Dame cathedral. It takes all day.

Along the way, I stop about every half-hour at an outdoor café, sit with an espresso or an aperitif, and read some of the book. And by the time I reach the cathedral, I've read Fitzgerald's *Tender Is the Night* once again. I've got eight copies on my shelf in Los Angeles that I've bought in Paris over a period of 20 years. In each one, I write "Paris 1998" and so on. This is my way of taking in the ambience of Paris and enjoying our greatest writer.

There are outdoor cafés everywhere, with people outside enjoying the sun and busy talking. The Parisians are great conversationalists, great aesthetes. As I walk from café to café, I like talking to people and getting engaged with the social life of Paris. When I came for the first time in 1953, it was to write the screenplay for *Moby Dick* for John Huston. We sat at an outdoor restaurant, La Fouquette, on the Champs-Élysées, discussing how I would adapt Melville's book. And along the avenue comes Art Buchwald, the columnist and a wonderfully funny man, who sat down with us.

So I have had a long relationship with Paris. I arrived one time and saw a French friend, who asked, "What are you doing here, Ray?"

"I've come to celebrate your failed revolution," I replied.

"What?!"

"Well, your revolution failed, didn't it?" I told him. "The French came to America during our revolution and helped us win it. But your people went home, they were inspired by our revolution, and they started one here. And of course it failed. It wound up with the guillotine. That was the final product of the French Revolution.

"In 1871 you had the Commune, when you fought yourselves in the streets of Paris and the Germans outside of Paris, and it was a failure. Then you lost the war in 1914, and General Pershing came from America to help you win against the Germans. In 1940 you lost that war, too, and General Patton came, and we rescued France from the Germans again.

The Eiffel Tower can be glimpsed from all over Paris.

"The fascinating thing is that out of all this despair, all this destruction, all this stupidity, what have you developed? The most beautiful country and the most beautiful city in the world!"

My friend threw his arms around me and embraced me—until then, he had been ready to kill me after the things I'd said—and all was well. The country is a perfect example of politics that don't work at all, but aesthetically, Paris is perfect.

Once I was traveling by train from Calais to Rome and had a stopover in Paris until 6 p.m. I took a taxicab with some friends to Les Deux Magots, the café where Hemingway used to go. Paris and the twilight seized and held me immediately. It was the blue hour, the hour of enchantment. As we motored past the Louvre, it was painted ancient gold by the sun. Every leaf on every bush and tree was bronzed with twilight illumination. As we rounded the Place de la Concorde, to our right the church of the Madeleine was a fiery temple, and yet farther on as we rushed, the Arc de Triomphe burned with fading light, and the Eiffel Tower was a great pure torch that showed our way to where we sat out in the cool dusk drinking aperitifs at Les Deux Magots.

By this time, I was exhilarated and in tears: I had died and been delivered to a place of golden coins that minted themselves by the tens of thousands from gods' mouths in fountains. All of the talk I heard, though I understood none of it, was wise and mythical and rare. All of the people walked or sat with faces bright and colored into masks by the last of the sun. The drink in my hand was a vintage two thousand years old. Among legions of young men, I thought I saw Caesar stride by in his pride! My friends, seated with me, were dipped in gilt and capable of living forever.

COMPASS POINTS

Where: Located on the River Seine, Paris is the capital of France. Its cityscape, museums, gardens, culture, and monuments draw 30 million foreign visitors per year.

Backdrop: Once a garden promenade, the Champs-Élysées, linking the Place de la Concorde and the Arc de Triomphe, has been called the most beautiful avenue in the world; filled with luxury shops, it is also the costliest ribbon of real estate in Europe. The literary, artistic, and intellectual patrons of the café Les Deux Magots have included Albert Camus, Pablo Picasso, and Simone de Beauvoir.

Visitor Information: Paris Convention and Visitors Bureau: http://en.parisinfo.com

Ray Bradbury is the author of more than three dozen books (including The Martian Chronicles, Fahrenheit 451, and The Illustrated Man), nearly 600 short stories, several screenplays, and numerous poems and essays. His accolades include the National Medal of Arts, an Emmy Award, a star on the Hollywood Walk of Fame, and an asteroid named in his honor.

SIR RICHARD BRANSON

NECKER ISLAND, BRITISH VIRGIN ISLANDS

I'm fortunate in that my favorite place on Earth happens to be where I live. I've traveled the world. I've been to Bali, Africa, South America—everywhere. And I've had lots of Boy's Own adventures, too, crashing in the Arctic and visiting Hawaii by mistake once in a balloon. I'm incredibly lucky that I've managed to create the place where I love to spend my time—a little island in the Caribbean called Necker.

At age 26, I stumbled across this deserted island in the British Virgin Islands and completely fell in love with it. Necker is sort of the last island before Africa, which is 4,000 miles away. The air is as clean as it gets, and so is the sea. The island was untouched by man, with a pristine coral reef all the way around it, and the most beautiful water. From the top of the hill, you can see rays and turtles swimming—the sea is that clear.

In the reef, there's just one small gap where you can enter from the rough seas outside into a perfect lagoon. There are masses of different fish and rays. Pelicans dive into the water, and oystercatchers nest on the island.

We have giant iguanas, which you find on only two islands in the world. They grow to be six or seven feet long, like mini-dinosaurs. We've also got giant tortoises as big as the ones on the Galápagos Islands. They don't do much—they just heave themselves up on the beach occasionally, to see if they can find other tortoises on the island and go make some little tortoises.

Recently we rescued two baby leatherback turtles who had headed into a pond instead of going into the sea. And a flamingo crashed into a prickly bush, so we had to pull it out.

I was brought up in the English countryside and like to be part of nature. And though I may have 200 companies around the world and 60,000 people out there doing things, what I'm good at is thinking up new ideas, planting the acorns. So the fact that I withdraw to the island and let other people run things—entrepreneurs are different than managers—actually benefits the company.

Because Necker Island is special, I have no difficulty attracting fascinating people to visit. Peter Gabriel and I conceived of a group called the Elders, and Nelson Mandela chose 12 of the wisest men and women in the world. They work to resolve global conflicts, using their moral authority. The group includes Kofi Annan, President Jimmy Carter, and Archbishop Desmond Tutu. They come to the island and are able to relax, at the same time trying to tackle some of the world's more intractable problems, such as Darfur. At the middle of the island, we have the Elders' Temple, where they meet.

Our world, this exquisite environment, is threatened by an enormous population explosion and global warming, a combination that could result in catastrophe for billions of people. Where I sit on Necker Island, I know that the sea level is going to rise—and this makes it very personal. It spurs me on.

We had a meeting here to put together a sort of environmental war room for the globe, to treat carbon as our greatest enemy and get a team to look at the best ideas and practices for tackling it. People like Larry Page from Google and former British prime minister Tony Blair came by for that.

An island is a microcosm of the world, and Necker will demonstrate how it—and a lot of the planet—can be 100 percent carbon neutral. We don't need air-conditioning here, because we've got a lovely breeze year-round, averaging about 16

Bali Hi, one of the guest cottages on Necker Island

Sir Richard Branson

> *We have giant iguanas, which you find on only two islands in the world. They grow to be six or seven feet long, like mini-dinosaurs.*

miles per hour. We're powering the island with wind and solar, with battery backup. So Necker has a serious side.

Of course, the island is also a vacation getaway. Quite a lot of celebrities come here, because they don't feel like they're under the microscope all the time. They can let their hair down and be completely private.

The island's houses are modeled on those in Bali, a place I love. On top of the hill is the main house. Rather than having people sit at their own tables for dinner, we normally have just one big table where everybody can join in, exchanging ideas and the experiences of the day. But they can then retreat to their own private areas. There are also houses for honeymooners in the middle of the island. And in the swimming pool there's a floating pavilion, Balinese style.

I come to the island to relax, too. I've never worn shoes here — ever. It's just lovely to be able to live without shoes and socks on! Now that our children have grown up, my wife and I have decided we're going to live on the island. I've always worked from home, never in an office, ever since I was a teenager — for example, I had a beautiful houseboat in London. I think it actually helps to work from pleasant environments. And obviously, it's not difficult to get the kids and their friends to come; the island is a big magnet.

I find it quite difficult now to leave Necker and go out into the world, traveling. But I'm lucky because I know the island is always there to come back to. When I'm in a business meeting in an office building somewhere, I can picture the island, the reef, and the turquoise sea with the cormorants diving. It's an Eden on Earth.

COMPASS POINTS

Where: Necker is in the British Virgin Islands, north of Virgin Gorda, in the Caribbean.

Backdrop: With an area of only 74 acres, Necker Island has a greener Caribbean side and a drier Atlantic side with thousands of cactuses. Flamingos have been reintroduced to two lakes. Island guests have included Princess Diana, Harrison Ford, and Oprah Winfrey. Guests can book the island exclusively or come during special weeks when couples share the island in house-party style. A stay includes accommodations in the great house or smaller Balinese-style houses, food and drinks (served anywhere on the island, anytime), and instructed activities such as tennis, kite surfing, sailing, and scuba diving (guests have found cannonballs from Spanish galleons). Prices start at $47,000 per night for up to 28 guests; shared weeks begin at $23,500 per couple.

Visitor Information: www.neckerisland.com

Sir Richard Branson is a British entrepreneur whose Virgin Group includes 200 companies, ranging from music and travel to health care and finance, in more than 30 countries. The travel brand includes Virgin Atlantic Airlines, the low-fare Virgin America, and Virgin Galactic, which plans to take tourists into space. Branson started in business at age 15 with a successful magazine, then founded a mail-order record business. He started Virgin Records; the label's first release was the hit Tubular Bells by Mike Oldfield, and it later signed the Sex Pistols. A competitive adventurer, Branson set records for the fastest Atlantic crossing by boat and the first by hot-air balloon. A high school dropout, Branson now has a net worth of $5 billion and was awarded a knighthood for entrepreneurship. In 2006, Branson pledged profits of his transportation interests to direct investments in clean energy, an amount estimated at $3 billion over ten years. Branson has established the Virgin Earth Challenge, offering a prize of $25 million for a commercially feasible method to remove greenhouse gases from the atmosphere and help to stabilize Earth's climate.

TOM BROKAW

TIBET

I went to Tibet in the 1980s because I was interested in human rights issues, and I was able to get around the country a fair amount. The combination of its topography, the culture, and the sheer mysticism of it all makes it the most exotic place I've ever been. Tibet remains for me an almost Zen-like experience—which is not something I had anticipated.

I went to a monastery in Shigatse in the interior of Tibet. At four in the morning, we sat in the main room with 150 monks ranging in age from 5 to 105. The air was filled with incense and smoke, and the monks chanted, in a steady drone, for 90 minutes. I felt like I was in a time machine, like I'd been transported back to the past.

There was nothing modern about the room. The windows were quite dirty, and there was a crack in the wall where the sun filtered through, making the atmosphere even more dramatic. The monks were dressed in robes of crimson and gold, and in the folds they had small wooden bowls for their yak-butter tea. Novitiates wearing elaborate headdresses would go out to enormous cauldrons, six feet high, in which the tea was being prepared. It would take two of them to pour it into pitchers. They would go around and fill the other monks' bowls, and then begin chanting again.

We headed back to the capital, Lhasa, on a meandering drive, and as we came over a pass at 19,000 feet, I got out of the vehicle—I was really well acclimated by then—and walked uphill. A pair of falcons didn't like me invading their turf and came flying out of their nest after me. They circled and circled, diving at me again and again. I stood there on top of the world and thought: *This is the true definition of wilderness.*

In Tibet, you feel as if you're looking down on Earth, like everything in the world is below you. The landscape is barren and snow covered, even in the middle of summer. Yet it's not unusual to see a kid walking barefoot. At one point, we ran into a family of nomadic herders. They pack up every three days and move with the herd, living on yak curd and yak-butter tea. The young people were beautiful, but they got old so quickly. The father was in bad shape, plainly dying of some respiratory illness. The family lived in a yak-hair tent, and the young woman went inside to put on her turquoise jewelry, which I imagine she had made. She was stunningly

Both young and old possess classic beauty.

beautiful. So was her husband. I think the Tibetans and the Somalis may be the most beautiful people in the world. It's their facial structure. Tibetan faces look a little more chiseled, though, and with their coal-black eyes, to me, they are the very definition of handsomeness.

What intrigued *them* most about *us* was when we shot video of them and showed them the tapes. They were absolutely wide-eyed. Then we got in our motorized vehicles and drove away, while they were riding yaks. To them, we might as well have been extraterrestrials.

I reported on a Kampa monk who lived up a sheer cliff at about 17,000 feet. The Chinese had destroyed his monastery during the Cultural Revolution, and the local villagers were rebuilding it. Meanwhile, he was living in a cave. To get up the cliff, I walked on a path so narrow it was like something out of a cartoon. A couple of people were living in caves on either side of the monk to tend to his needs. Everything was lit and heated by lamps fueled by dung.

Nearby there was a traditional burial site. Tibetans put their dead on remote high peaks, atop piles of rocks, and place prayer flags around them. And then the carrion birds come. It was remarkable to sit there in the clouds, talking to the monk and looking down on this burial site in a trackless mountain range.

Tom Brokaw

I have also traveled across the Tibetan Plateau with my close friend Yvon Chouinard, who owns Patagonia, the outdoor gear and clothing company. Near the Nepal border, we walked for a few days and visited another nomadic family. They served us yak-butter tea, of course, and I gave them some ballpoint pens with the NBC logo. As we were walking away, I said, "Yvon, you know what they're saying to each other right now?"

"No, what?"

"They're saying, 'That cheap bastard! We gave them a *lot* of yak-butter tea—and they just left us these crummy NBC pens!'"

COMPASS POINTS

Where: Located in Central Asia, Tibet is bordered by Bhutan, China, India, Myanmar, and Nepal.
Backdrop: The Tibetan Plateau is the world's highest and largest plateau, covering an area about four times the size of France (965,000 square miles). Its average altitude exceeds 16,000 feet, earning it the name "Roof of the World." The plateau includes Mount Everest (29,035 feet), on the border with Nepal, and many more of the world's highest peaks. Tibet has been under the control of the People's Republic of China since 1951. A Tibetan insurrection was crushed in 1959, and during the Cultural Revolution more than 6,500 Tibetan Buddhist monasteries were destroyed. Major anti-Chinese demonstrations took place in spring 2008. The Dalai Lama heads the Tibetan government in exile in Dharamsala, India. He no longer seeks full independence for Tibet but autonomous status, similar to that of Hong Kong. Tibet's situation continues to be a matter of international concern and tension.
Visitor Information: Foreign visitors need a visa and one or more travel permits that may be arranged through travel agencies and tour operators. The travel situation is subject to change. Tibetan government in exile: www.tibet.net; International Campaign for Tibet: www.savetibet.org

*From 1983 to 2004, television journalist and author **Tom Brokaw** was the anchor and managing editor of the* NBC Nightly News, *consistently ranked as the nation's top evening news show. He conducted the first American TV interviews with Mikhail Gorbachev and Vladimir Putin and reported many historic events, including the collapse of the Berlin Wall and the events of September 11, 2001. He was NBC's White House correspondent during Watergate and has covered every presidential election since 1968. Brokaw has received the Peabody Award, multiple Emmy and Alfred I. DuPont–Columbia University awards and the Edward R. Murrow Lifetime Achievement Award, and he is the only journalist besides Walter Cronkite to receive the prestigious West Point Sylvanus Thayer Award. Brokaw continues to present documentaries and other programming on NBC. His books include best-selling* The Greatest Generation *and* A Long Way from Home.

RINALDO BRUTOCO

PUAKEA BAY, BIG ISLAND, HAWAII

The first time I stepped off the plane in Hawaii, I knew I was home. It was the smell of flowers in the air, the breeze and the way it caresses your skin—and also something more profound, which I'd call *mana*, the Polynesian word for spiritual power, a kind of magic.

About 20 years ago, I decided to buy property there. On my wall at home in California, I put up maps of all the Hawaiian Islands. I looked for places where there would be no road between me and the ocean. Where would the trade winds be ideal? Where would the rainfall be right—not as wet as Kauai, but not so parched that the land would be barren? I narrowed down my search to the Big Island, between Kona and the northern tip.

I found a chunk of the huge Parker Ranch at Puakea Bay that had been divided into ten-acre parcels, right on the coast. The land gently slopes to the edge, then drops precipitously to the ocean. They used to load cattle onto waiting ships here, lowering them with a pulley 150 feet down the cliff to the deck.

At the shoreline, the drop continues underwater another 70 feet, and whales come with their calves to find safety here. They can swim in close and still be in deep water. The area is on the whales' migratory path, and you can sit on the property and watch them. Particularly in February, it's quite a parade.

Needless to say, I bought the property.

What I didn't know until after escrow closed was that this is the closest private land to the birthplace of Kamehameha the Great, the warrior-king who unified the Hawaiian Islands. He was born about 1758, near an ancient temple that is still the sacred spiritual center of the Hawaiian Islands. Once a year, the high *kahuna* rededicates the temple to keep it charged. I didn't know the story at the time. I just bought the property because I felt the *mana*. That's what pulled me in.

From my parcel there is a 180-degree view in front of you that's all ocean. About 18 miles across the water you see the island of Maui, where Haleakala volcano rises straight up out of the ocean. Almost every day a ring of clouds forms, like a halo, just below the top of the crater. It's a majestic sight.

After I bought the place, I was walking one day and saw a kiawe tree on a crown of land at a central point on the property. It was shady underneath, and I

A native tree frames a colorful Hawaiian sunset.

thought it would be a great place to meditate, to take in what it felt like to be there, to be interconnected with the *mana*. I sat there for well over an hour, and when it was time to go, I got up, turned around, and looked at the kiawe tree.

The branches spread out from the center, but where the central branch should be was a smooth rock about 15 inches long. It takes a certain type of rock tumbling in moving water to create such a shape, which Hindus call a *lingam*, an icon of the deity Shiva. The sacred Ganges river in India often creates these rocks.

The kiawe tree had a lingam in it. Where did it come from? How did it get there, near one of the oldest temples in the Hawaiian Islands? I don't have an answer for that. When I discovered it, I understood: *It's not my real estate, it belongs to the universe. I'm just a steward.*

Eventually, this piece of land will become the home of the World Business Academy, which promotes mindful business practices. I've been holding the property all these years, undeveloped, until the academy can take possession of it. And it still sits there to this day—the lingam, the tree, and the land.

COMPASS POINTS

Where: Puakea Bay is located near Hawi in the Kohala district at the northern tip of the Big Island of Hawaii.

Backdrop: Parker Ranch dates to 1847 and is older and bigger than many Texas ranches, covering 150,000 acres. Legend foretold that a king destined to unify the Hawaiian Islands would be born when a fiery light appeared in the sky, and Halley's Comet shone in 1758, the presumed year of Kamehameha's birth. Known as the "Napoleon of the Pacific," the 6'6" inch warrior outlawed human sacrifice and endeavored to ensure the islands' independence. The kiawe tree is a species of mesquite native to South America and was introduced to Hawaii in 1828.

Visitor Information: www.gohawaii.com/big_island

Business consultant **Rinaldo Brutoco** *founded the first pay cable television operation in the United States and serves on the board of the Men's Wearhouse, the nation's largest retailer of men's dress apparel. He founded the World Business Academy (www.worldbusiness.org) in 1986 as a network of business leaders creating "resources for individuals to be more effective, efficient, and responsible in commerce, society, and their own personal lives."*

Discoveries II

LANCE BURTON

LAS VEGAS, NEVADA

*D*uring my magic show I tell the audience: "I wasn't born here in Las Vegas. I'm originally from Kentucky. And I'm very well known there—I'm the only one with a tuxedo." As a kid, I spent summers on my grandfather's farm in Russell Springs, Kentucky. They didn't have indoor plumbing, so you had to get water out of a spring with a bucket and carry it back up to the house. There was an outhouse, too. It was from another era.

When you're a kid in Kentucky and think you want to be a magician when you grow up, it's an unusual career choice. But I wanted to be a magician since I was five years old. When I was 12, I saw Siegfried and Roy perform in Las Vegas on the *Merv Griffin Show*. Merv used to go there once a year to tape shows, so I also saw the other magicians who worked in Las Vegas in the seventies. I didn't know anything about gambling or tourism. I just knew there was this magical,

Las Vegas at sunset, from atop the Planet Hollywood Hotel

mystical place called Las Vegas, and that's where the professional magicians lived. So naturally, since I was a kid, I wanted to move there.

I was 21 years old the first time I went. I had just moved to Los Angeles, driving out from Kentucky in a broken-down car with a leaky radiator—just me, my tuxedo, and seven doves. I came to appear in a show put on by the Magic Castle in Hollywood. This was my big break in show business, and within a week I appeared on *The Tonight Show* with Johnny Carson.

Then I had a couple of weeks off, without any gigs, and my friend Johnny Thompson ("The Great Tomsoni") told me he was driving to Las Vegas. He had produced a magic show that was going to be taped for television there, and he had a U-Haul truck filled with magic illusions that he needed to drive to Las Vegas.

We headed across the desert, sharing the driving, and when we finally got off the highway and drove down the Strip, I was behind the wheel of the U-Haul. I was mesmerized by all the glittering lights, and I couldn't take my eyes off the marquees because I wanted to see where the magicians were working. I wasn't paying attention to the road, and when we got to the Aladdin Hotel, I actually drove the U-Haul right up on the sidewalk. John looked at me and said, "Kid, you better let me drive."

The good part of the story is that within four months I opened in Las Vegas at the Tropicana Hotel. It was my first job, in 1982. We did two shows a night, seven days a week. I worked for two years straight without a single day off.

After hours, Las Vegas has a couple of places where entertainers hang out after their shows. One is the Bootlegger Bistro, an Italian restaurant at the south end of the Strip. You see people you know: dancers, singers, comedians. I've also seen the Smothers Brothers and Clint Holmes. The restaurant is owned by Lorraine Hunt, a lounge singer who until recently was Nevada's lieutenant governor. Only in Las Vegas!

I didn't know anything about gambling or tourism. I just knew there was this magical, mystical place called Las Vegas, and that's where the professional magicians lived.

Las Vegas also has a magic club that has met on Wednesday nights for 40 years, lately at Boomer's, a bar off the Strip. It's a social thing where you can meet other magicians, exchange tricks, and talk magic. When you walk in, you see guys huddled in the corner, doing card tricks. It's fun.

But for me, here's the best thing about Las Vegas: After a show elsewhere, most entertainers have to pack up their act and travel to the next venue, living out of a suitcase. But in Las Vegas, the audience comes to you. So an entertainer can lead a normal—well, seminormal—existence. You drive to work, do your job, and then go home and sleep in your own bed.

I built a house nearby in Henderson, bordering the wilderness. Behind me is desert, and out the front I see the lights of downtown Las Vegas. It's a nice middle ground. Of course, I designed my house with hidden doors and secret passages. I'm still the kid who always wanted to be a magician and never grew up.

COMPASS POINTS

Where: Las Vegas is located in southern Nevada, in a basin of the Mojave Desert.

Backdrop: The "Welcome to Fabulous Las Vegas" sign was created in 1959; now world famous, its design was never copyrighted and appears on countless Las Vegas souvenirs. With more working magicians than any other city, Las Vegas is the unofficial magic capital of the world.

Visitor Information: www.visitlasvegas.com

Lance Burton has performed in Las Vegas for 25 years and presents a full-evening magic show at his own theater at the Monte Carlo Resort and Casino. At age 20, he was awarded the Gold Medal for Excellence by the International Brotherhood of Magicians, then two years later became the youngest person (and first American) to win the Grand Prix at FISM (Fédération Internationale des Sociétés Magiques). He has been honored for his charity work and especially likes the Shriners (www.shrinershq.org).

JACK CANFIELD

ASSISI, ITALY

*M*y wife and I were on our honeymoon in Italy, driving from Tuscany down to Rome, when we saw the road sign for Assisi. I'd always been very much impressed and moved by Saint Francis of Assisi. remember seeing a movie called *Brother Sun, Sister Moon*, and the way Saint Francis was portrayed was just profound to me. I consider myself to be someone who is an emissary of love and peace, and I admired his total commitment to those goals.

In Assisi, Saint Francis rebuilt San Damiano, the church and monastery that became home to Saint Clare and her order of "Poor Ladies." In the movie there's a song by Donovan:

Step by step, stone by stone,
Build your dreams up slowly.
Step by step, stone by stone,
Heartfelt dreams are holy.

That song meant a lot to me as a young man, so when we saw the sign for Assisi, I said, "We've got to go."

The town was just up the mountain. On the way, we passed through a valley with square fields and tall cypress trees—the classic Italian rural landscape.

When we got to Assisi, we went to San Damiano. It was here that Saint Francis looked at the crucifix and saw the figure of Christ come alive and speak to him. We took a tour, and the guide pointed out what the different rooms were—here's where the nuns slept, here's where the monks prayed, that sort of thing. The room where the monks ate was very stark—just a plank to sit on and a narrow wooden table. The only ornamentation on the wall was a word in huge letters: *Silenzio*, "silence." We left with a tremendous sense of calm.

Then we went into the small chapel, which had just enough room for two or three people on each side of the aisle. We sat down and meditated. That was our rule whenever we visited a church: We would do the tourist thing, but then we would meditate for maybe 20 minutes.

The hilltop village of Assisi in Italy's Umbria region

As we left the chapel, a tremendous downpour started, with thunder and lightning and rain. So we ran back inside and decided we would just meditate until the storm was over. And it was then that my wife and I had extraordinary experiences that were really quite profound.

My wife was claustrophobic and had always been afraid of being locked in a closet, the trunk of a car, or any similar enclosed space. A few nights earlier, I had told her about a woman I met, the wife of a bank president. One night, this woman and her husband had gotten home from a movie with their five-year-old daughter, and there were some people waiting for them wearing masks and carrying Uzis. The intruders ordered the man to take them to the bank the next day and hand over all the money. To keep him from trying anything heroic, they took his wife and daughter, put them in the trunk of a car, and drove away.

The mother told her daughter, "We're playing hide-and-seek from your daddy! He's going to find us." But soon the air in the trunk started to run out. The woman told me that she suddenly saw a hole open in the lid of the trunk, and that an angel had done it. I didn't know whether to believe her, but she seemed like a very logical person. Later, the police found the car and opened up the trunk. There was no hole in the lid, but the mother and daughter were both alive in this totally airless trunk. They should have been dead.

This story had really spooked my wife. "My god!" she said. "I couldn't stand to be locked in a trunk. I probably would have freaked out and killed my daughter by flailing around and hitting her!" But as my wife and I sat in this chapel, meditating, she had a release. Her claustrophobia was just gone! Later, when we were back home again, I asked her to get in the trunk of our car, and I pretended that I was walking away by making my footsteps softer and softer. And she was fine! Her experience in the chapel in Assisi had been a transformative moment.

That confirmed my belief in the concept of energy centers on Earth, and that Saint Francis and whatever else is going on at San Damiano is for real. It's not an accident that it is a holy place.

During my time in the chapel, I could feel the energy; it was palpable. I went into a deep, profound meditation and felt like I connected to the energy of Saint Francis. It was unbelievably powerful. It was definitely a heart energy, and I went into a state of joy. When I meditate, there are different states that I go to, very deep kinds of insightful places, but in this case I just couldn't help but smile the whole time. Also there was this huge expansiveness, as if my body were slowly extending outward, until it was as big as the church. The experience wasn't heavy or serious, just very joyful.

There was such a sense of peace in the chapel, as if you could touch it and feel it. You had this sense of the monks going in there every morning, chanting and praying. The Buddhists say that when people do that, they leave their energy there. And if you think of literally centuries of people praying and meditating, it builds up a field, and you can really feel it. We were very much moved.

COMPASS POINTS

Where: Assisi is located in the province of Perugia in the Umbria region of Italy.

Backdrop: Assisi was the birthplace of Saint Francis (ca. 1181), who founded the Franciscan order there, and Saint Clare, founder of the Poor Clares and one of Saint Francis's first followers. Saint Francis reported that Christ spoke to him from the San Damiano cross, repeating three times, "Francis, Francis, go and repair My house which, as you can see, is falling into ruins." Saint Francis first undertook repairs to San Damiano, but later realized that his mission was to repair the Church as a whole. The cross is now housed in the Basilica of Saint Clare in Assisi. Known as the patron saint of animals and birds, Saint Francis wrote the "Canticle of the Sun," a poem expressing love for Brother Sun and Sister Moon, and the "Canticle of the Creatures," which praises God for "all these brother and sister creatures." Legend says that Saint Francis once preached a sermon to birds he encountered along a road, and that the birds surrounded him without fear while he spoke. Each year on October 4, the feast day of Saint Francis, the Catholic church conducts ceremonies honoring animals.

Visitor Information: www.assisionline.com; www.italiantourism.com

*Motivational speaker and author **Jack Canfield** cofounded the* Chicken Soup for the Soul© *book series. The first book was rejected by 140 publishers, yet today the series has sold more than 112 million books in 41 languages. The series earned a spot in the* Guinness Book of World Records *in 1998 by having seven books on the* New York Times *best-seller list at once. Canfield's most recent book is* The Success Principles. *He supports the Pachamama Alliance (www.pachamama.org), which works with the Achuar people of Ecuador to preserve the rain forest and to create an "ecologically sustainable, spiritually fulfilling, socially just human presence on Earth."*

DEEPAK CHOPRA

OLD CITY OF JERUSALEM, ISRAEL

*I*n writing two books about Jesus Christ, I became obsessed by the places associated with his life, as well as the lives of the Old Testament prophets. It fascinated me, for example, that in Jerusalem you can actually see the hill where Abraham was about to sacrifice his son, Isaac, before the angel stopped him.

In visiting the Old City of Jerusalem, I wanted to re-create in my consciousness a history that goes back almost four thousand years. To enter the old walled city is to travel back in time. There are four separate quarters—Muslim, Christian, Jewish, and Armenian—all within walking distance. As you stroll from one place to another, despite what we hear about violence in that part of the world, the everyday scene is just the normal hustle and bustle of the marketplace. Everything from raw fish to carpets to antiques is being sold, and it's so crowded with people that there's hardly a place to walk.

You can drink Turkish coffee in the Muslim quarter, then within five minutes walk across to the Jewish or Armenian quarter, where the energy shifts, the atmosphere changes, and the smells and food and dress are different, along with people's faces.

There are pilgrims in the Old City from all over the world. They come to see places important to their religion, such as the Church of the Holy Sepulchre for Christians, the Western Wall for Jews, or the Dome of the Rock for Muslims. The pilgrims all have this look of absolute awe on their faces, and you can tell that they are transported.

One day I walked down the Via Dolorosa, the street in the Old City where Jesus carried the cross. The stations of the cross are marked out, and I began my walk where he was sentenced, at Pontius Pilate's court. The second station is where Jesus was flagellated, the third where he fell and was helped up. And I ended at Calvary, the hill where he was crucified.

People say, well, nobody really knows the exact route that Jesus took when he carried the cross. But if it's all within the area of the tiny Old City, you couldn't be more than a stone's throw away anyway, so it doesn't matter.

At a certain point, you realize that differentiating between history and mythology isn't important. As Joseph Campbell used to say, mythology becomes

Colorful East Market in Jerusalem's Old City

My Favorite Place on Earth

more important than history. This is because history is a form of journalism and so reflects the journalist's point of view. But mythology is what captures our collective imagination as human beings.

There's a practice called psychometry, based on the idea that a person can get information about an event by touching something related to it. You hold a rock or a relic and allow your imagination to go into the past. At one station of the cross along the Via Dolorosa, there is a handprint on the wall, supposedly the handprint of Jesus as he struggled to prevent himself from falling. I put my hand right into the handprint. And I felt great love, compassion, and pain, all at the same time.

When I first walked through Jerusalem, I thought, *Oh, if only this land could speak!* In the end, it did.

COMPASS POINTS

Where: The Old City covers an area of 0.35 square miles within the modern city of Jerusalem, which is located in the Judean Mountains of Israel.

Backdrop: With a history reaching back to the fourth millennium B.C.E., Jerusalem is one of the world's oldest cities. It is also Judaism's holiest city and the third holiest city of Islam. Jerusalem's Old City is a UNESCO World Heritage site, along with its walls. In Jewish tradition, it is said that the Messiah will enter Jerusalem through the walls' Golden Gate.

Visitor Information: www.goisrael.com

A leader in mind-body medicine, **Deepak Chopra, M.D.** *has written some 50 books with 20 million copies in print; they include the best-selling* The Seven Spiritual Laws of Success, The Book of Secrets, *and* Ageless Body, Timeless Mind, *as well as* The Third Jesus *and* Beyond Bethlehem. *Educated in his native India, he became chief of staff at Boston Regional Medical Center in Massachusetts, then left to follow his interest in Ayurvedic medicine, meditation, holistic medicine, and spiritual questions. He established the Chopra Center for Wellbeing in Carlsbad, California, to integrate Western medicine with natural healing traditions through public events and training for health care professionals. Dr. Chopra is a fellow of the American College of Physicians and a member of the American Association of Clinical Endocrinologists. He is president of Alliance for a New Humanity (www.anhglobal. org), a nonprofit organization supporting respect for life, human dignity, freedom, ecological sustainability, and peace. Dr. Chopra can be contacted at www.deepakchopra.com.*

YVON CHOUINARD

WIND RIVER RANGE, WYOMING

I'm not the kind of traveler who only goes and looks at stuff. I go places to *do* something. I'm there to fish or climb or kayak. And one of my favorite places is the Wind River Range, where I started climbing when I was 18.

I grew up in Burbank, California, where I learned to hunt with hawks and falcons. An adult in our little falconry club was a climber who taught us to rappel down the cliffs to the falcon aeries. In 1956, we all decided to meet up in Wyoming — I drove out by myself in my old car — to go into the Wind Rivers together to climb Gannett Peak, the highest one there. That was my first mountain climb.

I've spent years in that range. I love it much more than the Sierra. It's more remote, and it's easier to get around. In the Sierra, you have to go up and down to get from one valley to the next. But once you gain your elevation in the Wind Rivers, you can stay at 10,000 or 11,000 feet. You walk *around* the peaks, instead of having to go over passes. You're in high meadows, with peaks sticking up all over.

The Wind River Range runs parallel to the Tetons. And it's such a big range — 225 million acres — that I almost always go to new places. Now I go there mostly to fish; there are lakes and streams everywhere. The world record golden trout came out of there. Goldens were introduced to lakes that had no fish, so they grew very big, very fast. They also have rainbows, browns, cutthroats, brookies, and various hybrids.

It takes a few days in the Wind Rivers to get used to the altitude. But once you do, it feels great to be camping at 10,000 feet and breathing that brisk, clear air. The nights are cool, and the days are warm. But you have to be careful about going in there too early in the season, because the mosquitoes are unbelievable. It's like being in the Arctic at the end of June, when you can't even breathe without inhaling gobs of them. In the Wind Rivers, the first two weeks in July are like that. It's impossible — you can't concentrate on anything because of the deerflies, the horseflies, and the mosquitoes. But, you know, some of the best places in the world are guarded by insects.

If you go up there in September, you could have snow dump on you. Once I got caught and had to walk out in 15 inches of snow — in my running shoes!

Waterfall in Wyoming's Wind River Range

The Wind Rivers aren't wild like the Alps, which are the best climbing mountains in the world. These aren't serious mountains; there's an easy way up every peak. You do see people up there, but ten years ago it was much more crowded. I think it's due to the softening of America; the visitation in national parks is way down, too.

Also, if you climb in the Tetons—where I taught myself to climb and tie knots and everything after that first trip to Gannett Peak in 1956—you find that everybody is climbing the Grand Teton. The other peaks are empty. It's like Mount Everest—and it's the opposite of what climbing really is about. Climbing is about the process of climbing, and these people are just focused on the end result. It's kind of the opposite of Zen. They all want to get up the highest peak and put a notch on their belt.

I don't mind, though. I love it that I can go into the Wind Rivers and not see a lot of people. To me, those mountains are just a paradise.

Yvon Chouinard

COMPASS POINTS

Where: Located in western Wyoming, the Wind River Range is part of the Rocky Mountains.

Backdrop: The crest of the Wind River Range forms part of the Continental Divide. Gannett Peak, Wyoming's highest point, reaches 13,804 feet; the range has 35 other named peaks taller than 13,000 feet. The granite rock of the mountains was formed more than one billion years ago; the lakes and valleys were carved by glaciers during the ice ages.

Visitor Information: www.wyomingtourism.org

Mountaineer, surfer, and environmentalist **Yvon Chouinard** *founded the clothing and outdoor gear company Patagonia. He was a leading figure in the golden age of Yosemite climbing in the 1960s and began making his own climbing tools to save money. His first company's steel pitons helped enable big-wall climbing in Yosemite, but when Chouinard learned that they were causing damaging cracks in Yosemite's rock, he introduced new tools and started the "clean climbing" style. His 1978 book* Climbing Ice *launched the modern sport of ice climbing. Patagonia is known as a socially responsible company, giving 1 percent of its sales to environmental causes, a total of over $30 million so far. Chouinard supports the Atlantic Salmon Federation (www.asf.ca).*

ARTHUR C. CLARKE

SIGIRIYA, SRI LANKA

I call Sigiriya the eighth wonder of the ancient world. I visited it at the end of my first expedition to Ceylon (now Sri Lanka), in 1955. I'd already had a glimpse of this fantastic rock fortress from the air, and the stories about it fired my imagination, so I seized the opportunity.

Sigiriya (literally, "Lion Rock") rises 600 feet above the surrounding plain. It is a walled and moated royal capital of the fifth century, with a palace complex on top of the rock, elaborate pleasure gardens, extensive moats and ramparts, and well-known paintings on the western face of the massive rock. Kasyapa, the king of Lanka, ruled his land from there for 18 years. Originally, the rock was elaborated into the shape of a lion, with visitors making the last part of the ascent through its open jaws.

This complex has emerged as one of Asia's major archaeological sites, with a unique concentration of fifth-century urban planning, architecture, art, and engineering. Hydraulic technology created water gardens, complete with gravity-fed fountains, pools, and ponds.

Sigiriya has influenced my thinking about technological advancement in the ancient world, and I have often wondered where we might be today if those early advances had continued without centuries of interruption and neglect triggered by war, drought, and epidemics. It seems incredible that so vast an undertaking could have been carried out in a mere 18 years by a usurper to the throne who expected to be challenged at any moment.

Since my personal "discovery" of Sigiriya more than 50 years ago, I have made many journeys there, spending days and weeks exploring the 1,500-year-old ruins. I used to take my visiting friends and sometimes climbed the rock with them — as I did with L. Sprague de Camp, a fellow science fiction writer and the author of *Great Cities of the Ancient World.* I once chartered a small plane and took the visionary designer and inventor Buckminster Fuller on a quick aerial tour of Sri Lanka — and, of course, Sigiriya was a highlight.

The frescoes are Sigiriya's greatest glory. Originally there were close to 500 beautiful women, who were depicted rising from clouds, with flowers in their hair. But exposure to the elements for 15 centuries has taken its toll. Only two dozen

Cave fresco at Sigiriya archaeological site

images remain today. And in the mid-1960s, there was a horrible incident when unknown vandals destroyed some of the frescoes by applying tar on them.

One of the obliterated frescoes showed a woman clearly listening to a mysterious hinged box she is holding in her right hand. It remains unidentified, and local archaeologists have refused to take seriously my suggestion that it is an early Sinhalese transistor radio. (Or a mobile phone!)

One of my science fiction novels, *The Fountains of Paradise*, is partly based in Sigiriya (called Yakkagala in the story). I don't believe aliens were involved in turning Sigiriya into an archaeological marvel and cultural citadel—that credit goes to the maverick king and all those unknown men and women who toiled to make it happen. The site reminds me of the rich blend of aesthetics and technology that characterized Sri Lanka's past. It may well be a colorful aberration in the country's 25 centuries of documented history, but it indicates what could be accomplished through skill, determination, and focus.

Now that I'm in a wheelchair, my climbing (and even walking) days are over. Going up Sigiriya is now only a memory for me, albeit a very vivid one. I can still drive up the plains and look at the rock fortress from afar. Or I can fly over, which I want to do one more time.

COMPASS POINTS

Where: Sigiriya is located on the plains of central Sri Lanka, in an area of ancient settlement between the historic capitals of Anuradhapura and Polonnaruwa.

Backdrop: Sigiriya is built atop a magma plug, the remains of an eroded volcano. In the 1800s, the paintings were observed by telescope from the plains below. The first archaeological operations began in 1894 under H. C. P. Bell. His archaeological surveyor, John Still, noted, "The whole face of the hill appears to have been a gigantic picture gallery—the largest picture in the world, perhaps." Frescoes once covered an area about twice as big as a football field. Sigiriya's legendary history was brought to the screen by Dimitri de Grunwald in *The God King*, with Leigh Lawson as an impressive Kasyapa. The usurper Kasyapa killed his father by walling him up alive, then seized the throne destined for his brother.

Visitor Information: www.srilankatourism.org

The late **Sir Arthur C. Clarke,** *who died in 2008 shortly after this conversation, was the author of many classic science fiction novels, including* Childhood's End *and* 2001: A Space Odyssey. *Born in England, after 1956 he lived in Sri Lanka, where he avidly pursued scuba diving. He wrote about his adopted home in* The Reefs of Taprobane *and* The Fountains of Paradise. *In 1945, he was the first to suggest that satellites orbiting in fixed positions above Earth's surface could work as telecommunications relays. (One of Clarke's Three Laws: "Any sufficiently advanced technology is indistinguishable from magic.") Two spacecraft, an asteroid, and a dinosaur species have been named in his honor.*

Arthur C. Clarke

BARNABY CONRAD

PITCAIRN ISLAND

I had dreamed of going to Pitcairn Island since I'd first read *Mutiny on the Bounty* as a boy. Everyone knows the tale of Captain Bligh and the most famous of all mutinies. To me, it's the ultimate romantic sea story.

I have a further interest in the dramatis personae, having a distant family connection to the protagonist, mutineer Fletcher Christian. His first cousin married George Washington's step-granddaughter—who was my relative, the granddaughter of my great-great-great-great-grandmother, Martha Custis Washington. My family enjoyed being related to the wife of the first President of the United States, but I derived much more pleasure from the thought that I'm connected to a mutineer.

I resolved to go to Pitcairn Island one day and meet the descendants of the *Bounty* crew. People think that Pitcairn is near Hawaii, or near Tahiti, or near someplace. But it's not near anything. Pitcairn is one of the world's most remote islands. Yet somehow Fletcher Christian managed to find this tiny, uninhabited dot in the Pacific, roughly 3,500 miles from both New Zealand and Hawaii. No white man had ever set foot on it before.

I journeyed to Pitcairn by plane and cruise ship. Finally, early one morning, I climbed into a small inflatable boat piloted by Brian Young, a Pitcairn native and sixth-great-grandson of one of the mutineers. Ahead lay the island, rising a thousand feet out of the sea to a single peak. How exactly right it looked, this menacing monolith with long gashes of blood-red and ochre earth on its sides.

Since they have had so little contact with the outside world, their English is basically that of the time of Bligh and Christian.

The island has no beaches, so the only place to land is Bounty Bay—which is about the size of the average living room. Brian studied the breakers with squinting black eyes and waited. At last, he shouted "Now!" and gunned the outboard. The little boat sprang forward in front of a great swell; we caught it and surfed down the steep side of the breaker for a hundred yards and then shot into the little cove.

Waiting for us was the entire population of this one-mile-by-two-mile island—48 descendants of the original mutineers and their Tahitian women. With fewer than 500 visitors a year coming to Pitcairn, a ship's arrival is a great event.

As we drew up to the jetty, eager, friendly hands helped us out of the boat. "Weel-come to Peet-kern!" someone cried out. The islanders' speech is fascinating. Since they have had so little contact with the outside world, their English is basically that of the time of Bligh and Christian. For example, they refer to rifles as muskets, pronounced "moose-kits."

In spite of two centuries of inbreeding, the Pitcairners appeared to be the healthiest and happiest of people. Some of them are very dark and Polynesian, some are very light-skinned and English. A friendlier group cannot be imagined. We made the steep climb up the aptly named Hill of Difficulty to Adamstown. The islanders welcomed us into their homes—the oldest of which was made with actual planks from the *Bounty*.

Flowers and fruit were everywhere: bananas, guava, papaya, lemons, oranges, sugarcane, coconuts. And, of course, breadfruit. (The *Bounty* had been sent to gather breadfruit trees to take to the West Indies to supply cheap food for England's slave laborers there.)

Adamstown consists of a church, a small public square that displays the huge anchor from the *Bounty*, and the post office. Islanders sell postage stamps to collectors as their main source of revenue. (I'd heard that the Pitcairners had a good sense of

Pitcairn Island, home to descendants of the Bounty *mutineers*

humor, which was confirmed by a sign near the post office that read: "Don't forget the boat race on Sunday! Winner to receive a weekend on glorious Pitcairn Island.")

Another source of revenue for the islanders is wood carving, and I saw beautifully shaped birds, fish, canes—and, of course, replicas of the *Bounty*. I bought a fine model of the ship with wooden sails and received a bonus from Nig Brown, the island's only—and totally unnecessary—policeman: a square, salt-encrusted nail from the wreck of the *Bounty*.

"She lies right over there," said Nig, pointing down the rugged coast, "near where Fletcher Christian burned her." Shortly after arriving in 1789, Christian stripped the *Bounty*, then torched and sank the ship so that no passing vessel could spot it. Today what's left of the hull lies—tantalizingly, teasingly—just offshore in about 60 feet of water. Seeing it fulfilled my boyhood dream.

COMPASS POINTS

Where: A British overseas territory, the Pitcairn Islands lie in the southern Pacific Ocean; they consist of Pitcairn, Henderson, Ducie, and Oeno islands. Only Pitcairn is inhabited.

Backdrop: There have been some 2,500 works—articles, books, and movies—about the *Bounty* saga. Mutineer Fletcher Christian was 5'10", dark-haired, muscular, and bowlegged, with sweaty palms that soiled papers if he touched them. It took him weeks to find Pitcairn Island, which was mischarted 200 miles from its actual location. The remains of the *Bounty* were discovered in 1957 by National Geographic's legendary Luis Marden. An islander had warned him not to dive in the dangerous swells, saying, "Man, you gwen be dead as a hatchet!" Marden later wore cufflinks made of nails from the *Bounty*. The Adamstown museum displays Christian's Bible, issues of *National Geographic,* and postage stamps.

Visitor Information: www.government.pn. Because Pitcairn has no airstrip, reaching the island requires flying to Tahiti and then to Mangareva in the Gambier Islands, covering the remaining 330 miles by boat. (An alternative is the occasional commercial cruise ship.) There are no hotels, although some islanders take people in for a short time.

*A modern Renaissance man, **Barnaby Conrad** is the author of 34 books, including the classic* Matador, *which has sold three million copies, and he founded the Santa Barbara Writers Conference. During his tenure as vice consul to Spain, he studied bullfighting with Manolete and in 1945 appeared on the same bill with the great Juan Belmonte as the "California Kid." An acclaimed painter, his works hang in collections worldwide, including the National Portrait Gallery in Washington, D.C. Conrad is also a jazz pianist, woodcarver, and muralist.*

JEAN-MICHEL COUSTEAU

THE AMAZON, PERU

Twenty-five years ago, I had the privilege of going with our team to explore the Amazon. I had a lot of questions, and I came out 20 months later with more questions than I had when I went in.

We have no sense of how big the Amazon is and how much impact it has on every one of our lives every day. The Amazon Basin is as big as the continental United States. The Amazon River has ten tributaries that are as big or bigger than the Mississippi River, and the system pours out 20 percent of the world's freshwater. The Amazon has more fish species than the entire Atlantic Ocean, with about 5,000 discovered so far. And that's not to mention the area's insects, birds, trees, and plants.

We are all connected to the Amazon. The frame of the sofa you're sitting on may have come from the rain forest. The steak I eat in Paris may have been raised on soybeans from the Amazon, because trees are being cleared to raise cattle and plant soybeans. Every year, they clear-cut an area as big as the state of New Jersey. Who knows what medicinal plants are there to be discovered—if we can do it before we destroy them.

But beyond all this, I was totally blown away when I realized that there were thousands of native people in the Amazon who were not accounted for. They have no identity papers, no land ownership. These South American Indians roam the Amazon as they have done for thousands of years. They are human beings just like us, yet, I was outraged to learn, in the 1960s, "invaders"—we—used to hunt them for sport. Outsiders started going there to look for petroleum or to cut trees for export, and on weekends, when they had nothing else to do, those invaders would take off in airplanes and helicopters and go hunting Indians. They would come back at night and, over their six-packs of beer, ask each other, "How many did you get today?" "Oh, I got 17, what about you?"

The native people of the Amazon are in the way of big corporations, particularly the oil companies. They know that the territory was set aside for the Indians, but the companies don't even consider asking their permission to go into the rain forest. They just invade.

In total contrast to all this is a chief of the Achuar, a group of the Jivaro, whom I met in his remote village near the border between Peru and Ecuador. Chief

Kukus (*ku-koosh*) had nearly as much impact on me as my own father. He taught me his values. Yet in his own country, this gentleman was considered a strange human being, with no more rights than a tapir or a cockroach.

His village stood on a river in the deep forest. In order to avoid snakes and termites, the people cleared the area around their wooden houses, which were set on stilts because of the rain. The area below the floor sheltered the pigs and chickens they raised.

Young spear fishers on the Amazon River

There were a lot of birds in the trees, and monkeys all over the place. The people hunted with blowguns and poison darts, but in a sustainable way. They only killed what they needed, what Nature could provide.

Chief Kukus showed me some trees he had planted that were about ten feet tall. He told me: "I'll never see them grow big enough, and my children won't either—even my grandchildren, probably not. But my great-grandchildren, they'll be able to use those trees that I have planted." He pointed to one in particular and said, "That's going to make a good canoe."

Chief Kukus taught me his values. Yet in his own country, this gentleman was considered a strange human being, with no more rights than a tapir or a cockroach.

For me, the chief expressed the unwritten constitution of the future. In our modern culture, we deal only with the present—*now, now, now!* We *say* we care about our children and grandchildren, yet we do nothing about it. But the Jivaro people have the right concept. They know how to live in harmony with nature in a sustainable way.

Chief Kukus got to me very deeply, and I wanted his people to be recognized, to have identities. We tried to get him official papers, but had no success on the local level, so I took him to see the president of Peru, Fernando Belaúnde Terry.

When we got to the airport terminal in Iquitos, it was so strange: The chief had never seen stairs before. We went upstairs to wait for the airplane, and voices were coming out of the corners of the room, from black boxes. The chief had never heard loudspeakers. Then the DC-8 landed, roaring up the airstrip to the terminal. Chief Kukus said, "Ah, yes. I've seen it in the sky, but it was that small," and he made a gesture with his thumb and forefinger.

We flew over the Andes, where there are no trees, only glaciers and snow, and the chief was astounded at the sight. After we landed in Lima, I thought it might be a culture shock for him to be in a big city—about four million people then—so I took him to the beach first. The chief walked across the sand to the water, then suddenly stopped. He asked, "Where's the other side of the lake?" It was the Pacific Ocean.

We went to the hotel and had lunch. Several days before, I had invited Chief Kukus to try Champagne, which is part of the French way. I had opened the bottle and held up the cork and the wire that holds it, and said, "You know, chief, there is a tradition in my country where I give you the cork—that's the 'bird'—and I keep the 'cage.' We're supposed to keep them with us all the time. Next time we meet,

Jean-Michel Cousteau

you can show me the cork and say, 'Where is the cage for my bird?' or I can show you the wire and say, 'Where is the bird for my cage?' And if one of us doesn't have it, he has to buy a new bottle of Champagne!" During lunch at the hotel, Chief Kukus produced the cork and said, "Where is the cage for my bird?" He had carried the cork all the way from his village.

Chief Kukus painted his face and wore feathers and beautiful attire for his meeting with the president of Peru. But he did not get his papers. Belaúnde claimed, "Even the president cannot do anything against the institutions." It really hurt me, and we went back to the chief's village very disappointed.

In my whole life, only three or four people have had the impact of that Jivaro gentleman. Chief Kukus died in 1997.

COMPASS POINTS

Where: The Amazon rain forest covers 3.4 million square miles in South America and is shared by nine countries, including Brazil (60 percent) and Peru.

Backdrop: The Amazon rain forest is the richest, most varied biological repository on Earth, with millions of species of birds, animals, insects, and plants—many still unrecorded by science. At about 4,000 miles in length, the Amazon River could stretch from New York City to Rome. During rainy season floods, some sections of the river can be 25 miles wide. To obtain revenge and supernatural power, Jivaro warriors formerly took their enemies' heads and shrank them to the size of an orange.

Visitor Information: www.peru.info/perueng.asp

*Explorer and environmentalist **Jean-Michel Cousteau** has produced more than 80 films, winning numerous awards, including the Emmy and Peabody. He founded the Ocean Futures Society (www.oceanfutures.org) as a voice for the ocean in media and government and created Ambassadors of the Environment (www.aote.org), an education program operating in pristine natural areas, vacation resorts, and cruise ships. The Jean-Michel Cousteau Fiji Islands Resort proved to the business community the economic benefits of environmental awareness and design. When Cousteau screened his PBS documentary about the northwest Hawaiian Islands at the White House, it convinced President George W. Bush to declare the area a national monument, the largest protected area in the world. Cousteau was inducted into the International Scuba Diving Hall of Fame and received the first Ocean Hero Award from Oceana.*

CLIVE CUSSLER

MY HOUSE, PARADISE VALLEY, ARIZONA

A house is an expression of the person who lives there. Mine is comfortable, and everyone has fun there. The minute you walk in, you know no interior decorator has been here. "You can easily sit in it," as they say—not like a house that's been done up by a decorator, where you're afraid to sink in a chair.

My house is furnished in Mexican style with brightly colored furniture—and mannequins and dummies. One is a replica of me that sits on a bench in the front window. When people come to the door, they're surprised when the dummy starts talking. It has a microphone inside, and I'm hidden away talking as the dummy's jaw moves.

There's also a skeleton, a woman from the Mexican Day of the Dead celebrations with a man sitting next to her holding a bottle of Viva Villa tequila in one hand and the other hand on her knee. In my den, next to the TV there's an Indian whose middle is a slot machine. Then I've got a chef—for parties we set him out in the patio, holding a tray of hors d'oeuvres.

My office is a separate building done in Santa Fe style, with carved doors from an old Mexican cathedral and traditional round poles called *vigas* in the ceiling. I have thousands of books in there, along with paintings and models of the shipwrecks that I and my crew at the National Underwater and Marine Agency have found.

One painting is of the *Carpathia*, the ship that rescued the *Titanic*'s survivors. I was sitting here one day thinking that there's such a big deal about the *Titanic*, with people making movies and going down to the depths to shoot pictures—but whatever happened to the *Carpathia*? I did some research and found that it hadn't been scrapped, as I'd thought, but was torpedoed during World War I off Ireland. So I mounted three expeditions, and on the third one we found it, in 600 feet of water.

If we find a wreck, I don't stand in front of news cameras and make a big deal about it. I just write an archaeological report and pass it along to universities and governments. Then I move on to the next one. (Everybody thinks I'm crazy because I've never looked for treasure—in fact, my accountant thinks I belong in a rubber room under restraint.)

My office also has a large painting that attracts a lot of attention. Years ago when I was in advertising, an art director owed me a favor, so he said he'd paint my

The warm interior shows off a collection of folk art.

picture. My wife posed in a skimpy little dress with her hands tied. I'm holding her, and under her legs I've got a big Mauser pistol I'm shooting. My friend painted in a "Wanted" poster for my character Dirk Pitt and a model of the *Titanic*. Everybody stares in disbelief at this painting — and already my children are fighting over who gets it when I go! It's always good for a laugh.

Another thing that's fun is the bathroom. People come out dumbfounded because that's where I hang all my awards.

I enjoy my house so much. It's my own little sanctum sanctorum, and I intend to die here.

COMPASS POINTS

Where: Paradise Valley is on the outskirts of Phoenix in Maricopa County.

Backdrop: An upscale resort destination, Paradise Valley includes Camelback Mountain (2,704 ft.), a popular hiking spot and affluent residential area. The median home price in Paradise Valley is about $1.75 million, with houses ranging up to $20 million. Residents include rocker Alice Cooper, former Supreme Court justice Sandra Day O'Connor, and actor Leslie Nielsen; the late humorist Erma Bombeck also lived there.

Visitor Information: Arizona Office of Tourism: www.arizonaguide.com; Paradise Valley: www.ci.paradise-valley.az.us

Published in more than 45 languages and 100 countries, with a readership of 125 million, **Clive Cussler**'s *techno-thrillers include* Raise the Titanic!, Deep Six, Sahara, *and* Treasure of Khan. *An avid underwater explorer, he has discovered 60 shipwreck sites, including the U-20—the submarine that sank the* Lusitania—*and the* Cumberland, *which was sunk by the famous ironclad* Merrimack. *Cussler founded the National Underwater and Marine Agency (www.numa.net), a nonprofit organization dedicated to preserving maritime heritage through the discovery, archaeological survey, and conservation of shipwreck artifacts. He is a fellow of the Explorers Club of New York, the Royal Geographic Society, and the American Society of Oceanographers. His charitable causes range from juvenile diabetes to humane societies.*

HIS HOLINESS, THE DALAI LAMA

THE POTALA PALACE AND NORBULINGKA, LHASA, TIBET

The Potala Palace is said to be one of the largest buildings in the world. Even after living in it for years, one could never know all its secrets. It entirely covers the top of a hill; it is a city in itself. It was begun by a king of Tibet 1,300 years ago as a pavilion for meditation, and it was greatly enlarged by the Fifth Dalai Lama in the 17th century of the Christian era.

The central part of the building contained the great halls for ceremonial occasions, about 35 chapels richly carved and painted, four cells for meditation, and the mausoleums of seven Dalai Lamas—some 30 feet high and covered in solid gold and precious stones.

My own apartments were above the offices, on the top story—400 feet above the town. I had four rooms there. The one which I used most often was about 25 feet square, and its walls were entirely covered by paintings depicting the life of the Fifth Dalai Lama, so detailed that the individual portraits were not more than an inch high. When I grew tired of my reading, I often used to sit and follow the story told by this great and elaborate mural which surrounded me.

But apart from its use as office, temple, school, and habitation, the Potala was also an enormous storehouse. Here were rooms full of thousands of priceless scrolls, some a thousand years old. Here were strong rooms filled with the golden regalia of the earliest kings of Tibet, dating back for a thousand years, and the sumptuous gifts they received from the Chinese or Mongol emperors, and the treasures of the Dalai Lamas who succeeded the kings. Here also were stored the armor and armament from the whole of Tibetan history. In the libraries were all the records of Tibetan culture and religion, 7,000 enormous volumes, some of which were said to weigh 80 pounds. Some were written on palm leaves imported from India a thousand years ago. Two thousand illuminated volumes of the scriptures were written in inks made of powdered gold, silver, iron, copper, conch shell, turquoise, and coral, each line in a different ink.

In the spring I moved to the Norbulingka, in a procession which all the people of Lhasa came to see. I was always happy to go to the Norbulingka. The Potala

Part of the Norbulingka Summer Palace complex on the outskirts of Lhasa

made me proud of our inheritance of culture and craftsmanship, but the Norbulingka was more like a home. It was really a series of small palaces, and chapels, built in a large and beautiful walled garden. *Norbulingka* means "The Jewel Park." It was started by the Seventh Dalai Lama in the 18th century, and successive Dalai Lamas have added their own residences to it ever since. I built one there myself. The founder chose a very fertile spot. In the Norbulingka gardens, we grew a radish weighing 20 pounds, and cabbages so large you could not put your arms round them. There were poplars, willows, junipers, and many kinds of flowers and fruit trees: apples, pears, peaches, walnuts, and apricots. We introduced plums and cherry trees while I was there.

There, between my lessons, I could walk and run among the flowers and orchards, and the peacocks and the tame musk deer. There I played on the edge of the lake and twice nearly drowned myself. And there, also in the lake, I used to feed my fish, which would rise to the surface expectantly when they heard my footsteps. I do not know now what has happened to the historical marvels of the Potala. Thinking about them, I sometimes also wonder whether my fish were so unwise as to rise to the surface when they first heard the boots of Chinese soldiers in the Norbulingka. If they did, they have probably been eaten.

His Holiness, the Dalai Lama

In these days of overwhelming military power, all men and women can only live in hope. If they are blessed with peaceful homes and families, they hope to be allowed to keep them and to see their children grow up happily; and if they have lost their homes, as we have, their need for hope and faith is even greater. The hope of all men, in the last analysis, is simply for peace of mind. My hope rests in the courage of Tibetans, and the love of truth and justice which is still in the heart of the human race; and my faith is in the compassion of Lord Buddha.

COMPASS POINTS

Where: Tibet is located on the Tibetan Plateau, the planet's highest region, and contains most of the Himalaya range; Mount Everest stands at Tibet's border with Nepal. The Potala Palace and Norbulingka are located in Lhasa, Tibet's capital, one of the world's highest cities at 12,000 feet.

Backdrop: An independent realm dating to the seventh century, Tibet was invaded in 1949 by the People's Republic of China, which ten years later claimed it—a claim disputed by Tibet's government in exile in Dharamsala, India. China damaged or destroyed most of Tibet's important sites, including 6,500 monasteries, killing or imprisoning hundreds of thousands of Buddhist monks and nuns. Among the treasures of the Potala Palace is a stupa rising three stories high, sheathed in four tons of gold and adorned with semiprecious gems. Martin Scorsese made a 1997 film about Tibet's leader called *Kundun*, which means "presence" and is the title used to address the Dalai Lama.

Information: His Holiness the Dalai Lama: www.dalailama.com; International Campaign for Tibet: www.savetibet.org

The **Dalai Lama** *was born to a humble farm family as Tenzin Gyatso in 1935, recognized at age two as the reincarnation of the previous Dalai Lama, and enthroned in 1950. Forced to flee in 1959, he heads the Tibetan Government in Exile in Dharamsala, India, where he advocates internal autonomy for Tibet and promotes the preservation of Tibetan culture. The first Dalai Lama to travel to the West, he received the Nobel Peace Prize in 1989.*

TED DANSON

MARTHA'S VINEYARD, MASSACHUSETTS

To my eye, Martha's Vineyard is just perfection. If you stopped anywhere on the island and were handed a set of oils or a camera, you'd have the most amazing thing to paint or shoot.

I was raised in Arizona, but I went away to high school in Connecticut and spent seven years in New York, so there's a part of me that loves New England. And on Martha's Vineyard, New England meets the water in the best possible way. You have trees and ponds, big waves and sand dunes.

My wife, Mary Steenburgen, always went to the Vineyard in summer to visit friends. So one July we went there for our first holiday together as newly dating people. We stayed at the Beach Plum Inn in Menemsha, a teeny fishing village. It was the first time Mary's children and mine had spent any time together, and we did everything! We went clamming. We sailed. We walked and went surfing. We had the best time as a blended family. And we just fell in love with the island.

One evening each summer, on Illumination Night, all the cottages hang Chinese paper lanterns outside. At sunset they're lit, one by one. It's magical.

The people there are amazing, and it's a very democratic place. Native Americans live in a town called Aquinnah. Oak Bluffs is the oldest African American vacation spot in the country, going back to just after the Civil War. It has tiny gingerbread cottages that grew out of a Methodist tent camp. One evening each summer, on Illumination Night, all the cottages hang Chinese paper lanterns outside. At sunset they're lit, one by one. It's magical. There are probably—I don't know, I'm making this up—about 60 little gingerbread houses in a circle around this great outdoor tabernacle, where on Wednesday nights you can go sing hymns; you feel like you're back in the Midwest of Sinclair Lewis, in Columbus, Ohio.

The island also has the most talented, interesting people: artists, painters, writers, musicians. There's a shipbuilder whose family has been making beautiful boats for four or five generations. James Taylor lives there. In fact, he played guitar at our wedding while his sister Kate sang.

On our first visit, Mary and I had decided to look for property on the island, and we found this strange little 1950s house on a knoll overlooking Chilmark

Menemsha Harbor, Martha's Vineyard

Pond and the ocean beyond. It was not our taste, but we sat down in a room and looked at the view, and it was just like being hit between the eyes with a two-by-four. It was so relaxing; your body, your mind, everything, just went *Oooooohhhh*.

For our wedding, we made a lawn out of a big field on the property. There are huge boulders in the field that were left from way back when the island was formed by a receding glacier. One boulder is about six feet high and looks almost like an altar—something you should get married in front of.

We were outside, and it had rained, the tail end of hurricane weather in October. The lawn we'd planted had turned into a quagmire, and our idea of sitting out on quilts had gone right out the window. It stopped raining just about long enough for us to get married, and about 80 of us were all huddled under this one tent. It was so sweet, with lots of family and friends, including our parents and Mary's best friends, the Clintons, while Bill Clinton was president. The minister from Mary's church in Little Rock, Arkansas, came up, and he married us in front of the rock. It was beautiful.

Now we spend as much time on the Vineyard as we can. Near our house, there's a little lane that's lined with blackberries, and as you drive along you can just reach out the window on either side and pick them, because the lane is only one car wide. It leads down to Chilmark Pond, where you jump into your canoe. Swans float nearby as you cross the pond. You reach a big sand dune and can hear the ocean roaring, even though you can't see it yet. You climb some wooden steps to get to the top of the dune, and from there you can look a mile and a half to your left or right. You might see somebody walking a dog 300 yards that way, or a couple of people sitting on the sand—and that's a crowded day at the beach!

It's funny: I can't stand going on errands in Los Angeles, where I work. Who wants to fight the traffic? But on the Vineyard, if somebody sends me on an errand…*yes!* Let me run and get you half a cup of sugar, I don't care. Let me go! Let me just…drive around!

COMPASS POINTS

Where: Martha's Vineyard lies 3 miles off the southern coast of Cape Cod, Massachusetts.

Backdrop: The original (and still present) inhabitants were Wampanoag Indians. In the 19th century, the island had a prosperous whaling trade. Towns include Aquinnah, Chilmark, Edgartown, Oak Bluffs, and Tisbury. High-profile residents range from Walter Cronkite to Carly Simon; director Spike Lee has a house in Oak Bluffs, and Jacqueline Kennedy Onassis kept a home on the island. When Steven Spielberg filmed *Jaws* here in 1974, he cast locals in various roles.

Visitor Information: Chamber of Commerce: www.mvy.com; also www.mvol.com

Ted Danson's portrayal of Sam Malone on Cheers *earned him two Emmys for best actor in a comedy series; he also won the Golden Globe for his role in the television drama* Something About Amelia. *A longtime advocate for the environment, he was a founder of the American Oceans Campaign (now Oceana, www.oceana.org), calling the oceans "a mirror for the health of the entire planet."*

JOHN DAU

DUK COUNTY, SUDAN

*I*n 1987 I was uprooted from my village during the Second Sudanese Civil War and became one of the "Lost Boys of Sudan." We crossed sub-Saharan Africa on foot, pursued by armed soldiers and wild animals. We chewed grasses and ate mud to stay alive. Travel was always a disaster, running from one place to another. There was no good place.

After 22 years of separation, I went back to southern Sudan when the peace agreement was signed in 2005. I have never had such an emotional feeling. I could see the place where I grew up, the place where I was young and used to play. I felt like I was back home.

Also, there was no snow! I live in Syracuse, New York, now and it is very cold and gray. There is no sun. So I like Duk County—there are 12 hours of daytime and 12 hours of nighttime year-round, and no winter!

Let me just pretend I'm filming my village for you. It is early in the morning, and I can see all these different birds wandering around and flying about everywhere. They are eating, digging down in the earth to get something, pecking on a tree, or eating something in a flower. In one day you can see maybe 50 different types of birds. There are cranes, hawks, two types of crow, and many other birds whose names I know in Dinka, but not in English.

Now people are wandering around. They are milking cows. It's very natural. This is land that nobody claims. No one says, "Hey! This is my place! Don't touch it!" You may have your little piece of land where your home is, which is okay, but you can't claim anything else. In America people claim this or that tract of land. In Duk County, no. When you let your cows go for grazing, they can just wander anywhere.

Now the children are playing with their grandparents or great-grandparents. The mother and father are working in the garden. It's mixed agriculture; people keep cows and grow crops.

The elders are gathered under the shade of a tree. Maybe they are judging between two people who have a dispute. It's like a courthouse under a tree.

People here don't wear watches. You don't say "We've got to meet at such-and-such time." You might say, "When the sun is right here, or when the shade of that big tree is in this place, we are going to meet." There is no time. You're not enslaved, running to appointments. You don't have to worry that the grocery store is closing and you've got to hurry.

You don't worry about getting gas, either. There is no gas! Everything is done by foot. You can run from one place to another.

Children are not only for one family. They are brought up by the village. For example, anyone who sees a child misbehaving must discipline that child. The parent will come later and be very happy that the problem has been dealt with. You don't have to worry; there isn't anybody who would kidnap your children.

The only thing you do worry about is animals, such as hyenas or lions. But it's not a big deal; they are scared of people, so they don't come close. And they are the only problem. In America you always make sure your door is locked; anything can happen to you. In Duk County you never worry.

At the time I lived there, there were no schools. Children would sit together, somebody would tell a story, and the group would guess what the moral of the story is. Parents and grandparents would tell folklore tales. It was an informal education: no classes, no assignments.

When I went back in 2005, things had changed. First, everything was destroyed. There was nothing there. The few people who were there had come back from Kenya and Uganda, carrying stuff. I saw paper bags—like you get when you go to the grocery store in America—scattered around everywhere.

You don't worry about getting gas, either. There is no gas! Everything is done on foot. You can run from one place to another.

I saw that the number of cattle had been reduced, and some people did not have sheep and goats that they used to have. The number of people is reduced, too, because some were killed.

But people are returning to southern Sudan from Kenya, Uganda, Ethiopia, Eritrea, Egypt, and of course northern Sudan. I go back to Duk County every year for about a month and a half. I see not only my family, my relatives, but also the guys from my boyhood. Some of them look very old, and others very short (I am tall now—6'8"). They were starved for so long. I was not able even to recognize some of the boys. But when we talked about what happened and the stuff we went through, then I started knowing them again.

There are many changes happening. For one thing, people are doing a monetary kind of business now. Before, it was barter trade; you exchanged your goat for grain or corn. But now people are using money.

John Dau

Youths in a market in Kuda, southern Sudan

People have started wearing clothes in the Western world style. Some are going by watches; they know just when they need to be somewhere. There are cars running around. There are businesses selling things like sweets—called candy in America—and some people drink wine or other alcoholic beverages. People talk in different languages—some speaking English, some Arabic, and others Swahili. They were refugees in other countries and learned these other languages.

Today, people are drinking not from the stagnant water but from the water tap. They are talking about the government and taxes, about getting a job and sending children to school. They talk about the new stuff of the modern world. But women still do the same jobs they were doing before, taking care of children, fetching water, and cooking food. They are not looking for jobs outside their homes—although a few, maybe one percent, are breaking that mold.

Weddings are still the same, but they now also include money. Before, it was only an animal dowry; you gave cows, goats, and sheep. But now it is combined with money.

I have mixed feelings about all this. I welcome the basic changes—having children go to school, making sure there are medicines, and other advancements. I raised money and built a medical clinic in my village, which is good. But there is some cultural erosion taking place, which I don't like. I want to keep Sudanese culture.

I am seeing that maybe we've lost some good things because of modernity. Our people may think you've got to do away with your old culture entirely so you can have all those good modern things. They need to be informed that there's nothing wrong with their culture. Culture maintains your identity. It makes you respected and makes you respect others. Your culture becomes your color. It is who you are.

COMPASS POINTS

Where: Sudan is located in northeastern Africa. Duk County is in the southeastern part of the country.

Backdrop: The Second Sudanese Civil War (1983-2005) killed 1.9 million people and forced 4 million people from their homes. The "Lost Boys of Sudan," largely from the Christian south, were orphaned or separated from their families during attacks by Muslims from the north. Girls were raped, murdered, or enslaved, but boys often were away tending herds and could flee. They traveled to refugee camps in neighboring countries, and eventually thousands were brought to the United States. Sudan is ranked as one of the most unstable countries in the world on the Failed States Index and has suffered warfare in Darfur since 2003. It is the largest country in Africa, with a population of 11 million but only one doctor for every 100,000 people.

Visitor Information: http://sudan.net

During the Second Sudanese Civil War, **John Dau** *fled with other "lost boys" on a journey that spanned more than 1,000 miles and 14 years. At one point, he recalls, "Rebels were shooting at us, so we had to dive into water infested with crocodiles. Thousands of boys were eaten, drowned, shot, or captured." Dau began his education in a Kenya refugee camp, writing the alphabet in the dirt with a stick. When a U.S. church sponsored Sudanese refugees, he was brought to Syracuse, New York. "On my first trip to the supermarket I couldn't believe there was an entire aisle of food for cats and dogs," he says. "At home, even people have no food." The story of his cultural relocation and assimilation is traced in the 2006 Sundance Film Festival award-winning documentary* God Grew Tired of Us *and in the National Geographic book of the same title. Today Dau has earned an associate degree at Onondaga Community College and is pursuing his bachelor's degree at Syracuse University. He established the John Dau Sudan Foundation (www.johndaufoundation.org), which builds clinics and supports programs in southern Sudan. The foundation's Duk Lost Boys Clinic opened in 2007; until then, villagers had to walk or be carried 75 miles to the nearest medical facility.*

John Dau

Discoveries III

BO DEREK

SEVILLE, SPAIN

*n*early 30 years ago, I picked up a book called *All Those Girls in Love with Horses* by Robert Vavra and saw photos of a girl at the famous Andalusian riding school just outside Seville. She was very beautiful, with long black hair to her waist, and as she effortlessly asked the Andalusian stallion to leap and dance, her hair was always in sync with the flying mane and tail of the horse. I just wanted to *be* her.

Years later, my husband and I wrote a film, *Bolero*, around the photos I had seen. To make the movie, we traveled to Seville. I remember late one night checking into the Alfonso XIII, a grand hotel in the old part of the city. I was terribly jet-lagged and woke up about three in the morning with a sick, bleary feeling. I went to the window, opened the drapes and shutters—and got a wonderful whiff of orange blossoms.

Orange trees were in bloom all over the city, the streetlights outside were a beautiful amber color, and I had this overwhelming feeling of being in love with Seville. And I hadn't even seen it yet! I just knew—for no reason at all—that I had an affinity for this place. I don't believe in reincarnation, but if I lived anywhere in a past life, it was here.

The next day, I went to the nearby city of Jerez de la Frontera and met Alvaro Domecq, the director of the Royal Andalusian School of Equestrian Art, which is like the Spanish Riding School in Vienna, but older. I watched a demonstration of his magnificent gray stallions dancing and performing incredibly athletic movements.

Alvaro looked and me and said, "Which one do you want to ride?" I couldn't believe he would let me on one of those magnificent creatures. Sheepishly, I pointed to the one I thought was the prettiest, and within minutes the horse was leaping and rearing and dancing, with me as a grateful passenger. I immediately fell in love with these horses, the Andalusians, and I've been riding and breeding them on my small California ranch ever since.

The Andalusian is the oldest saddle horse known to man; it was the warhorse of the Greeks and Romans. It's more receptive to communicating with people than other breeds are, which is very rewarding. We human beings, as predators

Spanish horse and rider at the fair of Seville

and pack animals ourselves, relate very well to dogs. Cats, on the other hand, are a little more difficult, so they're more rewarding. Then you take a horse—a herd animal, a flight animal, not like us at all—and it's gratifying to have it even acknowledge you.

I love everything about Spanish horses, as well as the workmanship of the saddles, bits, and spurs. You can look at paintings by Velásquez from the 17th century and see the same tack on the horses that riders use today. And—typical of me!—on my first trip, I went nuts and bought a *traje corto*, a country riding outfit with high-waisted pants and a short jacket (I can still get into it).

Each year, I go back to Seville for the Feria, a spring festival, and stay at the Hotel Alfonso XIII. It feels like home because I lived there for so long when we were making *Bolero*. The hotel looks Moorish, with lots of arches and arabesques. During one Feria, I remember, two crazy horsemen rode their horses up the marble steps and right into the lobby.

Bo Derek

The hotel stands in the old part of the city, where I like to go out with friends and drink sherry—*jerez*—and eat cheese, olives, and Iberian ham. Of course, everything happens late in Spain; you don't eat dinner until midnight.

On my first trip to Seville, I strolled back to the hotel late one night after being out with some really fun people and having a great time. It was probably three in the morning, and I was walking through a narrow street in the old town. On one side, I could feel the heat radiating off the wall, where the sun had been, and on the other side of the street, the wall was icy cold from the night. Gypsy music poured out of the bars. I could smell orange blossoms. It was simply beautiful.

COMPASS POINTS

Where: Seville is the artistic and economic hub of southern Spain, as well as the capital of Andalusia.

Backdrop: Seville was occupied by the Moors in the eighth century and still shows many Moorish features. The city cathedral occupies the former site of a mosque and is the world's largest Roman Catholic cathedral. Hotel Alfonso XIII was built to house visiting heads of state at the 1929 Great Ibero-American Exposition. The royal riding school in Jerez de la Frontera is on the grounds of the Palacio de las Cadenas, a 19th-century baroque-style building designed by Charles Garnier, who also designed the Paris Opera. In the school's equestrian "ballet," horses perform high leaps, pirouettes, and other moves timed to music. The Seville Spring Fair (Feria) began in 1847 as a livestock fair, but has become a grand spectacle, with a parade of carriages and riders, all-night dancing of traditional Sevillanas, and a riverbank filled with decorated tents where party guests eat tapas and drink sherry.

Visitor Information: www.spain.info/TourSpain/?Language=en

Bo Derek gained national attention in the Blake Edwards movie 10, *earning her a Golden Globe nomination as well as launching a fashion trend with her hairstyle of cornrows and beads. Other credits include the film* Tarzan, the Ape Man *and television's* Fashion House, *and she was appointed a trustee of the Kennedy Center for the Performing Arts. Derek works on behalf of disabled veterans, tours with the USO, and is an honorary Green Beret. She is also a spokesperson for the Animal Welfare Institute, working to end horse slaughter.*

SYLVIA EARLE

THE DEEP OCEAN

*T*he ocean is the biggest ecosystem on the planet, and I love taking the plunge into any piece of it. My favorite part is below the "twilight zone," where light completely disappears—the deep sea.

Down there it's night all the time. Yet you're surrounded not by absolute darkness but by firefly light—living light, the light that is emanated by 90 percent of the creatures that live in the deep sea: jellyfish, sea cucumbers, little fish, bacteria. Most of the life in the deep sea has the capacity to flash or sparkle or glow. It's like diving into the Fourth of July.

There are luminous creatures even in shallow water, but they are especially abundant in the deep sea because there is no natural light. They use their luminescence for a variety of purposes. To see where they're going, flashlight fish actually shine a light ahead. Angler fish use illumination as a lure to tempt prey to come close enough to eat.

Other creatures use light to communicate with their pals out there in the dark. Among the little crustaceans called ostracods, the males perform a brilliant blinking sequence to attract females. The females will sit in the sand and look for males flashing a particular pattern—different species have their own signature flashes. If a female sees a male that she really can't resist, she leaps up out of the sand and they go do what it takes to make more ostracods.

Some creatures use light to evade predators. It wouldn't help octopuses that live in the deep sea to squirt out a puff of black ink to confuse would-be pursuers, as they do in shallow, light-filled waters. Instead, in the deep sea, octopuses squirt luminous ink. It's beautiful.

I love all the creatures in the deep ocean. So many people think of life on Earth as being only terrestrial. When we think of animals, we think of cats and dogs and horses, maybe birds and turtles and alligators, and some people even include fish. All are vertebrates, animals with a backbone. But people don't realize that most of life on Earth is in the ocean, and most of it is invertebrate, without a backbone or lungs.

To visit the deep sea, you take a submarine—that is, unless you want to do it just once. I love all subs (the Beatles' *Yellow Submarine* was my song; it just strummed my heartstrings). A small, one-person sub is like a diving suit that happens to be made of metal and acrylic instead of material. It's the closest thing to diving that you can have in a machine.

One of my favorites is the *Deep Worker*, the descendant of a sub that I helped develop called the *Deep Rover*. Your body is encased in a metal cylinder, and there's a bubble over your head that offers great visibility. Your hands are free because you drive the sub with your feet. The right foot is the accelerator and reverse pedal; to turn, you swing your toes back and forth. The left foot is for going up and down.

You get lowered over the side of a boat, and away you go. You're free in the sea! It takes only about five minutes to reach 500 feet. At the surface, the water is sky blue, but as you descend the blue goes through every shade you can imagine: sapphire blue, violet, indigo. Finally the blue becomes blue-black—and then just black.

Sometimes I like to simply drift, like a piece of plankton, looking at the light show that's all around. I may switch on the lights to see who is creating the bioluminescence. It may be long chains of salps, which are like sea squirts, each about two inches in length. They live in colonies, gelatinous chains that may stretch for 50 feet.

Seeing things like this makes me want to encourage other people to go down and see for themselves. You have to know about something before you want to protect it. Knowing is the key to caring. But as a species, we are woefully uninformed about the nature of the ocean. It's no wonder that we care so little, and love so little.

Most people don't realize that the ocean drives the climate, that most of life on Earth is in the ocean, and that we should care about it—because the ocean in turn is what generates most of oxygen in the atmosphere, absorbs carbon dioxide, and makes the planet hospitable for the likes of humankind and all the rest of life on Earth.

In the last fifty years, we have lost 90 percent of the big fish in the ocean. I say "lost," but we know where they went; they went into our stomachs. We ate them. In a few decades, we have also disrupted the nature of the planet through what we've put into the ocean—literally hundreds of millions of tons of noxious materials—and through what we've allowed to get in from the air, the carbon dioxide that is stimulating an acidification of the sea. It really is profoundly bad news.

An increasingly acidic ocean damages obvious systems such as coral reefs, but it also harms anything with calcium carbonate in its makeup—and that includes the backbones of fish or anything with a shell. Among these are tiny creatures

Jellyfish are among the glowing creatures of the deep sea.

Sylvia Earle

called coccolithophorids. We rarely hear toasts praising coccolithophorids, but if we knew more about them, we'd care about them and be inspired to see that they stay healthy—because they generate a lot of the oxygen we take in with every breath. They also produce food that takes up a lot of carbon dioxide and sustains other forms of life in the sea. They are the cornerstone of our life and our survival.

The good news is that we haven't lost the chance to turn things around. But we don't have a whole lot of time left to get back on track. I believe we have ten years—the most important period in the next 10,000 years—to take action that will secure an enduring future within the natural systems that sustain us.

This is one reason I'm driven not only to go into the ocean as often and as deep as I can but also to encourage others to go and see for themselves. Less than 5 percent of the deep ocean has been seen at all, let alone explored. And that's another reason I love it so. You never know what you're going to find.

I once had a memorable encounter in the ocean off the island of Lanai in Hawaii, at a depth where I could just barely see—light above, dark below. On the surface, the sun was shining and people were swimming, sailing, and doing all the things people do in the sunlit blue waters of Hawaii. But I was far below, 1,300 feet underwater.

I noticed something out of the corner of my eye that at first I thought was a piece of trash (you often see trash drifting around). But when I turned my little submarine and put my lights full on this thing, it turned out to be a big octopus, about six feet long.

The good news is that we haven't lost the chance to turn things around. But we don't have a whole lot of time left to get back on track.

It just kind of hung out, clearly looking at me. And for the next hour, this octopus and I literally danced. It would move back a bit, then move gently toward me. I would turn, and it would come over to me and stop. At one point, the octopus actually plastered itself on top of the submarine and looked at me through the bubble—it was a bit like a Gary Larson cartoon. It was mesmerizing, magical, a wonderful ballet with a creature from the deep.

I hope more people will go into the deep sea and look around. Little one-person subs are a wonderful way to get there. They're so simple to drive that even a scientist can do it! I look forward to the day when there's a Hertz or Avis Rent-a-Sub, where you can check out the submarine of your dreams and just take off into the sea.

COMPASS POINTS

Where: The "twilight zone" typically begins at 500 feet, but is sometimes as deep as 1,500 feet, depending on the clarity of the water.

Backdrop: The deep sea holds 90 percent of the total volume of the world's oceans. Cold, dark, and inhospitable to humans, the deep sea can be compared to outer space, and its exploration involves similar difficulties and expense. Water pressure increases with depth, and the pressure 2.5 miles down is 400 times greater than at the surface. The deepest point in the oceans, the Marianas Trench, is seven miles below the surface. Most organisms living in the deep sea depend on organic matter that falls down from the illuminated zones above.

Visitor Information: Many ocean resort areas offer submarine rides to tourists. Professional scuba training is available worldwide. And anyone can snorkel.

Called "Her Deepness," **Sylvia Earle, Ph.D.,** *has logged nearly 7,000 hours underwater; she set a record for solo diving to a depth of 3,300 feet. An oceanographer, explorer, author, and speaker, she was chief scientist for the National Oceanic and Atmospheric Administration and has led more than 60 expeditions, including the first team of women aquanauts and the Sustainable Seas Expeditions, a study of the United States National Marine Sanctuary sponsored by National Geographic. She has appeared in hundreds of television productions. Her books include* Exploring the Deep Frontier *and* Wild Ocean: America's Parks Under the Sea; *for children she has written* Hello Fish *and* Dive! *She was named* Time *magazine's first "Hero for the Planet" and honored with knighthood in the Netherlands Order of the Golden Ark, inclusion in the National Women's Hall of Fame, and medals from the Explorers Club and the National Wildlife Federation. Dr. Earle supports the International Union for the Conservation of Nature* (www.iucn.org), *representing 1,000 organizations devoted to conserving the diversity of nature and its resources.*

WILL FERRELL

A SUMMER COTTAGE, SWEDEN

My wife, Viv, is Swedish and has cousins who live in Stockholm. They have a little summer cottage out on a working farm about an hour southeast of the city. One of the farm's previous owners parceled off parts, built these little places, and now there are about 80 cottages.

We've been going to Sweden every summer since 1999, and we'd always go out to this farm for part of our visit. It's such a spectacular place that after four years we said, "Hey, if one of these little summer cottages ever comes up for sale, we'd be interested." And sure enough, about a month later Viv's cousin called and said there's one available.

So here we were, buying a place sight unseen—looking at photos from the Internet and having Viv's cousin check it out for us. And when we got there—well, it's definitely one of my favorite places on Earth. Our cottage is up on a hill and looks over a lake, a field, and the old main farmhouse.

A place to relax during Sweden's long hours of summer light

Our place is very traditional. Like all of the cottages, it's painted red with white trim. I don't know where they get that red, but I've heard that there's a specific clay in Sweden that gives them this pigment. It's close to fire engine red, but a little dirtier. The roof is red tile, but we have a little one-room guest cottage that has a grass roof.

It's kind of insane that we live there, because Viv is 5'10" and I'm 6'3". We're these huge people in what is essentially a dollhouse. Every summer, I try to guess how many times I'm going to hit my head. This last summer was pretty good: In five and a half weeks, I only hit my head five times.

The cottage has a combination living room and kitchen, a small bathroom, and two small bedrooms. That's our whole house. I don't think it's more than 600 square feet, maybe 800. But we love it that we're all kind of on top of each other. It's such a different experience. It's real family time.

A funny thing is that after we purchased the cottage, the owners said, "Oh, by the way, there's a Viking burial mound behind the property." And sure enough, we have this archaeological wonder in back of our house—just 20 feet away.

The Swedes are so low-key. In America it would be a selling point: "*Viking burial mound adjacent!*" In Sweden they didn't even mention it until after the sale. It was like, "Oh yeah, one more thing . . ."

In Swedish a cottage like ours is called a *stuga* or a *summar hus*. My wife is totally fluent in Swedish. So are our two boys. And I'm at the three-year-old comprehension level. I understand just enough to know if someone is saying something bad about me.

On a typical day there we might pack up our bikes and ride to a little lake nearby, which has a tiny beach and is popular with the local kids, and hang out there for the day. Or maybe we'll pick blueberries—and that's it! If we do one activity a day, we're doing good.

In Swedish a cottage like ours is called a stuga or a summar hus.

There's a really old beat-up tennis court on one of the farm fields near our cottage. We know just where the dead spots are, so we play this weird game of tennis where we try not to hit the ball into certain areas because it will bounce strangely.

We love having friends visit us from the States. They either love the place or they're like, "Okay…this is nice…but, uh, is there a city close by? Where's the Internet?!" It either drives people crazy or completely relaxes them.

Will Ferrell

Our friends who visited us last summer were fortunately of the "we love it" type. They described where we live as being like the Shire in *The Hobbit*.

One day we took them to see a thousand-year-old tree, which we visit on a walk every summer to see how it's doing. You know, it *is* kind of Lord of the Rings-ish there. It's really neat.

COMPASS POINTS

Where: The province of Södermanland is on the southeast coast of Sweden.

Backdrop: During the Viking Age (700–1066), Norsemen explored Europe and sailed as far as Newfoundland. Sweden has many Viking burial sites; the deceased and various grave offerings were covered with stones and soil to create a burial mound. The Swedish language has 29 letters with 9 vowels, and various dialects employ different intonations, stresses, and tones—all making it fairly difficult for English speakers to learn. Some words, though, look close enough to English to guess correctly—for example, *mannen* ("the man") and *en stinkande fisk* ("a stinking fish").

Visitor Information: www.visitsweden.com

*Actor, comedian, and writer **Will Ferrell** gained fame during seven years on* Saturday Night Live *with his memorable characters, such as Spartan cheerleader Craig Buchanan, and impressions of crooner Robert Goulet and TV host Alex Trebek. One of his sketches became the basis for the movie* A Night at the Roxbury, *and he went on to starring roles in* Old School, Elf, Anchorman: The Legend of Ron Burgundy, Stranger Than Fiction, Talladega Nights: The Ballad of Ricky Bobby, *and* Blades of Glory. *He has earned Golden Globe and Emmy nominations, as well as the James Joyce Award from University College Dublin's Literary and Historical Society. Ferrell supports Cancer for College (www.cancerforcollege.org), which provides scholarships for current and former cancer patients, and the Natural Resources Defense Council (www.nrdc.org), which works to protect wildlife and wild places.*

CARRIE FISHER

LONDON, ENGLAND

There are places you visit where—for some unexplainable reason—you feel at home. London has always been such a place for me. Certainly, there are tangible reasons why a city appeals to you, whether it's the kindness and humor of the people, the history, the theater, or the antiques markets. London has all these things, but something else, too—a thing that can't be put in words, a feeling that you've finally arrived after a long journey, that you've returned to a place where you belong.

I've loved London ever since I went to drama college there when I was 17. Its boroughs are familiar to me, having lived in many of them over the last 34 years. I attended the Central School of Speech and Drama in Swiss Cottage, North London—my first semester spent in a flat near the school, the next two semesters in Chelsea.

When I began filming the *Star Wars* series, I was living just off Kensington High Street. For the sequels, I lived first in St. John's Wood at Eric Idle's house. One night I woke up and there was a lot of noise downstairs. I descended to the living room only to find Eric partying with the Rolling Stones.

Town houses in London's Notting Hill neighborhood

Eric had returned for the weekend from Tunisia, where he was filming *Monty Python's Life of Brian*. He'd brought with him this horrible stuff he called the Tunisian Death Drink. Harrison Ford dropped by, and we stayed up drinking this wretched booze until dawn, when Harrison and I were picked up for our early call out at Elstree Studios in Borehamwood.

Having had no sleep, we could not be called hungover—in fact, we were still drunk. There's a scene in *The Empire Strikes Back* where you can actually see the effects of our debauched high jinks from the night before. It's when Han and Leia arrive in Cloud City to meet Han's old pal, Lando Calrissian—or Billy Dee Williams, depending on your point of view. It's the only time when Harrison and I actually smile during the entire trilogy—after our drunken arrival in the *Millennium Falcon*, fresh from the planet of Monty Python and the Rolling Stones.

Since then, I've returned to London at least once a year, usually staying with friends in their flat in Notting Hill, a place I consider a second home. I hope to move to London once my daughter goes off to college in a few years. To that end, I subscribe to *Country Life* magazine, and each month I pore through its pages of houses. It's my Sears, Roebuck catalog. I dream of one day owning a home with a thatched roof, hundreds of years old, and inviting my friends for tea.

COMPASS POINTS

Where: London is in southeast England.

Backdrop: Students of the Central School of Speech and Drama have included Laurence Olivier, Judi Dench, and Vanessa Redgrave. The design of the *Millennium Falcon* was inspired by a hamburger, according to *Star Wars* creator George Lucas, with the olive on the side being the cockpit. Notting Hill, a hub for artists and alternative culture, has been a setting for movies such as *Performance* with Mick Jagger and *Notting Hill* with Julia Roberts and Hugh Grant. Comic actor Eric Idle describes himself as the "sixth nicest Python."

Visitor Information: www.visitlondon.com

Carrie Fisher is an actress (Shampoo, When Harry Met Sally, *and most famously the* Star Wars *series, playing Princess Leia Organa), a novelist (*Postcards from the Edge, Surrender the Pink, Delusions of Grandma*), and a screenwriter, as well as one of the most sought-after "script doctors" in Hollywood. Fisher has toured the country with her one-woman play,* Wishful Drinking.

FANNIE FLAGG

FAIRHOPE, ALABAMA

When I was eight years old, my father and mother and I were driving down from Birmingham to Gulf Shores for a beach vacation. Around eight at night, we passed through a little town on the Mobile Bay. It was called Fairhope—a name that is still magical to me. I remember this one street, with a park overlooking the water. Spanish moss hung from the oak trees. Across the street were houses, and everybody had a little lamp on their porch. Wisteria vines and azaleas were blooming. I felt like I was inside of a painting.

We didn't stay, just passed through. But I remember thinking—you know how kids are—"When I get rich, I'm going to come live here!"

Years later, I moved to New York City, where I was appearing on talk shows, writing for *Candid Camera*, and acting in plays. I was doing too much and working too hard. It was a time in my life when I was very mixed up. I didn't know whether to stay in show business or to try to write.

I needed to think, so I went down to Fairhope and rented a little place. Every night, I'd sit by the water on the Orange Street Pier and watch the sun go down. In the little church behind me, at six o'clock, the bells would ring. And somehow, sitting there calmed me down. I don't know if I had been getting ready to have a nervous breakdown or whatever, but Fairhope healed me. It was very restorative.

About 20 years ago, I bought a tiny place there, on the water. I go every year and spend the spring or fall. When you walk outdoors, the temperature is the same temperature as you are; it's like you're literally part of nature. I sit out on my porch and watch the pelicans fly by, and the blue herons, ducks, and swans. The whole town is a bird sanctuary.

Despite what people think when they hear my Alabama accent, I didn't grow up in the country. I grew up in a city apartment in Birmingham, which was like Pittsburgh—very industrial, urban, fast paced. So I didn't come from a small town. I found one—which makes you love it even more. People who move to a small town are like religious converts; they're much more passionate about it than the people who grew up in it.

Fairhope is a sweet place, gracious without being saccharine. People are nice, and they make life easy. It sounds like a cliché, but nobody locks their doors. In many

Resident gulls on a Fairhope pier at sunset

ways, though, Fairhope is not a typical Alabama town. It was always very progressive, with lots of artists and writers. Upton Sinclair lived there. Winston Groom, who wrote *Forrest Gump*—he's my neighbor. So is Mark Childress, who wrote *Crazy in Alabama*. The first thing I ever wrote, I wrote in Fairhope. It sparks my imagination.

When I was in New York City working in show business, I had lost contact (and this sounds terrible) with "real" people—the people I wanted to write about. But in Fairhope, I thought: *Oh, okay! This is how people live.* They're nice to each other. They're not so frantic. In New York, people are trying to kill each other. I didn't want to step over somebody to get ahead.

A lot of these feelings came out in my book *Welcome to the World, Baby Girl!* The main character experiences very much what I did in getting back to a small town and kind of finding myself again.

I have a lot of old friends in Fairhope, including kids I went to school with. (So now they're *really old* friends.) There's a woman everyone adores named Betty Jo Wolf, who started a bookstore and art supplies shop called Page & Palette. She is like the heart of the town. (One of her twin granddaughters runs the store now.) Betty Jo gave me my first book signing in 1980.

When I wrote my latest book, *Can't Wait to Get to Heaven*, the store wanted me to do a signing. Because it was my birthday, they surprised me and took over a bed-and-breakfast inn on a beautiful acre of land. They had a thousand people there dressed in white, as angels. They had little girls dressed as angels, up in the trees. That's what the people of Fairhope are like.

I fall in love with places like I do with people, and I think I may be in love with Fairhope. They may have to call a psychiatrist on me. I am just attached to it. When I'm lonesome, I think: *Oh! I've got to go home*. It's a magical little town, and you feel a special something there that you don't feel in other places.

Sometimes I think about that drive I took with my parents when I was a little girl, passing through Fairhope in the night. The town impressed me so much that I spent my whole life trying to get back there. And here is what's so wonderful: I live on exactly that same street I saw when I was eight years old.

COMPASS POINTS

Where: Fairhope is in southern Alabama, on the eastern shore of Mobile Bay.

Backdrop: The town was founded in 1894 by followers of economist Henry George as a utopian community they felt offered "a fair hope of success." In 1907, educator Marietta Johnson founded the progressive School for Organic Education in Fairhope, offering nature study, crafts, folk dancing, and a lack of tests and grading; the school is still in operation.

Visitor Information: City of Fairhope: www.cofairhope.com

The author of Fried Green Tomatoes at the Whistle Stop Cafe, **Fannie Flagg** *was nominated for an Academy Award for her screenplay adaptation of the novel. Her other books include* Daisy Fay and the Miracle Man, Standing in the Rainbow, *and* A Redbird Christmas. *She has acted in Broadway shows such as* The Best Little Whorehouse in Texas *and films, including* Five Easy Pieces *and* Grease, *as well as appearing on game shows, notably* Match Game.

JEFF FOXWORTHY

CAMP SUNSHINE, DECATUR, GEORGIA

One of the cool things about my job is that I've literally been to all 50 states numerous times. I've seen everything there is to see in our country—but this camp in Georgia for kids with cancer is one of my favorite places.

Everybody has some kind of fear in their life, but you can't imagine being eight years old and scared that you're not going to make it through the next school year. To me, the counterbalance of fear is hope. And when you take all these kids who have been fighting this monster by themselves, in a hospital room or at home, and you send them to camp, it works wonders.

Camp Sunshine is out in the Georgia woods. They have little cabins and a big mess hall where the kids beat on the tables and sing silly songs every night. It's so funny: If you go down to the swimming pool on day 1, you see a bunch of kids all sitting very prim and proper around the pool. By day 4, the side of the pool is full of wigs and prosthetic arms and legs, and there are just kids playing in the pool. They get together and realize, *Hey, I'm not alone in this thing.* The camp is kind of a magical place.

The kids get to be kids. They may have chemo in the morning, but by afternoon they're out horseback riding. In the middle of the night, they sneak out and stick pink flamingos in front of other cabins. Parents aren't allowed, although they can come to Talent Night at the end of camp.

I've hosted the show many times. The kids are short on talent but very big on enthusiasm, and they don't get embarrassed easily. When kids are sick like that, they're kind of old souls anyway. They've learned what's important in life and what's not.

I always humiliate myself in front of them and dress totally goofy—like in shorts with a top hat and cowboy boots. I sing every stupid song I've ever known. The kids do a skit and always put shaving-cream pies in the counselors' faces. And the counselors always act like they don't know what's coming. This has been going on for 30 years!

Everybody has fun—and some of these kids haven't had any fun or laughed in a long time. To me, the appeal

> *When kids are sick like that, they're kind of old souls anyway. They've learned what's important in life and what's not.*

Campers sing after each meal—"Lean on Me" is a favorite.

of comedy in every form is that it's like a release valve. We all get stresses and worries built up inside us, but when you hit that little "laugh" button, you relieve some of the pressure for a little while.

At the talent show, I try to make every kid feel at ease enough to do *anything*—including, in one case, burping the alphabet. One time, a camper of Korean heritage sang a Korean song, which seemed to be out of tune and went on *waaaay* too long. When he finished, I told him that that was my *very favorite* Korean song.

All the kids know I'm the host of a TV show called *Are You Smarter Than a 5th Grader?* Once I asked a five-year-old, "So, tell me, Danielle, is your mommy smarter than a fifth grader?" She answered, "No! She *never* gets that far when she plays!" I shook my head and told her I'm not smarter, either.

I particularly remember one little boy at the talent show. He was the last to come on at the end of the night. He was just the cutest little thing, but he was tiny for his age—probably eight or nine years old, but not much above three feet tall. He had some type of brain tumor; they'd done radiation on it, and it had made him blind. And he gets up there with all the confidence in the world. I hand him the microphone, and this little kid starts singing: *"This little light of mine, I'm gonna let it shine!"*

Jeff Foxworthy

You look out in the audience, and everybody out there has tears rolling down their faces—and they're smiling at the same time. And you realize: That's it! Right there! This boy has been dealt a hand nobody should ever have to be dealt, especially a little kid, and he has not let it subdue him in any way. You can see this great little spirit shining through all of it.

To me, Camp Sunshine is a celebration of life, instead of the fear of dying. It's a place of hope.

COMPASS POINTS

Where: Camp Sunshine takes place in Rutledge, Georgia, about 50 miles east of Atlanta.
Backdrop: Camp Sunshine allows children with cancer to participate in the same activities found at traditional summer camps—swimming, archery, horseback riding, tennis, pottery, fishing. Campers publish a daily newspaper and take part in evening dances and shows. Each summer about 375 children attend the camp, which is overseen by a full medical staff and 200 volunteers.
Visitor Information: www.mycampsunshine.com

One of the country's most respected comedians, **Jeff Foxworthy** *is the largest-selling comedy recording artist in history, as well as a multiple Grammy Award nominee and author of more than two dozen books, including* Jeff Foxworthy's Redneck Dictionary *and the* New York Times *best-sellers* Dirt on My Shirt *and* How to Really Stink at Golf. *He hosts the television quiz show* Are You Smarter Than a 5th Grader? *and* The Foxworthy Countdown, *a top-25 country music radio show.*

MORGAN FREEMAN

THE CARIBBEAN

*T*he British Virgin Islands may be the most beautiful set of islands anywhere in the world. I'm a sailor, and I love the channel that stretches about 30 miles between the islands of Virgin Gorda and St. John, like a little inland sea. The water is perfectly clear. And the color! It's mostly deep blue, but in the shallows the water turns aquamarine because of the white sand below. In some places, the water is green.

I'm your basic warm weather person, and the median temperature in the Virgin Islands is 86 degrees Fahrenheit—right up my alley. When you step outside in the morning, you're already relaxed because you're not cold. And usually you've gone to the Caribbean on vacation, so there's nothing, really, to stress yourself over.

Another place I like to sail is the Grenadines, starting at the island of Grenada and heading north to St. Vincent. I gunkhole the islands (to *gunkhole* means to go from anchorage to anchorage). You just stop where you like, throw out a hook, and catch your dinner. Or maybe someone comes along in a little boat and offers you a fresh catch.

I don't like to cook, but a sailor who wants to eat has to cook. If I can get crew who are willing to do the cooking, why, they're very welcome—although I'm so much of a loner that this doesn't happen very much. Most of the time, I sail solo. It's terrific, the best way to live.

I have a special spot I love—but I don't want to tell anyone about it. That's the problem with idyllic spots: You talk about them, and they don't last. Let's just say it's an island with a bay that has a series of deep inlets. The water shallows out so you can have a pretty good anchorage in just 14 feet of water. The swimming is delightful. And the water is always calm, because you're so protected up in those inlets.

One year, I had an unusual guest there. My grandkids and I were swimming. I had gotten out of the water, but they were still splashing around when suddenly they rushed out, saying there was this "big thing" in the water. I went overboard and looked, and sure enough there was a barracuda—maybe a four-footer, no more, just a small one.

Aqua-blue Caribbean bay lined with white sand, perfect for anchoring

I tried to chase it away, but apparently it had a sense of humor: It would always swim just ahead of me. The barracuda stayed around, and every morning we'd get up and look under the dinghy where there was shade. There it would be! We nicknamed him Barry. We'd always check: Is he there? Yep, there's Barry!

I guess the life lesson to learn in a place like the Caribbean is how to relax. Nowadays people are in stressful situations a lot, and the hardest thing to learn is to just let it all go. I've found a place that lets me do that.

COMPASS POINTS

Where: The Caribbean Sea is a part of the Atlantic Ocean that lies southeast of the Gulf of Mexico. The Virgin Islands are located east of Puerto Rico in the Leeward Islands, while the Grenadines are northeast of Venezuela in the Windward Islands.

Backdrop: The Virgin Islands archipelago is divided into the British Virgin Islands (a British overseas territory) and the U.S. Virgin Islands (an insular area of the United States). In 1493 Christopher Columbus became the first European to sight the islands, naming them Santa Ursula y las Once Mil Virgenes (St. Ursula and Her 11,000 Virgins)—later abbreviated as Las

Virgenes. Supposedly, he named one island Virgin Gorda ("Fat Virgin") because it looked like a plump, reclining woman. The Grenadines chain is divided between two island nations: St. Vincent and the Grenadines, and Grenada. Called the Spice Isle, Grenada produces one-fifth of the world's nutmeg, as well as cinnamon and cloves. In 2004, 90 percent of Grenada's homes were destroyed or damaged by Hurricane Ivan. Some species of barracuda can grow to six feet in length. Barracudas can swim at 27 miles per hour during bursts of speed. Although they are predators, they very rarely bite human beings—and they bite only once, because human beings do not resemble their typical diet.

Visitor Information: British Virgin Islands: www.bvitourism.com; Grenada: www.grenada explorer.com; St. Vincent and the Grenadines: www.svgtourism.com

Highly regarded actor **Morgan Freeman** *has received Oscar, Golden Globe, Screen Actors Guild and Obie awards. Starting his career in off-Broadway theater and on the children's television show* The Electric Company, *he broke into film and created memorable characters in* Driving Miss Daisy, Glory, The Shawshank Redemption, Along Came a Spider, Bruce Almighty, Million Dollar Baby, Batman Begins, *and* The Bucket List. *The Grenada Relief Fund that he helped establish to rebuild that island after Hurricane Ivan has been restructured as Plan!t Now* (www.planitnow.org), *which provides information to help communities in high-risk regions protect themselves from the effects of storm and hurricane disasters.*

ARTHUR FROMMER

UBUD, BALI, INDONESIA

The town of Ubud lies in the central highlands of the island of Bali — and at the epicenter of the island's life and culture. Far away from the big resorts along the coast, Ubud is largely unaffected by the harsher, more commercial forms of tourism. The shoreline has been inundated with beach-loving, nightclubbing sorts, a hard-drinking, hard-living crowd. But Ubud is away from all that. It gets a gentler sort of tourist who is genuinely interested in absorbing the culture, the religion, the life of Ubud.

And, of course, Bali as a whole is away from the life of Indonesia, being a Hindu island in a huge Muslim country. The Balinese try to maintain their Hindu traditions, and Ubud's visitors include a great many backpackers fascinated by Hindu traditions and respectful of them. At night in the village squares of Ubud and neighboring towns, Balinese dances are frequently performed for tourist and resident alike, without distinction between them.

You often see religious processions, with children all dressed up and the beautiful Balinese people walking along. They're very happy to be witnessed and don't resent the presence of tourists. The Balinese are so confident about their own culture, and so in love with it, that they actually want you to take part in it. As a traveler, you are constantly invited to ceremonies. On my first visit, in just a short while, I was invited to a cremation ceremony (funerals in Bali are joyous occasions) and to a wedding. I went to both of them and never felt that I was an outsider.

The Balinese are a lovely people who have very limited material possessions. Bali has no heavy industry, but there are little crafts villages surrounding the town of Ubud, almost like gems on a necklace. Each village specializes in a different craft, and the people earn a hard living by making wood and stone sculptures, oil paintings, wood furniture, and batik.

At the end of the long day, many of them go to a nearby stream to wash away the sweat of their labors. On my first afternoon in Ubud, I went to a river where about a hundred men, women, and children had doffed their clothing, without any self-consciousness at all, and were bathing in the fresh waters — laughing, conversing, and smiling at one other. They immediately waved to me and my wife, inviting us to plunge in. Little children shouted *Hello! Hello!* — their one word of English.

Traditional wooden carvings at temple in Ubud, Bali

All this makes Ubud a lovely place to stay. If you drop in to the tourist office, they will recommend various little hotels—or if you wish, you can opt to stay with a private family. There are a great many homes in Ubud that accept overnight guests, including some where they put you in a hammock on the porch! It is one of the cheapest destinations in all the world, but it's a joyous atmosphere.

It makes me remember an experience I had many years ago that eventually led me to write *Europe on $5 a Day*. I was in the U.S. Army in Germany and had a short leave, so I went to the beautiful city of Copenhagen in Denmark. But I had failed to make reservations, and when I arrived at the railroad station, they told me there wasn't a hotel room to be had in all of Copenhagen. It was high season, and therefore I'd have to stay in a private home.

I was extremely upset, because I was a young GI and had heard that Copenhagen was the center of all the vices in the world—and I wanted to be right in the heart of it. Instead, I was being sent to this bourgeois neighborhood. I took a bus, got off at the right street, and knocked on the door of the house. I was so depressed that I was scarcely civil to the people who greeted me.

Arthur Frommer

They showed me my room and told me that if I got up early in the morning before they did, I could make my own coffee, and they showed me where the bread was, and so forth. I got up the next day and made myself coffee and toast. Then I went outside to a bus stop and waited with some Danes who were taking the bus to go to work downtown. And suddenly it dawned on me: For the last 12 hours, I had lived like a resident of Copenhagen, not a tourist. I was viewing a totally different life, one that was unseen by most tourists. This was an important lesson, and I began to value authentic experiences when I traveled abroad.

You get this same feeling when you go to Ubud. The Balinese whom you meet away from the coastal resorts and in their own authentic setting, like Ubud, are gracious and welcoming. They invite you to attend their gatherings. They seem to enjoy your presence. They are among the most generous and outgoing of all the people I've met in a long life of travel, and their culture is a beautiful one, of which they are justifiably proud, and without the slightest show of arrogance.

They are a model for all of us.

COMPASS POINTS

Where: Ubud is located in the central foothills of the island of Bali, in Indonesia.

Backdrop: More than 90 percent of the Balinese people are Hindu. A major center of art and culture, Ubud appears to be a single town but actually consists of more than a dozen villages, flanked by terraced rice fields, steep ravines, and rivers. Ubud is the home of the Balinese royal family. Its name comes from the Balinese word *ubad* ("medicine"); originally, the town was known for medicinal plants. When German artist Walter Spies settled there in 1927, he and other foreign painters entertained Noël Coward, Barbara Hutton, H.G. Wells, and Charlie Chaplin. They also trained local artists and co-founded an artists' cooperative, leading Ubud to become Bali's cultural hub. Today the town has many galleries and several museums, including Museum Rudana, which reflects the Balinese philosophy of Tri Hita Karana, in which art is meant to help create world peace, brotherhood among peoples, and prosperity. Among Balinese arts are *batuan* (painting), *mas* (wood carving), *celuk* (jewelry), and *batubulan* (stone carving). The dances of Bali are based on stories from the *Ramayana* and other Hindu epics, and they include the well-known monkey dance. The Ubud Monkey Forest, a nature reserve and temple complex, is roamed by two hundred long-tailed macaques.

Visitor Information: http://bali.my-indonesia.info; www.balitourismboard.org

Acknowledged as the nation's foremost travel authority, **Arthur Frommer** changed the way Americans travel when he wrote Europe on $5 a Day in 1957. Aiming to help travelers see more for less, his book introduced itself as a guide "for tourists who own no oil wells in Texas." The write-ups showed the joys of traveling cheaply and offered smart, sometimes provocative asides, such as: "Here the beds are somewhat narrow and suitable only for couples, to whom this book sends best wishes," and "I like the hotels on Rue de Buci, a block away from all the existential activity." Frommer's travel guides have since grown to more than 350 titles. The Yale-educated lawyer also founded Frommer's Budget Travel magazine, writes a widely read newspaper column, and is the host of a radio show syndicated nationwide. He offers travel opinions and budget tips regularly at www.frommers.com/blog. Frommer supports the Community Service Society of New York (www.cssny.org), the American Civil Liberties Union (www.aclu.org), and the Smile Train (www.smiletrain.org).

JANE GOODALL

GOMBE, TANZANIA

I was 26 and just arrived at Gombe. I can still remember going along Lake Tanganyika in a little boat, looking up at the shoreline and the thick forest and the valleys, and thinking: How on *earth* am I ever going to find a chimpanzee here?

It was July, so it was the dry season. There was that very special smell of dried grass and dried earth. There had been a couple of fires, so a faint tang of smoke hung in the air.

At our camp, we got the tent set up with help from the game scouts. I was there with my mother, who had volunteered to accompany me because British authorities resisted the idea of a young woman living alone among wild animals in Africa. We had a cook, and I was told I had to employ one of the local people as a guide because I wasn't allowed to be out in the forest on my own.

Back then, girls didn't do that sort of thing. At home I was a person who didn't care about clothes and parties and hairdressers and things like that. Well, I did like the parties, but they were not important. But on an earlier trip to Africa, I had met Louis Leakey, who decided I was the person he wanted to go out and look for chimps.

Once the tent was up, I set off on my own up the slope. I can never forget the extraordinary feeling of being up there, looking down over the lake and hearing birds, particularly the mourning doves, and then baboons barking in the distance. The air was hot. I was in khaki trousers, a shirt, and tennis shoes, sitting there and not believing that this could possibly be happening to me. It was just so amazing.

Later we had supper, Mum and I, by a fire. Then I pulled my little camp cot out under one of the palm trees. I could see the stars and hear the trees swaying above me. It was like a dream; none of it seemed real. I fell asleep, as I would for many nights, under the rustling palm fronds.

It took a while before I saw any chimps, and even longer to get them habituated to me. I would sit on a peak—the Peak, I called it—with my binoculars, wearing the same-colored clothes each day. And gradually, the chimps got used to me. It just took a lot of patience.

The breakthrough came after about five months when one of the chimps, David Graybeard, came to my camp to feed on the ripe fruits of an old nut palm.

He noticed some bananas on the veranda of my tent and took them. He returned each day while the palm was ripe—and we left bananas out for him.

He began to bring others with him—Goliath, Flo, Olly, and Mike—and when Flo became sexually receptive, all the community males followed her! They were scared of coming to this place with the tent, but Flo was so attractive they just had to.

In October came the rainy season, and a very different world. The first rains bring with them the smell of parched earth receiving the water. It's like an awakening; little flowers come up from the ground, and the smells are rich as rich can be. Walking through the forest when it's damp, you no longer have dry leaves rustling underfoot, and the air is smooth and soft.

The breakthrough came after about five months when one of the chimps, David Graybeard, came to my camp to feed on the ripe fruits of an old nut palm.

The pitter-patter of raindrops on the forest canopy is absolutely fantastic—until it starts *really* raining. Then the branches and palm fronds sway wildly, you hear the growling of thunder, and lightning comes down among the trees. It's exciting, and you absolutely understand why the chimps do their rain dances. All through the rainy season, they put on these wild displays at the start of very heavy rain. It's as if they're defying the elements. I don't think they like the rain, because then they get wet and cold, especially at night.

These rain displays are spectacular. The chimpanzees charge over the ground, with bristling hair, lips bunched in a furious scowl, stamping their feet, slapping their hands. They're roused, stimulated. They sometimes run upright. They drag huge branches, throw rocks. And this may last for ten minutes or more. Afterward, they sit huddled, looking cold and miserable. And they push out that great long lower lip to catch the raindrops that trickle down over their noses.

I went out from camp every day, unless it was absolutely pouring early in the morning. But it never seemed to do that; it waited until I had climbed up the Peak, and *then* it poured. So I seldom had a lazy morning. I was up at six every day, including weekends. (How would I know it was the weekend, anyway? The chimps didn't.) By 3 p.m., you feel very weary because of spending a lot of the day on your tummy, crawling, with vines catching your hair.

The forest is for me a temple, a cathedral under the skies, made of tree canopies and dancing light. And I especially love it when it's raining gently and everything is quiet, save the soft pattering of falling drops. That's heaven on earth for

A young chimpanzee plays in a tree at Gombe Stream National Park.

My Favorite Place on Earth

me. I can't imagine going through life without being tuned in to the mystical side of nature. So many people are too busy nowadays.

Today, the Gombe National Park headquarters has been built more or less where my first camp was, with staff housing and so on clustered down near the beach. But once you get past that—which I do as fast as possible—you're back in the same old magical forest.

Nothing has changed there, except that the trails are wider. And they went and put a little bench up on the Peak for tourists to sit on. That really upsets me. To me, it was sacrilege to put it there. I used to go up on the Peak and could so easily feel 26 again, exactly how I felt back then. But now the bench is a sort of looming presence; I can't get it out of my mind. It's a log, nothing fancy, but I don't like it being there.

Outside the park, though, the trees are all gone. When you fly over, you see this little jewel of a forest surrounded by cultivated fields. The park is small, only 30 square miles—although if you ironed it out, it would be more than double that size. It's all steep up, steep down.

As you travel along the lake by boat from the nearest town, Kigoma, you pass the devastated slopes. Sometimes I arrive late, and then suddenly on the dark air comes this unbelievable smell, just the most poignant smell of vegetation and flowering plants. And immediately I am transported to the Gombe that I love, a wilderness of beauty.

COMPASS POINTS

Where: Gombe National Park is located in western Tanzania, 10 miles north of Kigoma on the eastern shore of Lake Tanganyika.

Backdrop: Of the original group of chimpanzees that Jane Goodall studied in Gombe, all are gone. Fifi, a tiny infant in 1960, died in 2004. But their offspring live on. In the wild, chimpanzees can live to be 50 years old, maybe longer. They are human beings' closest relatives, with about 98 percent of their genes in common with ours. A chimp, however, has about five times the upper body strength of a man. While perhaps two million chimpanzees lived in West and Central Africa at the turn of the twentieth century, today only about 220,000 survive in all of Africa, due to loss of habitat, poaching of infants, and hunting for meat. U.S. laboratories house some 1,300 chimpanzees, and most conduct invasive research; around 500 chimps have been retired from lab use and live in sanctuaries in the United States and Canada.

Jane Goodall

Visitor Information: www.tanzaniatouristboard.com; www.tanzaniaparks.com/gombe. htm. Accommodations in Gombe Stream National Park include a luxury tented lodge, a self-catering hostel, a guest house, and campsites.

When **Jane Goodall** began studying chimpanzees in 1960, she had no college degree, but subsequently got a Ph.D. in Ethology at Cambridge University. She changed primatology with her observations of chimps using tools and hunting, and her insistance that animals have distinct personalities, minds, and emotions. She later found that chimpanzees engage in a primitive form of warfare. Her awards include the Medal of Tanzania, National Geographic's Hubbard Medal, and Japan's prestigious Kyoto Prize. She is a UN "Messenger of Peace" and a Dame of the British Empire. The Jane Goodall Institute (www.janegoodall.org) continues researching. It initiated Tacare ("Take Care"), a program for community-centered conservation and sustainable development in Africa, and founded Roots & Shoots (www.rootsandshoots.org), whose student groups in 100 countries work on projects for people, animals, and the environment. Goodall travels more than 300 days a year to lecture, meet with decision makers, and spend time with youth, and since 1986 has remained nowhere for longer than three weeks consecutively.

JOSH GROBAN

SOUTH AFRICA

*E*ver since I was a kid, I've been interested in African music. I grew up listening to people like Youssou N'Dour and Baaba Maal, as well as Paul Simon singing with Ladysmith Black Mambazo on *Graceland*. So when my band and I got word that we were finally going to tour South Africa, we were absolutely beside ourselves.

We had all been touched by the music that comes out of that part of the world. There's something about the rhythm — the way the guitar sounds and the bass drives the song and the sounds flow. South African pop music just had a visceral effect on me and always made me feel good.

When we finally got to South Africa, so many things happened in a three-week trip that it left us all completely awestruck. First, the fans were so welcoming, and the concerts were everything we'd hoped. I had heard that the fans in South Africa had taken to my music before people in any other country.

Second, I listened to as much music as I could. I walked around Cape Town, one of my favorite cities in the world. It's a natural wonder, with beautiful weather, beaches, and Table Mountain in the background. I found some great small record shops that had all sorts of CDs you can't find at home, even in places like Amoeba in L.A.

I came across a song called "Weeping," by a group called Bright Blue, that was kind of controversial when it first came out. It's about Nelson Mandela, the end of apartheid, and moving forward and embracing our common humanity during times of conflict. I was really taken by the song, and I realized that the message, unfortunately, is still relevant today.

The third and most important thing that happened in South Africa was being invited to meet Mr. Mandela in Johannesburg. I went to his office, which also acts as something of a museum, with memorabilia such as his prison uniform and his diary, opened up to a page about understanding and compassion that was written about halfway through his enormous sentence.

What can you say to Nelson Mandela? Anything I said would be a moment wasted, instead of hearing what he might have to say to me. So I took in everything I could, and told him that I was in his corner for anything he wanted me to help with. I've been very honored to be an ambassador for his foundation ever since.

Cape Town's Victoria & Alfred Waterfront, set below Table Mountain

After the meeting, we got into a car and went to see firsthand one of his feeding shelters in Soweto. There is so much beauty in South Africa—nature, the music, the people—and yet there is so much poverty, the likes of which I had never seen in my life. It made me realize, in a very different way from just hearing about it or seeing it on TV, what's going on there.

All the kids were lined up outside the shelter and singing a song when we drove in. It was right in the neighborhood where the kids lived, and many of them got their one meal a day at the shelter—a concrete building with a hole in the wall where someone would pass out two slices of bread with peanut butter in the middle, and a glass of powdered milk.

The kids could also do arts and crafts there. Most of their fathers were gone, having either left or died, but the mothers were there learning to do things like garden and make crafts. It was a twofold project—feeding the kids and also teaching the mothers how to sustain their families and make money.

The head of the shelter talked about the cost of doing what they do, and it's minuscule. I realized that the money I had in my wallet, in my back pocket, could feed these kids for a month. It made me see that in a place where the main thing is just keeping people alive, a little bit goes a very long way.

That trip to South Africa inspired my own foundation. My fans and I together have raised almost $2 million. We try to find places that fall through the cracks, where a little bit of money can do an extraordinary amount of good. One is Zamimpilo, an orphanage in South Africa where we've brought in running water, beds, a jungle gym, and other things.

Another place we visited on our trip was a perfect example of the contradictions in South Africa. It's called Sun City, and to get there we drove among people living in tin shacks. Eventually we found ourselves at an enormous man-made resort, more luxurious and palatial than anything I'd ever seen in my life. From there, we went on a safari and saw cheetahs and lions.

All over the country, every time you drove somewhere that was majestic and wonderful, you had to drive through such depths of despair. Seeing the two sides together, we realized South Africa's potential for prosperity, but were also saddened that this very new free country has so much work to do.

On our trip, we took in the great things South Africa has to offer, and we also walked away feeling like we wanted to give back to the country that had given so much to us.

Back home, I decided to record two songs for my *Awake* album with African musicians, and I thought I'd be going back to South Africa to do it. It turned out that a lot of the people we wanted to work with happened to be in New York, so we went there. I got to meet musicians who were my heroes, like Joseph Shabalala, who founded Ladysmith Black Mambazo. He told me how much music means to him and to his country.

There is so much beauty in South Africa—nature, the music, the people— and yet there is so much poverty.

Going into the studio to record "Weeping" with these musicians reminded me of being in choir in elementary school. When you sing with people whose musical style is different, you have to try not to lose track of who you are vocally but at the same time to blend in with the other voices.

It was a master class, and just being with the musicians from South Africa was a childhood dream come true. I worked on that track with many of Paul Simon's *Graceland* musicians. By coincidence, Paul was rehearsing next door and came in to hear the song. And so everything—from my early love of South African music to my trip there—came full circle.

Josh Groban

COMPASS POINTS

Where: The Republic of South Africa is located at the southern tip of Africa.

Backdrop: The South African constitution recognizes 11 official languages, English ranking first in government and business but only fifth among languages spoken at home. Nelson Mandela spent 27 years in prison during the anti-apartheid struggle; later he helped lead the country's transformation to multiracial democracy and served as president. His 46664 Campaign, named after his prison number, fights HIV and AIDS in Africa. South African musician Joseph Shabalala had repeated dreams in which he heard certain Zulu harmonies, inspiring him to form Ladysmith Black Mambazo. Visitors to Cape Town can reach the top of Table Mountain by foot or cableway.

Visitor Information: www.southafrica.net; www.southafrica.info/travel

Josh Groban is a Grammy-nominated singer-songwriter whose album sales total more than 23 million. They include his self-titled debut Josh Groban, Closer *(featuring the hit "You Raise Me Up"),* Awake, *and* Noël. *He has had two PBS specials—the first of which became the top-selling DVD of 2002—and has sung at the Super Bowl, the Oscars, and the closing ceremonies of the 2002 Winter Olympics with an audience of two billion people. He also performs at numerous charity events. The Josh Groban Foundation (www.grobanitesforcharity. org) focuses on efficient, underfunded organizations that benefit children in need around the world through the arts, education, and health care.*

MATT GROENING

KAUAI, HAWAII

I grew up in the fern-filled forests of Oregon, where my pals and I trudged through gentle downpours and made our fun by kicking soggy pinecones down muddy trails. So for me, the rest of the world feels pretty much like a parched desert.

My father, Homer (named after the poet), was a filmmaker obsessed with water and everything water-related—from frozen (skiing) to salty (diving) to leaky (turning a faucet into a musical instrument for one of his movies). In the 1960s, Homer made a bunch of short films about surfing and the beauty of undersea life, and I used to wonder, "Why the hell are we living in *Oregon?!*"

It's not as if my dad didn't know about life in a tropical paradise. Before I was born, he was an Air Force pilot, and in the early 1950s the family had lived an idyllic life on the north shore of Oahu. A decade later, I got to start going on trips back to Hawaii, when my dad shot surfing movies, and about 25 years ago I discovered the island of Kauai.

It's the wettest of all the Hawaiian islands, and Kauai's daily rainfall reminds me of the moisture soaked into my bones from my Oregon youth. The sweet little north-shore town of Hanalei, where I often rent a house, sits in a valley below Mount Waialeale, which is reputedly the rainiest place on Earth. I love staring up at the cliffs where a dozen waterfalls seem to spring out of nowhere after a storm. A few years ago, I found myself blissing out by floating lazily a hundred yards offshore in Hanalei Bay with my pal Mark, and I pointed up to the mountain and declared, "That's the wettest place on Earth." Mark looked around at the ocean in which we were bobbing and said, "I thought *this* was."

Kauai is the oldest of the major Hawaiian islands and also the one most affected by erosion. You can see it in action at Waimea Canyon—"the Grand Canyon of the Pacific"—which is a mile wide and 3,000 feet deep, with red and orange walls cut by what looks these days to be a trickle of a river.

Another wet place is the roadless Na Pali Coast, with stunningly high cliffs and countless amazing landmarks, including Waiahuakua Cave, the second longest sea cave in the world. Every time I visit the island, I drive to Ke'e Beach at the end of the road and hike the fairly steep two-mile Kalalau Trail to Hanakapiai

Jumping from the rocks is one way to reach the water.

Beach. The trail continues another nine occasionally treacherous miles, but so far I've left that to less wimpy campers and wild goats. If it starts to rain, I turn back, because the path gets slippery, and even on dry days I somehow invariably return with mud-filled shoes.

It generally rains about a half-hour a day on Kauai, but in the winter I've seen it rain 12 out of the 14 days I was there. As consolation, you do get a rainbow or two every day, and the tourists jump in their cars when it rains, leaving the beaches empty and gorgeous.

My favorite spot is Lumahai, just around the corner from Hanalei. It's famous as a backdrop for the movie version of the musical *South Pacific*, and lots of fashion spreads are shot here. A short, narrow trail from the highway leads to a crescent bay, where people ignore the warning signs and leap into the ocean from a big rock. My kids do it over and over again, although I haven't yet gotten the nerve. I just wait in the water and hope that no one gets conked on the head.

I also like a snorkeling beach a few miles to the north called Tunnels. Scuba diving there is easy and inviting, with lots of fish and eels, and the occasional harmless whitetip reef shark. There's nothing like swimming into an underwater cave, seeing a sleeping shark, and realizing: *There's no way out of here except past him.* You just try not to bother anybody.

I also have enjoyed diving at Niihau, a tiny island 18 miles west of Kauai. It's a privately owned island, so you can't land on it, but with dive operations such as Bubbles Below, you can snorkel and dive offshore. The first time I went to Niihau, I asked the boat's skipper how things were looking in the water. "Kind of sharky," he said. Another time, my pals and I frolicked in a bay while a few dozen dolphins swam by. They weren't paying much attention, just mocking us with their ability to swim fast.

Just off Niihau is one of my favorite dive spots, Vertical Awareness, a vertical reef that drops 400 feet in crystal clear water, with black corals that look like small trees. Diving there was one of the great experiences in my life—the water was so clear I felt like I was hanging in space.

Kauai is full of secret treasures, and every year I discover a few more. The thing that sold me on the island so many years ago was a north-shore wet cave with a secret room. Off an unmarked trail, you clamber down some rocks into the cave to find a large pool filled with rainwater. Very *cold* rainwater, as you discover when you swim the 50 feet across the pool. Then you slip through an indentation in the rock and end up in what they call the Blue Room. Somehow the sunlight shining down through the clear water reflects off the bottom of the pool into this chamber. It creates an otherworldly blue light. The experience is eerily quiet and dreamlike.

I've been coming to Kauai for 25 years, and each visit astounds me. The staggering beauty of the island forces my brain to slow down, and I think someday I won't leave.

COMPASS POINTS

Where: Kauai lies northwest of Oahu in the Hawaiian Islands.
Backdrop: Kauai is called the Garden Isle for its abundant vegetation. Mount Waialeale (5,148 ft.) is shrouded by clouds 300 days a year and receives some 460 inches of rain annually (an average of 1.5 inches a day). Despite claims by locals on Kauai, the mountain is the second rainiest place on the planet, edged out by Mawsynram, India, by just 7 inches. More than 70 movies and television shows have scenes shot on Kauai, ranging from Elvis

Presley's *Blue Hawaii* to *Raiders of the Lost Ark* and *Jurassic Park*. The town of Hanalei was the animated setting for 2002's *Lilo & Stitch*. The beach at Hanalei stretches for two miles. Waimea Canyon is ten miles long and was cut by the Waimea River, which flows with rainfall from Mount Waialeale. Some cliffs along the Na Pali Coast rise 4,000 feet above the ocean. The coast has no automobile road and is accessible only by boat or foot. The often treacherous Kalalau Trail crosses five large valleys in just eleven miles on the way from Haena State Park to Kalalau Beach. The trail is often eroded, with muddy puddles, crumbling rock, and narrow stretches perched above cliffs hundreds of feet high.

Visitor Information: Kauai: www.kauai-hawaii.com; Hawaiian Islands: www.gohawaii.com

Interviewee **Matt Groening** *is the writer and cartoonist who created* The Simpsons, *which has been on television since 1987, making it the longest running American sitcom. He also created the Emmy-winning* Futurama. *Since 1980, Groening has drawn the weekly comic strip* Life in Hell, *which is collected in books such as* Love Is Hell *and* The Big Book of Hell. *He enjoys all things ocean-oriented, and the moment he ducks his head underwater, he stops thinking about cartoons.*

TONY HAWK

MY HOUSE, ENCINITAS, CALIFORNIA

I travel at least half my life, if not more. So being at home is how I get away—from crowds, the press, and the hectic lifestyle of being on the road.

I grew up in San Diego, so I feel at home here. My wife and I bought a house a couple of miles from the beach, and in back I built my own skate park.

We gutted the house because we wanted to make it feel like a really cool modern hotel. We travel so much that we decided to mimic our favorite places to stay: Chateau Marmont in L.A., W hotels, Morgans Hotel Group. We actually took pictures of the furniture in lobbies and in our rooms, and we had a furniture designer imitate it. It's modern-type furniture, with clean lines and things that are sort of perpendicular to each other. The furniture looks pretty warm—a lot of browns and earth tones.

A skate park resembles an empty swimming pool with added features.

My younger sons are nine and seven, and their room is sort of a big playroom. They have a giant bunk bed with a slide, all the main video-game systems, and a pinball machine. In my office, for editing skate videos, I've got this giant Mac desktop with a big monitor—and two terabyte hard drives, because video is all about storage.

We have a traditional swimming pool with a diving board, a Jacuzzi, and all that. And behind our guest house is the 4,000-square-foot skate park. It's very well rounded, with bowl elements as well as elements of an actual urban landscape, like benches and handrails for grinding. The skate park looks like an empty swimming pool with all these street features rising up in the middle.

There's exactly one neighbor family who can see the skate park from their house, and only from their upstairs. (I went to them with the plans to make sure they were okay with it.) So I can just try new moves at home and not feel self-conscious that a crowd is watching me learn—and fall. I can goof around and not worry about spies!

The park is right on the edge of a canyon, and you can see the ocean from there, with sunsets right on the water. I can't complain: I get to skate for a living, and I can play video games and say that I'm working!

COMPASS POINTS

Where: Encinitas is 25 miles north of San Diego, California.

Backdrop: The city of Encinitas has 58,000 residents, its average daily high temperature is 72°F, and its primary industry is growing ornamental flowers, particularly poinsettias. Among its districts are Leucadia, Cardiff-by-the Sea, and an old-town section by the beach. Local surfing spots include Swami's, a beach below the bluff-top meditation gardens of the Self-Realization Fellowship, a spiritual organization founded in 1920 by Paramahansa Yogananda. The first skateboards, probably created in the late 1940s or early 1950s, were wooden boxes or boards with roller skate wheels attached. Surfers used them for fun away from the beach, hence the name "Sidewalk Surfing"; in 1964 Jan and Dean had a hit record of the same name, having reworked the lyrics of the Beach Boy's "Catch a Wave" to make it a song about skateboarding. A terabyte of stored computer information is one trillion bytes. The first one-terabyte hard drive was marketed in 2007. Videos submitted by online users to YouTube.com—among them skate videos—fill 600 terabytes, or 600 trillion bytes, of storage.

Visitor Information: www.encinitaschamber.com

Skateboarding's primary icon, **Tony Hawk,** turned pro at age 14 and brought the sport to mainstream attention. He is best known for his "900"—making two-and-a-half rotations (900°) in the air before landing back on the pipe—a trick that existed only in theory until he landed it at the 1999 X-Games. He has also invented many tricks, including the Stale Fish and the Airwalk. The Tony Hawk's Pro Skater series is one of the most successful video-game franchises of all time. His autobiography, Hawk: Occupation Skateboarder, was also a best-seller. He has received ESPN's ESPY Award as Best Alternative Athlete and is a repeat winner for Favorite Male Athlete in the Nickelodeon Kids' Choice Awards. Touring arenas nationwide, Tony Hawk's Boom Boom HuckJam presents top skateboarders, BMX riders, and freestyle motocross riders in a choreographed extravaganza with live music. The Tony Hawk Foundation (www.tonyhawkfoundation.org) has awarded more than $2 million to help finance public skate parks in low-income areas.

Discoveries IV

TONY HILLERMAN

SHIPROCK, NEW MEXICO

I got back from World War II, carried off a hospital ship on a stretcher. There was no place to go home to, because my dad had died and our farm in Oklahoma had been sold. My mother, a nurse, had moved to Oklahoma City to work, so I headed there. And, since Mom was the only person I knew in the city, I went down to the USO.

There I met a pretty red-headed girl, whose dad had drilled a well out on the Navajo Reservation in New Mexico. Of course, during the war, you couldn't get any gasoline, or anything else, so the well had just sat there, but now he wanted to go back and reopen it. He needed somebody to drive a truck out there for him.

I didn't have a job—I didn't have a driver's license either, and according to the Army my left eye was blind, so I had a patch over it—but I told the girl, Hell, I'd drive the truck out West…if she'd go along.

So her dad hired me, and I drove the truck out to the reservation. The well was way out in the boonies on the rez, and one day we had to stop because a bunch of Indians on horses were coming through, and we let them go by. I was impressed; these guys were really fancily dressed, and they were carrying all sorts of stuff, including a decorated bow and some arrows.

When we got to the place where the well was drilled, I asked a rancher about them. He said it was a Navajo family, and that both sons were Marines who were shot up in the Pacific. Now the boys were home again, and they were having a Blessing Way ceremony for them, to cure them. I asked if I could go see it, and he said sure, as long as you behave yourself.

So I went to the ceremony, and it made a tremendous impact on me because they weren't curing the boys of their wounds—they were trying to restore them to *hozho*, the Navajo word for harmony. They shot arrows at symbols of evil, the same arrows I had seen. The goal was to help the boys forgive and not be mad at the Japanese or anybody anymore. I thought this was a wonderful thing.

One of the Navajo boys' grandmothers had brought some food, and I got invited in. I ate a lot of freshly cooked mutton—which I must say wasn't very tasty, even when you're hungry. But it all made a hell of an impression on me. I thought: This is quite a tribe.

New Mexico's towering Ship Rock is sacred to the Navajo.

I had grown up in Potawatami County, Oklahoma. Our friends were Pota-watami and Seminole and Sac and Fox; they were farmers, too. But none of them reminded me of the Navajo, and the Navajo stuck in my mind.

I knew I didn't want to be a farmer anymore, having grown up in the great American dust bowl—and we didn't have a farm left, anyway. I decided maybe I could be a writer, because all my life I did love to read. So I thought, I'm going to learn more about the Navajos, and maybe I'll use them as characters and the rez as a setting. I imagined a Navajo policeman, and away we went. I started to write *The Blessing Way,* which was my first book.

I haven't got over my hang-up with the Navajos. I still think they're wonder-ful people, and I'm full of stories about them. For example, the Navajo have their own police department, and once I asked one of the detectives, a sergeant I knew,

What do you guys do when the victim of the crime thinks it was done by a witch? How do you find a witch?

And he said, Well, it's pretty easy. Out here, witches are the epitome of evil, and you look for a person who is relatively wealthy, who has more than he needs, and who isn't helping his friends and kinfolk. In other words, you look for somebody who's greedy. I know you urban Americans don't consider that as being evil, he said, but we do.

I liked that idea. I'm really fond of that culture, always will be.

One of my favorite spots in Navajo country is Shiprock. It's a strange mountain. It's volcanic, and the Navajos have a wonderful story about it. In the old days, they lived west of where they are now. They had an enemy that was really giving them a hard time, and they called on the Holy People to help them. And the Holy People did: The earth started heaving under the Navajos like a tidal wave, moving them eastward. When it finally stopped moving, it left them where they are now. And this mountain popped out of the ground — Shiprock.

When I'm starting a book, I usually go out there and hang around, smell the air, all that sort of thing. When you write, you need to get to quiet places where you can sit and think and produce some ideas.

Practically everywhere you go on the rez, if you talk to people you'll get a story of what happened up this canyon, or why that is a holy place. I'm a born and raised Christian, so I believe in God. And I believe that the good Lord who created us likes us all, whether we're Navajo or black or Chinese or whatever. I have no doubt that He helps the Navajo along. So I respect their holy places.

One thing that appeals to me about Shiprock is that the volcanic eruption created a great long crack in the earth that runs northward from the actual pinnacle. It produced a kind of Great Wall of lava rock that's four or five feet thick in some places, and it's high. Because it's lava, it breaks up; there are places where there are holes through it, and the winds whistle through.

When I'm starting a book, I usually go out there and hang around, smell the air, all that sort of thing. When you write, you need to get to quiet places where you can sit and think and produce some ideas. So I drive on the dirt road that runs out along the volcanic wall, and see what is going on. And nothing is ever going on! Because nobody lives anywhere near there. That's the beauty of it. There's always lots and lots of silence.

COMPASS POINTS

Where: Shiprock is located on the Navajo Reservation in the Four Corners area. It is 13 miles southwest of the New Mexico town of Shiprock, off U.S. 491 (formerly designated U.S. 666).

Backdrop: The Navajo name for Shiprock is Tsé Bit' A'í, or Rock with Wings. In the 1870s, Anglo-Americans named it Shiprock because they thought it resembled a 19th-century clipper ship under sail. Towering 1,800 feet above the desert plain, the pinnacle is the eroded throat of a volcano that erupted some 30 million years ago. Tony Hillerman's novel *The Fallen Man* is set around Shiprock.

Visitor Information: www.newmexico.org

The late **Tony Hillerman,** *who died in 2008 shortly after this conversation, wrote mystery novels that take place in the Four Corners and are imbued with a deep understanding of the landscapes and native peoples of the Southwest. His books include* Dance Hall of the Dead, Skinwalkers, *and* A Thief of Time. *Hillerman was honored with Edgar and Grand Master awards from the Mystery Writers of America, as well as the Navajo tribe's Special Friends of the Diné Award. He supported St. Bonaventure Indian School* (www.stbonaventuremission.org) *in Thoreau, New Mexico, which works to lift Navajo students out of poverty through education.*

JEAN HOUSTON

AMERICA BY TRAIN

We were always being called. The phone would ring in New York, and when my comedy-writer father hung up, he was likely to say, "Okay, everybody, off to Hollywood." Or Chicago. Or New Orleans. And the packing would begin. My hero's journey was a very literal one that took me to 43 states before I was 12. We were always on the train—traveling to shows, from shows, with shows.

The 1930s through the early 1950s were the golden age of radio, and comedy writers were racing around the country through a continental turnstile. They were the migrant workers of showbiz, following the laughs wherever they took them: New York, Chicago, St. Louis, Los Angeles, Dallas, New Orleans, Miami, Washington, New York.

Cross state lines—cross counties even, in those days—and the world shifted. America had not yet melted; the pot was still brimming with many different and distinct cultures and ways of speaking, eating, worshiping, relating. Back then, before television was in every household, America was not yet homogenized.

My itinerant family was always traveling through different realities, in unexpected circumstances. A mom-and-pop roadhouse (so different from today's characterless franchise highway inns) was invariably a unique place to stay, filled with characters right out of a 1930s movie—men who gave long-winded disquisitions like W. C. Fields, pranksters and tricksters and con men and con ladies, people who made their living on the road.

Characters were everywhere. In the early 1940s, when I was just a tiny kid, we were somewhere in the South where they still had Fourth of July parades that featured the ancient remaining soldiers of the Civil War. An old Confederate man, who was probably a drummer boy back in the Civil War, came over to me. He was a long, lanky fellow in his gray uniform, and he leaned down and shook my hand: "Young lady, I want you to know you're shakin' the hand that shook the hand of my pappy—and my pappy shook the hand of Thomas Jefferson!" I've always remembered him.

To the people who worked on the train, I was known as the "little little girl with the big big voice." My mother was from Sicily and her family all sang opera,

Mid-twentieth-century passenger train engine

Jean Houston

so I was trained in it. I would sing "Ah, Sweet Mystery of Life" and other tunes. One time in the middle of the war, a very drunken sergeant came down the train aisle and said, "Hey, tha'sh no little girl right there, no little girl has a voice like that: That's a *midget*!"

When you change realities as often as we did, reality itself gets to seem very fluid— astonishing, bizarre.

Because we traveled constantly, my father felt he needed roots, so he brought our animals along. We took our dog, Chickie, who had a brief career in the movies playing one of Daisy's puppies in the Dagwood and Blondie series. We took the cats. We took two ducks named Louella and Hedda, after the gossip columnists.

And we had a great big turtle, named Somerset after novelist Somerset Maugham, whom he greatly resembled.

At one point, we even had a swan. As my father brought the swan into our stateroom, he told my mother: "Oh, Mary, don't worry. You can hypnotize a swan like you do any bird. You just put its head under its wing." Of course, the swan woke up and started biting everybody, and when it bit the conductor, we all got thrown off the train in Albuquerque.

I think those early travels gave me an ability to adapt pretty quickly. They prepared me to deal with different cultures and peoples, which is what I do now; I've lectured or taught in a hundred countries and worked intensively in 40 cultures. So the "train trip" has been going on through my whole life, giving me a sensibility for different people and ways of seeing.

By the time I was 12 years old, I had attended 20 schools, from Biloxi, Mississippi, to Bemidji, Minnesota. They were very different from schools today. One week it would be the friendly drone of a one-room schoolhouse, then a few weeks later the lock-lipped terror of a "religious" school, then a progressive school where it was all finger-painting and dancing (which I loved), or a school for Army brats.

Needless to say, my real education took place on the train. My mother believed in the classical dictum that the mind's muscles are built up through memorization. "Jeanie," she said to me one day shortly after my third birthday. "We're going to put biceps on your cortex. Now repeat after me, 'To be or not to be. . . .'"

"Be not be. Buzzzzzzz. Look, Mommy, I'm a bee. Buzzzzzzz. I'm gonna sting you."

"That is the question," my mother persisted.

"What is the question, Mommy?"

By the time I was ten, I had been made to learn by heart whole scenes from Shakespeare's plays, sheaves of poems, great chunks of Dante's *Divine Comedy*, and (from my father) all 67 stanzas of "The Face on the Barroom Floor."

The rest of my education went apace. I was always on a collision course with history, and geography was something that sped by at 80 miles an hour. "Jeanie, quick, look out the window! There goes the Continental Divide, and it was there that Chief Stony Foot captured the traveling minstrel show and put them to work tanning buffalo hides."

When you change realities as often as we did, reality itself gets to seem very fluid—astonishing, bizarre. Quite simply, reality shows you its real face and becomes mythic. Each phone call that sent us "on the road" and into the train was for me an open door to a mythic life.

Whenever I dream about my childhood, there is often the accompanying score of a train moving along the tracks. Today I live in Oregon, not far from the train tracks. To hear the train going by in the night…*whooo, whooooo*…is hugely comforting to me. (The plane I'm on nearly every week just doesn't do it.)

For me, the train represents the long voyage—not home, but to many homes. Because we moved so much and were on the road so often, every place became a home. But the continuity of it, my ultimate home, was the journey itself.

COMPASS POINTS

Where: Amtrak has several long-distance routes that carry passengers across America from coast to coast and on north–south journeys.

Backdrop: In 1941, there were 414,414 miles of railroad track in the United States, but today there is less than half that number at 171,061 miles. The last documented Civil War veteran died in 1956. "Ah, Sweet Mystery of Life" has music by Victor Herbert and lyrics by Rida Johnson Young: "Ah! Sweet mystery of life / At last I've found thee / Ah! I know at last the secret of it all!" Among America's most famous trains was the *Twentieth Century Limited*, an express that ran between New York and Chicago from 1902 to 1967, covering the 960-mile route in just 16 hours. To board the train, passengers walked on a crimson carpet that was rolled out at both ends of the journey, giving rise to the term "red-carpet treatment." The train boasted such amenities as a barbershop and secretarial services. Its streamlined locomotive and passenger cars, designed by Henry Dreyfuss in 1938, made the *Twentieth Century Limited* what many consider the greatest American train in history. Another popular train, the *California Zephyr,* ran from 1949 to 1970 between Chicago and Oakland, California, scheduled so that passengers traveled through the dramatic western scenery during daylight hours. The train's dome car enabled viewing in all directions.

Visitor Information: For U.S. train travel: www.amtrak.com; for Amtrak and private rail tours: www.vacationsbyrail.com

Jean Houston, Ph.D., is a founder of the Human Potential Movement. Her 26 books include the autobiography A Mythic Life *and* A Passion for the Possible, *which was also a PBS special. With her husband, Dr. Robert Masters, she established the Foundation for Mind Research, and she is the founder and principal teacher of the Mystery School, a program of cross-cultural, mythic, and spiritual studies. An advisor to UN agencies in human and cultural development, she also worked with the Dalai Lama and served as advisor to several U.S. presidents and first ladies. Dr. Houston has taught philosophy, psychology, and religion at universities around the world and presented the William James Lecture at the Harvard Divinity School.*

JIANG ZHI

PAVILION—BEIJING, CHINA

This pavilion is in a neighborhood of Beijing called Tongzhou. In China, where there is a garden there must also be a pavilion. The pavilion is a very important part of Chinese architecture and landscape. It reflects one unique aspect of Chinese culture: From the small, you see the grand.

The culture also places great emphasis on the balance between "the emptiness" and the soul. A pavilion is small and empty, and its "emptiness" holds the vastness of the universe. As the scholars of ancient China described it: "When inside a pavilion, there is nothing else. And this is how one owns the view to the universe."

The pavilion has always been a favorite subject for poetry, and it is also a place where romantic affairs take place. Therefore, a pavilion is a place for action, whether that action takes place physically or emotionally.

Is the woman being pulled into the spotlight, or is she pursuing it? There is no right answer. The viewer can decide what he wants to make out of it. What I am

"Things Would Turn Unbelievable Once They Happened 1, 2006" by Jiang Zhi

trying to do here is to describe a mysterious event and attempt to turn the viewer into the narrator.

COMPASS POINTS

Where: Tongzhou is in southeast Beijing, in the People's Republic of China.

Backdrop: Tongzhou district lies at the end of the Grand Canal; as the water and land approach to central Beijing, its name means "The Place for Passing Through." Jiang Zhi's photograph is titled "Things Would Turn Unbelievable Once They Happened 1, 2006." The photographer used a wire to hold up the model (a technique common in filmmaking to lift an actor), and then erased the wire from the image. Otherwise he employed no special effects and created the image on the site, using a low shutter speed in the dark. The photograph is part of a two-year project studying illumination. "Light and darkness are relative," he says, "and they coexist. Light, just like darkness, is an original power or strength of life."

Visitor Information: China: www.cnto.org

Jiang Zhi was born in 1971, graduated from the China Academy of Fine Arts, and currently lives and works in Shenzhen and Beijing, China. He has exhibited his work in China, Europe, Thailand, Brazil, and the United States, where he is represented by DF2 Gallery in Los Angeles (www.df2gallery.com).

CHRIS JOHNS

WILD DOG RESEARCH CAMP—
OKAVANGO DELTA, BOTSWANA

My journey with African wild dogs began in the late 1980s when I was working on a magazine story in the Serengeti for *National Geographic*. One day I came across a pack of dogs hunting a wildebeest. I didn't know much about them, but I was fascinated. They just struck me as animals I'd like to spend a lot of time with. I am a longtime lover of dogs and have five at home on our farm in Virginia—my own pack.

Seeing the African dogs started me on a quest. Eventually I met wildlife biologist John McNutt, nicknamed "Tico," and went out to his Wild Dog Research Camp on the edge of the Moremi Game Reserve in the Okavango Delta. The camp has nice double-roofed tents and a community kitchen outdoors. During the day, baboons wander through, and a lot of nights we'd have lions.

My tent folds out on top of my Land Rover, so I sleep up there and some nights I'd hear this *BDRRRbdrrbdrr* sound, quite loud. I'd wake up, look out through the bug netting in my tent, and be eye to eye with an elephant—literally inches away. Occasionally, elephants would bump the Land Rover and rock it a little bit while I was sleeping. The Okavango is truly a wild place.

I'm a mountain guy; I grew up in Oregon, in the Cascade Range. The Okavango Delta, on the other hand, is one of the flattest places on Earth, but I still find it to be a gorgeous landscape, with floodplains and forests. In a week, you can identify 130 different kinds of birds. At a place called Black Pools, you might be in the middle of 250 elephants as they're drinking.

My assistant David Haman and I would get up at first light and spend the morning with one of Tico's research packs, photographing the dogs. In the evening, we'd go with another pack. African wild dogs are second only to elephants for fascinating social behavior, and they have family values we should all aspire to. When they make a kill, the weaker, older dogs and puppies are always fed first. I enjoyed watching the dynamics as the alpha male kept the pack working together, not being overly strict but not too lenient, either.

The dogs' interaction with humans is fascinating, too. They came to know Dave and me well, and we had quite a deep connection. If a visiting scientist or

Two pups play tug-of-war over animal skin

student went out with us in the Land Rover, the dogs noticed it right away—and took issue with it! They seemed suspicious and were wary, almost like they were saying, *We didn't give you permission to bring this new person to our den.*

The dogs have a playful manner about them as well. As the morning heated up, I would often relax and take my hat off my head. Twice I had a wild dog sneak up behind me, grab the hat out of my hand, and take off, flipping it in the air. Then they'd play chase and tug of war with it. They're absolutely delightful animals.

The wild dog is the most endangered large carnivore in Africa, so it was an incredible privilege to be with them. The danger is mostly through loss of habitat, although many of them are killed by lions. Also, because wild dogs are very efficient hunters, they have a bad reputation with farmers and a lot have been shot.

Over the years, Tico and I have gotten to know the cast of characters in the packs. We'll be looking at a yearling dog, and Tico will say, Well, that's the great-grandson of Belle—a female we used to see often in the late 1990s.

African wild dogs are impossible to domesticate, and that's part of their appeal. Their metabolism is so high, and they're so smart, it would be an travesty to try.

Physiologically, they're running machines—and incredibly graceful animals.

I remember one dog I just loved, named Zermatt, who was beautifully colored. He was a magnificent hunter and made about 70 percent of the pack's kills. Sometimes I think of him now that I've stopped being a field photographer and work in an office. On a hectic day, my mind calls up a picture of him on the hunt. I see him running toward a huge sage bush about five feet high—and as he jumps at 35 or 40 miles an hour, he turns and spins in midair and comes down on the other side. The grace of that!

When they're running, African wild dogs have this blissful look on their faces, like this is what they're meant to do—and this is where they're meant to do it.

COMPASS POINTS

Where: The Okavango Delta is in Botswana, in southern Africa.

Backdrop: The Okavango is the world's largest inland delta, a green oasis of life in the Kalahari Desert. The delta includes floodplains with knee-deep water, forests, grassy plains, and papyrus-lined waterways. African wild dogs have a patchwork coat of black, yellow, and white; their scientific name, *Lycaon pictus*, comes from the Greek for "painted wolf." No two dogs have the same markings, which makes individuals easy to identify. The dogs' vocal communications include a sharp alarm bark, a rallying howl, and twittering and whining as part of their greeting ritual.

Visitor Information: www.botswana-tourism.gov.bw/attractions/moremi.html

As a field photographer for National Geographic *magazine,* **Chris Johns** *traveled all over the world shooting more than 20 stories, including eight covers. In 2005, he was named editor-in-chief, and under his leadership the magazine has been extensively redesigned to attract a new generation of readers and has won six National Magazine Awards, including the award for General Excellence for large-circulation magazines in 2006 and 2007. His acclaimed books include* Wild at Heart: Man and Beast in Southern Africa, Valley of Life: Africa's Great Rift, *and* Hawaii's Hidden Treasures. *Johns supports Save the African Wild Dog (www.save-the-african-wild-dog.com).*

JACK JOHNSON

PIPELINE—OAHU, HAWAII

I grew up near the Pipeline, and in high school I'd be out there surfing just about every day. When it was flat, we'd just go snorkeling and look around the reef. When it got really big and stormy, four or five friends and I would band together—safety in numbers!—and see what we could do.

There were really beautiful moments. When the waves at the Pipeline get to a certain size, they break about half a mile off the shore. You're out there looking back at the island, and it's a view that's completely different—in a humbler way, it's like an astronaut looking back at Earth. It feels like you've stepped out of your day-to-day life.

When the Pipeline is really firing, you can get deep into the tube of the wave. You sit out in the channel and watch your friends take off over the ledge. They lose their weight for a second as they drop in on a huge wave. Then they position themselves just right and disappear into the tube. Finally the wave shoots all this spray out the end, and your friend comes flying out. What he did seems impossible.

Then almost by muscle memory you do the same thing. Riding inside the tube makes you feel more connected to everything around you, and in harmony with nature.

When I'm on tour I like to get out surfing, and it could be anywhere. If I go for a few weeks without using those muscles, I stop feeling like myself, so we always find a spot. We were in England in summer and surfed at a beach with stormy little waves in Cornwall. Even in Germany, we surfed in the Rhine River.

After I've been home for about a month, I just fade back into my daily routine, surfing at the Pipeline. The Pipeline has taught me a lot of lessons. When I was 17, I got pretty badly hurt there. That was definitely a changing point in my life. I'd been invited to surf in the Pipe Masters, which still is probably the most prestigious surf event. I made the finals and was feeling pretty high on myself. At that age it's easy to start thinking you're indestructible.

Then about a week later I smashed my face into a coral head. Looking back, it was scary how close I came to dying. I was knocked out underwater for a second. I knew I'd hit my head really hard, and I thought, I just need to relax and get some energy before I swim. But I started dozing off. It reminded me of mornings when

Surfer gets barreled at Hawaii's Pipeline.

Jack Johnson

you're so tired that you can't stop pushing the snooze button. You know you're late for work, but you keep thinking, *I'll just get five more minutes' sleep, and I'll still make it in time.*

I kept trying to give myself a few more seconds. Eventually, I dozed off to the point where I tried to take a breath, swallowed a bunch of water, and woke up. I realized, *Whoa, I'm drowning here.* I was really lucky to get to the surface and make it to the beach. I lost three of my teeth—I've got fake teeth in the front now—and needed about 150 stitches in my face from hitting the coral.

Getting hurt out there really humbled me at an age when I probably could have used a little humbling. It also taught me the power of nature. I had taken it for granted. I'd been sort of toying with it and thinking I was indestructible. After that, I felt very mortal.

COMPASS POINTS

Where: The Pipeline (aka the Banzai Pipeline) is a reef break off Ehukai Beach Park on the North Shore of Oahu.

Backdrop: The name Pipeline was first used in a 1961 Bruce Brown surf movie. Surfers who made names there include Butch Van Artsdalen and Kelly Slater. It is one of the world's most dangerous surf breaks and has claimed more lives than any other (partly because it is so crowded).

Visitor Information: www.gohawaii.com

Singer and songwriter **Jack Johnson** *began surfing at age five and launched his musical career with* Brushfire Fairytales *in 2001. Other albums include* On and On, In Between Dreams, Sleep Through the Static, *and the sound track for the film* Curious George. *He directed the surf films* Thicker Than Water *and* The September Sessions. *Jack Johnson's All At Once Community* (www.allatonce.org) *is a social action network that connects people with nonprofit community groups, enables discussion, and promotes change.*

ROBERT TRENT JONES, JR.

MOSCOW COUNTRY CLUB, RUSSIA

*O*n the day in 1994 when Russia's first golf course opened, I taught a soldier in the Red Army how to hold a golf club, and he took a few practice swings. He hit some balls down the fairway, and I remember thinking: *The Reds are on the greens! The Cold War is over!*

Opening the Moscow Country Club had taken 20 years of discussions, political delays, and construction. As the course's designer, I had a mission. I wanted to bring the Soviets the game of golf, which I'd been involved with all my life, hoping that it would act as a goodwill measure to enable Russians and Westerners to compete on playing fields, not through war.

I had traveled to the USSR in 1974 with my father and Dr. Armand Hammer, who early in the era of Détente offered Soviet leader Leonid Brezhnev the idea of having a golf course. Brezhnev wanted to attract Japanese and Western businessmen, but there were no golf courses in the Soviet Union.

The first property we looked at was on the Volga River. The Soviets entertained us there, and we drank vodka. We toasted our mothers, we toasted the river, we toasted everything. I was in my 30s, but that was too much vodka even for me. So we went and took a sauna nearby in the traditional Russian way, where they slap you with switches from birch trees to get your blood moving. Then we all jumped in the Volga together, skinny dipping. The Americans looked pretty happy, the Russians a little solemn, but it was an afternoon of bonding.

Five years later, the Soviets finally settled on a beautiful property called Nahabino, out past the Moscow Ring Road. They wanted the course to be somewhat hidden, because they didn't want to show golf to the people, so the site was in a deep forest.

For years, nothing happened on the building of the course, but we persisted. As historian Alistair Cooke said, I was trying to take an individualistic sport to a collective society. When Mikhail Gorbachev came to power, the plans were dusted off again and—after 14 years of discussions and negotiations—we finally signed a deal to start construction. It was formally announced at a U.S.–Soviet

As we were building the third tee, we actually did find a World War II Russian bunker used to hold the perimeter against the Nazi invasion.

Water hazard, hole 15, at the Moscow Country Club

missile summit on June 1, 1988. President Reagan and Secretary of State Schulz wanted something peaceful to announce, so while the politicians were talking about ICBMs, we were talking about golf balls.

During construction, we had a problem getting approvals from the U.S. Department of Defense. The guy reviewing the contract didn't play golf and thought that "bunkers" had military significance, which held things up. As we were building the third tee, we actually did find a World War II Russian bunker used to hold the perimeter against the Nazi invasion. We left the bunker there, next to the tee, as an artifact of history.

For our course superintendent, we hired a Russian who had been a missile expert. At the time, the government was reorganizing the Red Army and many of its support facilities, and he wanted to convert titanium from ICBMs to peaceful purposes. He used some decommissioned titanium to make a putter and a driver, which he gave to me. It was truly turning swords into plowshares. I still have the putter, but eventually I gave the driver to President Clinton. He swung it around, joking, "I hope it's not radioactive, Bob!"

When the course opened in 1994, we played the first Russian Open—or as I called it, the "Russian Closed" because the officials decreed that although there were 50 of us playing, only Russians could win. But none of them were good golfers yet.

During the opening ceremonies at Nahabino, I was very moved. There in the forest of fir, larch, and birch trees, I could feel the deep Russian soul expressed—Tchaikovsky's passionate lyrical music, Dostoyevsky's early existentialism, the great poets like Gorky, and the feeling they convey of the Russian landscape. But it's hard to explain unless you've literally had your hands in Russian soil, as I did.

At the ceremony, Deputy Foreign Minister Ivan Ivanovich Sergeev, who was instrumental in getting the golf course built, said: "I have spent my whole life as a civil engineer, trying to better my country for my countrymen. Now that I can speak freely because of *perestroika*, I can tell you that my entire country is an ecological cesspool. But here in Nahabino, one garden is growing. There is hope!"

COMPASS POINTS

Where: The Moscow Country Club is located off the Volokolamskoe Highway past the Moscow Ring Road, near Novo-Nikolskoe village.

Backdrop: The club offers residential leases on "dacha-miniums." Moscow's playing season is short, running from mid-May to mid-October, but in June the "white nights" make it possible to play golf all day and all night. The father of Communism, Karl Marx, and free-market economist Adam Smith both played golf; Marx learned while he was working on *Das Kapital* at the University of London.

Visitor Information: Russian National Tourist Office: www.russia-travel.com; Moscow Country Club: www.lemeridien-mcc.ru

*Golf course architect **Robert Trent Jones Jr**. designed the Princeville Golf Resort on Kauai, the Links at Spanish Bay in Pebble Beach, and 250 other courses in locations from China to South Africa, from Kashmir to the Caribbean. He is known for breaking down political, climatic, and geographical barriers to golf course development and has been called "the father of modern environmental golf course design." During the Clinton administration, he installed the White House putting green. A poet, Jones wrote of the Moscow Country Club: "Celebrate the essence of Nature / Not the victory of temporary games." His book* Golf by Design *teaches players how to lower their scores by reading the features of a golf course. He supports Refugees International (www.refugeesinternational.org).*

CALVIN KLEIN

TANZANIA

*W*hen I went to Tanzania, my goal was to visit the Maasai. In my work, I have been influenced by the way they dress—the colors they use, the jewelry. So I wanted to meet them in person, and I hoped to visit them in a place that wasn't overrun with tourists.

First, I had some other adventures. I stayed at Kikoti Camp at the edge of Tarangire National Park. It's a traditional tent camp, with lots of canvas and a washbasin; it's not luxury. But the views of the savanna and the wildlife are amazing. Then we went on to the Serengeti. There's nothing in the world like the animal migration there. You'll see a million wildebeest and a couple hundred thousand zebras, and it goes on and on.

Next we drove into Ngorongoro Crater. The inside of the crater is its own world—the light, the sky, the reflections on the lakes—and it's all constantly

Roadside shop with traditional shukas

changing. It's like looking at abstract art come to life, a canvas spread over a hundred square miles. As you drive, you see herds of animals: gazelles, giraffes, elephants. What makes this place so special is that human beings don't arrange things. The animals do what animals do. And if a tree gets knocked over, it stays on the ground. I believe that man can't do anything as beautiful as what nature has done in this part of Africa.

At last, I saw the Maasai. I flew to a remote village called Emboreet, where the people live in mud huts with no electricity, no running water, nothing. They still kill lions and drink blood. The environment is harsh, but they are beautiful people. Their height! Their faces! Their sense of style! The clothing ranges through every shade of red and pink and orange. And they mix things: You'll see blacks and navies, stripes, plaids, and checks—all these patterns and colors wrapped around one black beauty. And all sorts of beadwork and jewelry hang from their necks and ears.

Back in the early eighties, I did a collection based on photographs I'd seen of the Maasai. They wear vibrant colors, while I usually like more muted tones, but their sophistication was inspiring. The mix of color and pattern was something unique. Thirty years later, it was so exciting to meet the Maasai in person—to see their incredible style come to life.

COMPASS POINTS

Where: Located in East Africa, Tanzania is bordered by Kenya and seven other nations and the Indian Ocean.

Backdrop: Tanzania was created through a union of two former British colonies, its name blending Tanganyika (mainland) and Zanzibar (offshore islands). Tanzania boasts Africa's tallest mountain (Mount Kilimanjaro, 19,340 feet) and largest lake (Lake Victoria, 26,560 square miles). Being only lightly visited, Tarangire National Park retains the air of undiscovered Africa. Just outside, Kikoti Camp has en suite tents set on platforms for wide views and offers beds with linens, verandas, and solar-powered electricity; the camp is located along the annual elephant migration corridor. The Serengeti is the scene of the world's largest land migration, with a million wildebeest moving in columns that may be 25 miles long; their mating leads to a "population explosion" of more than 8,000 calves a day. Ngorongoro Crater—the largest unbroken, unflooded caldera on Earth—is home to grazing animals such as zebras, gazelles, and elands, and perhaps the highest density of predators in Africa— some 25,000 animals in all. They include all the "big five:" rhinoceros, lion, leopard, elephant, and buffalo. The Maasai traditionally wrap themselves in a piece of cloth called a *shuka,* usually red, although pinks and floral prints aren't uncommon even among warriors. The colors of beads used in making jewelry have symbolic meanings: red (blood, warrior, bravery), white (peace), blue (water). The Maasai pierce their earlobes and stretch them with everything from bundles of twigs to empty film canisters.

Visitor Information: www.tanzaniatouristboard.com

The preeminent American among fashion's modernist designers, **Calvin Klein** *has created one of the world's best-known brands. He launched his company in 1968 and within weeks had sold $50,000 worth of clothing to the chic department store Bonwit Teller. Soon his sleek designs were being featured in* Vogue *and* Harper's Bazaar. *In the 1970s, he created "designer jeans," and his brand has expanded to include underwear, fragrances, swimwear, accessories, and eyewear, with annual sales of more than $6 billion. He has received seven awards from the Council of Fashion Designers of America and three Coty Awards, the youngest designer ever to win that honor. He also received the President's Medal from the Art Directors' Club for his creative advertising. Calvin Klein supports the Gay Men's Health Crisis* (www.gmhc.org), *fighting AIDS.*

SHERRY LANSING

VENICE, ITALY

I've never met a trip I didn't like. My favorite moments include sitting on an elephant in Botswana while watching the sun come up, and snorkeling in Fiji, where the fish look like beautiful exhibits in a museum.

But Venice tops them all—any area of the city, any time of year. My favorite view is being on the Giudecca and looking across the water at the Doge's Palace and St. Mark's Square.

In Venice, there are no cars, so you walk everywhere, which I love. I love being able to turn any corner and see beautiful buildings and people who are filled with life. I love the way the light changes. I love going into one of the museums, from the Accademia to the Guggenheim, and realizing that art and culture endure.

I always laugh when people tell me to be sure to go to this or that restaurant. It's irrelevant! Any restaurant in Venice is the best single meal you've ever had in your life.

The Campanile and Doge's Palace

You never have to get dressed up in Venice or worry if you have the proper clothes. The Italians do everything with this incredible feeling of relaxation. There is no pretense. If you go for a walk, you make a new friend—whether it's the person who gives you a cup of coffee and takes time to talk to you, or someone working in a museum who shows you a painting they love.

It's the most welcoming culture. I fell in love with Venice instantly, and it's a love affair that has lasted. When I go too long without visiting it, my heart actually aches. And when I'm there, a peace comes over me, a sense of what's important. You know how sometimes you go through a day and you don't know where it went? You never really looked at the sky or talked to anybody—you were just rushing through life. In Venice, the simplest things give you pleasure. You take time for them, and they have great meaning.

Every moment feels authentic and real. In Venice, you always have a sense of history, but also the feeling of being alive in that particular moment.

COMPASS POINTS

Where: Venice is located on the Adriatic Sea in northern Italy.

Backdrop: Venice is made up of 118 islands in a saltwater lagoon; they are linked by some 150 canals and 400 bridges. St. Mark's Square is the lowest spot in Venice, so it is the first to flood during storm swells or severe rain. At the Doge's Palace, the architectural device of using arcades makes the building seem to float free of gravity. The Peggy Guggenheim Collection fills an 18th-century palazzo with 20th-century European and American art, including works by Picasso and Magritte.

Visitor Information: www.italiantourism.com

Sherry Lansing became the first woman to head a major film studio (20th Century Fox), and as chairman of Paramount Pictures she oversaw the production of Academy Award winners Forrest Gump, Braveheart, and the highest-grossing film of all time, Titanic. Today she heads the Sherry Lansing Foundation (www.sherrylansingfoundation.org), which supports cancer research and education, art, and culture. Lansing is a regent of the University of California and sits on numerous boards, including the Carter Center and Teach for America. She received the Jean Hersholt Humanitarian Award at the 2007 Academy Awards ceremony.

GEORGE LUCAS

MONUMENT VALLEY, ARIZONA & UTAH

I first came in contact with Monument Valley when I was in college and won a scholarship to work on *MacKenna's Gold*. They gave the students a Land Rover and a camera, and we were supposed to make documentaries about the making of the movie.

I had seen Monument Valley in John Ford westerns, and it was beautiful. After the documentary, I decided to stay on and make my own movie about the desert. So I spent two months sitting out there, pretty much by myself, watching the sun rise and the sun set, and the clouds go by and the shadows on the mesas, and the bugs crawling across the ground, and the wind blowing through the grass — every conceivable sensual element of that environment. And I fell in love with it. It was peaceful; it was meaningful.

I had grown up in farm country, on a walnut ranch in Modesto, California, next to vineyards and a peach orchard. The ranch in front of us had horses and alfalfa fields. So I was outdoors a lot, and I like fresh air.

But the desert is like a multiple of ten of the place where I grew up. It's just a picture-perfect environment, all the time. I loved watching everything change with the sun. So I made a short, abstract film, called *6-18-67* because that was the date when I started shooting it. It's kind of a tone poem, showing all the things I saw out there.

> *Monument Valley was very moving. It was one chance I had to just be at peace.*

There's a certain kind of peace that comes over you when there's nothing happening, or at least very little. If you stand in the desert for only a second, you don't see much. But if you stand there for a long time, you get to see all the details—all the little things going on, the movement and the changing shadows, the changing light, the different smells. There's a certain smell in the desert. It's hard to describe, but it's basically fresh air. And then there's the smell right before it starts to rain.

Monument Valley was very moving. It was one chance I had to just be at peace. By that time, I was a crazed student, doing stuff and running around and having a busy life. But fortunately, for a couple of months, it just stopped. I was able to observe and to capture various images and thoughts on film.

In my later films, the desert comes up quite regularly. If I have a choice of shooting in the snow or the desert, I pick the desert. A lot of people like to be in the mountains, and that's their place of peace. My peace is the desert. I sort of communicate with it.

I think part of it is the desert's expanse. And the simplicity of it. I have a bit of an Asian-Japanese sensibility about space. I like minimalist reality, and that's kind of what the desert is. A lot of horizontal lines, not many verticals. Maybe a well-placed rock in the middle of the landscape, or some cactus standing up here and there. The landscape is a combination of Buddhist and *Krazy Kat*—two of my favorite things.

At one point, I was up on a hill, shooting clouds, and I could look *down* on a lot of the mesas. They were so beautiful. When you're down on the desert floor, you don't get much of a perspective on it. But that one image always sticks in my head—up high where you can see for miles and miles, just mesa after mesa, and it seems like it goes on forever.

East Mitten, Monument Valley

I think the most significant part of being in a special place is that it allows you to get inside yourself. It puts you in a restful, peaceful state, where you're not threatened and you don't have anxiety, but the beauty just washes over you in a very quiet way. It's not that it gives you that much; instead, it allows you to give yourself something. And that is how I would define a special place: It allows you to be yourself.

COMPASS POINTS

Where: Monument Valley lies on the border of Arizona and Utah, within the Navajo Indian Reservation.

Backdrop: A traditional Navajo prayer asks the blessing of the Holy People who created Monument Valley: "May it be beautiful before me. May it be beautiful behind me. May it be beautiful above me. May it be beautiful below me. May I walk in beauty." Monument Valley has been a location for numerous movies, starting with John Ford's *Stagecoach* (1939) and since then ranging from *2001: A Space Odyssey* to *Mission: Impossible II*. Gregory Peck and Omar Sharif starred in *MacKenna's Gold* (1969). The valley's great monoliths were formed during the past 1.5 million years; caps of hard rock protect the softer sediments underneath from erosion.

Visitor Information: Monument Valley Navajo Tribal Park: www.navajonationparks.org; www.utah.com/monumentvalley

By fusing timeless storytelling with advanced technological innovation, **George Lucas** *has created some of the most successful movies of all time, including* American Graffiti *and the* Star Wars *and* Indiana Jones *films.* Star Wars *set new standards in visuals and sound, winning eight Academy Awards. His company, LucasFilm, includes Industrial Light and Magic, whose pioneering visual effects created the dinosaurs of* Jurassic Park, *the skeletal buccaneers in* Pirates of the Caribbean, *and other memorable digital images. Lucas has received the Irving G. Thalberg Memorial Award from the Academy of Motion Picture Arts and Sciences, the American Film Institute's Lifetime Achievement Award, and the National Medal of Technology, the nation's highest award for technological achievement. The George Lucas Educational Foundation (*www.edutopia.org*) encourages innovation in schools.*

George Lucas

LORETTA LYNN

HURRICANE MILLS, TENNESSEE

*H*urricane Mills is just a little town. If you blinked your eye as you passed, you'd miss it for sure! But I like it. It's home.

My husband, Doo, and I moved in about '66, and I've been here ever since. He loved our farm. When I'd come home—I don't care if I'd only been gone two days—he'd take me to the cornfield just to see how high the corn had gotten. I couldn't tell the difference! He was something.

You know what's funny: Hurricane Mills looks exactly like Kentucky, where I grew up. It's green. Trees everywhere. People come here to ride horses, and there's all kinds of things they can do.

Doo and I always went riding on Sundays when I was home. We'd just go to the countryside and ride. One time, we'd been out all day, looking around, and we passed this place. I looked up and saw a big white house, like in *Gone with the Wind,* and I said, "I want that house, right there!" We lived in that big house for years. It was built back around the Civil War sometime, and we say it's haunted.

Doo farmed corn and soybeans. One time I did a commercial for a tractor

Grist mill located on the ranch.

company, and he got all his tractors and stuff free. He planted 1,200 acres, so he worked hard.

Now I live not far from that big house. You can bet that anybody who comes into my house could live in it. I don't want anything I can't put my feet up on, you know? I want to be comfortable when I'm home. I've got a sectional couch and a big old drum that I bought from the Indians that have a powwow here every year. I took a drum that four guys played, put a glass top on it, and made it into a coffee table in the living room. Everybody looks at it and says, "Well, what is *this*?"

My house is real homey. People that come here to do TV—you know, like *Entertainment Tonight*—they don't ever want to leave.

But it's been so hard since Doo's been gone. When he passed away, we were married for 48 years. Now I let the neighbors farm the land, and it's better than just letting it sit there; that would bother me. There's a hundred-acre field of corn right down from my house. When the corn's just about over, they'll cut it all down, get the fodder, and then they'll plow it up and put it in grass again. And then springtime, we'll start all over. Life goes on…!

COMPASS POINTS

Where: Hurricane Mills, Tennessee, is located 65 miles west of Nashville.

Backdrop: The main attraction in Hurricane Mills is Loretta Lynn's Ranch, which includes her plantation home, a museum, and a re-creation of the cabin where she grew up in Butcher Holler, Kentucky.

Visitor Information: www.lorettalynn.com/ranch

Country music icon **Loretta Lynn** *has recorded 70 albums and written more than 160 songs. Some feature feisty women narrators, such as "Don't Come Home A-Drinkin' (With Lovin' on Your Mind)," or confront social issues of the day ("Dear Uncle Sam" was about the Vietnam War). Lynn's singing style has been described as a "fusion of twang, grit, energy, and libido." Her rags-to-riches life story is summed up in* Coal Miner's Daughter—*a hit single and album, a best-selling biography, and an Oscar-winning film. Sixteen of Lynn's singles and seventeen albums reached number one on the country charts. She was the first woman named "Entertainer of the Year" by the Country Music Association and has received four Grammy Awards and ten Academy of Country Music Awards. Lynn has been inducted into the Country Music Hall of Fame and Songwriters Hall of Fame, and she was a recipient of the Kennedy Center Honors.*

LEONARD MALTIN

TELLURIDE, COLORADO

*M*y wife Alice and I first went to Telluride in 1979 for the annual film festival—but we had already seen the town without knowing it. It was used as the location for a movie called *Butch and Sundance: The Early Years*, the not-very-memorable sequel to *Butch Cassidy and the Sundance Kid*. They used a saloon and a lot of storefronts on Telluride's main street, which needed very little camouflage to pass as period locations.

We were living in New York City then and had never seen the American West; we were flyover people. So we flew to Denver and rented a car to drive around Colorado. The climax was the ride into Telluride. The scenery changes every few minutes: aspen trees, rivers, mountain peaks, gullies, abandoned miners' cabins from a century ago. On the last stretch, you make a turn and suddenly there it is before you, a little town nestled amidst enormous peaks, like Brigadoon.

We bought a postcard that shows the main street in 1880, when Telluride was a mining boom town. It looks exactly the same today, except there are no hitching posts. Telluride is in a box canyon, and the main street dead-ends into a mountain with a waterfall. Although we've seen many changes in the town over the years, including the construction of entire condo villages, there's one thing no one can spoil, and that's the feeling of that street. When you're standing there, you know you're in Telluride.

Adding to the fun is that the home base of the Telluride Film Festival is the old Sheridan Opera House, lovingly restored to the way it looked in 1913 when it was built for vaudeville shows and touring theater companies. There's something special about being in that theater, maybe because it's easy to imagine stars like Sarah Bernhardt performing there—which she did.

Telluride is located at 8,750 feet above sea level, so the air is thin. Early on, I learned that you should never run to see a movie, even if you're late. You'll regret it! One time I was staying on the second floor of the Sheridan Hotel. I went downstairs to a movie and realized I'd forgotten something, so I bounded up the one flight of stairs—and fell to the floor, gasping.

I don't learn easily. The next year, they showed Les Blank's documentary film about the polka, called *In Heaven There Is No Beer?*, and they had a polka party afterward. I danced briefly with a friend—and believe me, it was brief. I couldn't take it. The altitude is something you always have to keep in mind.

Funny and unexpected things happen in Telluride. A few years ago, I interviewed Peter O'Toole on stage, following a selection of excerpts from his long film career; he's a charming man and a wonderful raconteur. As we drove away from the session, O'Toole noticed one of the festival's codirectors, Bill Pence, riding a bike. I explained that that was how he chose to get around town. When we got out of the car O'Toole walked over to Bill and said, "Can I give it a try?" I have a wonderful photo of Peter O'Toole riding around on a bicycle, at nearly 9,000 feet above sea level.

I don't think you'd see that at the Cannes Film Festival, but you would at Telluride. People let their guard down, because it's not a gawking festival, nor a marketplace where deals are being made. It's a festival for movie lovers.

In fact, the organizers don't announce the guests of honor or the film program ahead of time. If you're coming only because of a particular star or film, they don't want you there. They want you because you love movies and you trust them to put on a good show.

Louis Malle used to attend on a regular basis. One year, he flew in from the Venice Film Festival, which runs simultaneously, with the print of his newest film, *Au Revoir, Les Enfants*. The screening was held in the Opera House on Saturday afternoon, and I was lucky enough to be there. It's a very emotional film, and when it was over, there was silence. People didn't feel right applauding. As everyone filed out of the opera house, Malle was standing outside on the lawn. I think he questioned whether the film had played well; he had shown it only once before, and he was nervous. It was, after all, a very personal story from his own childhood. Somehow everyone lingered on the lawn; people didn't walk away. Finally, Bill Pence spoke up and said, "Louis, we just want to thank you for your movie"—and everyone burst into applause! It was an unforgettable moment, and he was very touched. It could happen that way only in Telluride.

One more thing that sets this event apart from the others is the fact that you spend so much time outdoors; it's the only film festival where I've ever gotten a sunburn.

Another thing that's fun about the festival is that once the movies start, the buzz begins. As you walk around town, you talk to other people: *What have you seen? What's good?* And that becomes part of the fun, picking up on the word of mouth. The programmers deliberately leave slots open on the schedule, so films that get particularly strong reactions or that sell out can be shown again. That's a wonderful idea.

Many years, the films that become the end-of-the-year prestige films are launched at Telluride. I remember being there the year of *Sling Blade*. Billy Bob Thornton, the director, writer, and star of the film, was in town. Very few people knew who he was or what the film was about. It came out of nowhere, so to speak, and knocked everyone out. No one was surprised that it went on to enjoy great success, winning Thornton an Academy Award for his original screenplay.

When my wife and I first started going to the festival, the town was populated largely by trust funders—what they called trustafarians. We like to say that we were in Telluride before Oprah and Tom Cruise discovered it (and we only wish we'd bought property then). I remember talking to the proprietor of a café, a lawyer from Denver who dropped out and came to Telluride to pursue her dream. Two years later, she was gone, presumably having dropped back in, and someone else had taken her place. I imagine that's a cycle in Telluride.

The core of Telluride is still rustic, but maybe this is just the rose-colored observation of a visitor. The truth is, over the years the town has become more gentrified and expensive. The old-timers can barely afford to live there now, and many workers have to commute in every day from Montrose. Some of the rough edges still show, however, which adds to the charm. There is a constant stream of visitors throughout the year who ski, participate in business conferences, and attend one of the many other festivals that dot the calendar (bluegrass, poetry, hang-gliding, and so on).

But it's the Labor Day film festival that keeps my wife and daughter and me going back. One more thing that sets this event apart from the others is the fact that you spend so much time outdoors; it's the only film festival where I've ever gotten a sunburn.

I can't tell you how many times I've photographed the exact same shot outdoors, looking down the main street to the mountains and Bridal Veil Falls. The peaks have so many facets, and the play of the light and sun and clouds on them creates an ever-changing landscape. The only thing consistent about it is its beauty.

Someone taught me the word *alpenglow*, which I like. Moviemakers call it the "magic hour"—that last hour or so of golden sunlight. It's spectacular when it hits the mountains in Telluride. I'll always have that picture in my mind.

Gondola pictured against the backdrop of golden aspens

Leonard Maltin

COMPASS POINTS

Where: Telluride is located in southwest Colorado, 127 miles south of Grand Junction. Its airport is 9,078 feet above sea level.

Backdrop: A mining town, Telluride boomed in 1878, went bust in 1893, and rose again as a ski town in 1973. The average annual snowfall is 309 inches. The downtown core is a National Historic District, with hundreds of Old West buildings. In Telluride in 1889, Butch Cassidy robbed his first bank, making off with $24,580. During the film festival over Labor Day weekend, the town's population of 2,200 residents triples. Notable films that have premiered at the festival include *The Crying Game*, *Lost in Translation*, *Capote*, and *Crouching Tiger, Hidden Dragon*.

Visitor Information: Telluride: www.visittelluride.com; film festival: www.telluridefilm festival.org

One of the country's most respected film critics and historians, **Leonard Maltin** *has been the resident movie reviewer on* Entertainment Tonight *for more than a quarter-century. He is the author of the perennial best-seller* Leonard Maltin's Movie Guide, Of Mice and Magic: A History of American Animated Cartoons, *and other books. His television specials include* Fantasia: The Creation of a Disney Classic *and* The Making of High Noon. *He has been president of the Los Angeles Film Critics Association and serves on the National Film Preservation Board. Maltin also teaches in the School of Cinematic Arts at the University of Southern California.*

MANUEL

THE ROSE PARADE, PASADENA, CALIFORNIA

We all have one place that makes us think *Wow! What happened to me there changed my life!* When I was 21, destiny brought me to Los Angeles. I had been making clothes in Mexico since I was seven years old, and I came to the United States to chase that big old rainbow of design. I didn't know I'd have it in my hands so quick, but within 18 months I was working for the tailor to the stars, Cy Devore, making clothes for Frank Sinatra and the Rat Pack.

But before long, I got bored to death making gray sharkskin with narrow lapels. And tuxedos—some were black and some were white, but it never went anywhere from there. I thought: *This isn't my idea of designing. This is just monkey see, monkey do. I need to find something different.*

In the early fifties, a girlfriend asked me to go to the Rose Parade in Pasadena. She said we'd sleep there on the sidewalk the night before. I said, "Excuse me? I don't sleep on sidewalks! Let's get a nice hotel." She told me they're booked months ahead of time. So we bought the Cadillac of all camping beds, just to keep my pride up, and we slept out on the sidewalk on New Year's Eve.

In the morning, the parade started. There were people riding horses, and I had never seen anything so flamboyant in my whole life. The colors! The glitter! The embroidery! To see macho men dressed up in clothes with flowers on them, wearing hats all adorned with rhinestones—it just freaked me out. I thought, *Oh my god! That's what I want to do!*

After that, I worked for Nudie's Rodeo Tailors, the famous glitzy western store in North Hollywood. Then I went out on my own and got crazy making clothes for the rock 'n' rollers, from Ricky Nelson to the Rolling Stones, from the Jackson Five to the Grateful Dead.

What are you going to do? If you sell candy, all the kids from the neighborhood come to your store! The same thing happened with my rhinestoned and embroidered suits. Most people have a peacock inside of them, that ready-to-bust-out pride. After a while, I learned how I could wake them up and say *Hey, let's not think halfway! Just go for it!*

> *To see macho men dressed up in clothes with flowers on them, wearing hats all adorned with rhinestones—it just freaked me out.*

One of many flamboyant floats in the Tournament of Roses Parade

I made some clothes for the Beatles. They were so English, those kids, especially John, so I decided to make them some colorful outfits. I used leftover fabrics—can you imagine that? I did it as a joke, thinking they were never going to like them. But they loved them! These ended up as part of the Sgt. Pepper uniforms that the Beatles wore on the album cover.

More than anything else, designing clothes has been fun. It led me to a beautiful, textured world full of truly fascinating people. And it all goes back to the Rose Parade. The parade filled me up, man. It just knocked me out. I heard my calling, and it changed my life.

COMPASS POINTS

Where: The Tournament of Roses Parade takes place on January 1 in Pasadena, California, located 15 minutes north of downtown Los Angeles.

Backdrop: The parade was started in 1890 by new residents from the East Coast who wanted to showcase California's warm winter weather. The parade is never held on a Sunday, a policy that was set in 1893 "to avoid frightening horses tethered outside local churches and thus interfering with worship services." Parade rules require that every square inch of a float be covered with flowers or other plant materials such as bark, seeds, and leaves, and float decorators often end the day covered in glue and petals. Recent floats have depicted King Kong stomping through a floral jungle, a guitar-playing dinosaur, pigs dancing the hula, a robotic chef, and a working roller coaster.

Visitor Information: www.pasadenacal.com; www.tournamentofroses.com

*Custom clothier Manuel Cuevas—known to everyone as **Manuel**—is the designer who put Elvis in a jumpsuit, turned Johnny Cash into the "Man in Black," and originated the inflated lips insignia for the Rolling Stones. Aiming to define performers' images through their apparel, Manuel made James Dean's jeans in* Giant, *transformed Glen Campbell into the Rhinestone Cowboy, and created Dwight Yoakam's lean look. His clientele has ranged from Ronald Reagan to Salvador Dalí to Dolly Parton. He created wardrobes for 90 films and for television shows such as* The Lone Ranger *and* Bonanza. *For his achievements in fashion design, Manuel has received a Coty Award, a Moda Award, and a Country Music Association Award. He lives in Nashville, Tennessee, and is establishing the Manuel Foundation to train fashion students from around the world.*

Discoveries V

STEVE MCCURRY

ANGKOR WAT, CAMBODIA

I've been to Angkor Wat more than ten times, starting in 1988, before there were any tourists. The Khmer Rouge were lurking in the jungle, and you couldn't be one hundred percent sure that the place wasn't mined.

What struck me immediately about Angkor was its emptiness. Once, this had been a thriving civilization, with all the temples intact and people worshiping there. Now it was a lost civilization, a place in ruins, and I felt a sense of loneliness and loss that this place full of sublime structures had fallen into obscurity—ignored and uncared for.

I also felt a great sense of adventure and was transported back to another time. The temple walls were carved with wonderful sculptures—transcendent faces, gods and kings, lovely nymphets called *apsaras*, and dancers carved in stone.

All these amazing monuments and statues were hidden away in a thick, hot jungle, with serious vegetation swallowing many of them. Among the leaves, the

Buddhist monks in the rain at Angkor Wat

temples were crumbling. It was a place that exuded poetry. Here were all these deities and demigods and dancers, but nobody to look at them, appreciate them, and draw inspiration from it all.

I saw that although Angkor Wat is made of stone, its beauty is fleeting. The Buddhists say that things are transitory, that there's an ephemeral quality to life, an impermanence to everything—to us, to all things in the world. Things live and die. And at Angkor you see a place that was born, lived vibrantly, and now is dying. It is being overgrown by the jungle, and that will be the end of it.

But even though all the carved figures are disappearing, they are smiling. Despite the ravages of time, and the fact that they are unappreciated and unseen, they still manage to have serene, compassionate expressions on their faces. They have a wonderful sense of joy. They're above it all.

COMPASS POINTS

Where: Angkor Wat is a temple complex at Angkor, located near Siem Reap in northern Cambodia.

Backdrop: Angkor Wat has been a major religious center—first Hindu, then Buddhist—since Angkor was built in the 12th century as King Suryavarman II's state temple and capital. The familiar outline appears on Cambodia's flag—concentric galleries around a temple "mountain" whose peaks evoke Mount Meru, mythological home of the Hindu gods. The encompassing walls and moat symbolize surrounding ranges and the ocean. Today Angkor Wat is a UNESCO World Heritage site, and temple restoration efforts are under way.

Visitor Information: www.tourismcambodia.com

Steve McCurry's indelible images include "Afghan Girl," which appeared on the cover of National Geographic *in 1985 and is perhaps the most recognized photograph in the modern world. His career was launched when he dressed in native garb and crossed into rebel-controlled Afghanistan just before the 1979 Russian invasion, emerging with rolls of film sewn into his clothing—images that won the Robert Capa Gold Medal for Best Photographic Reporting from Abroad. He has also received the Magazine Photographer of the Year award. McCurry has covered many conflicts, from Iraq, Afghanistan, and Lebanon to Ground Zero on September 11. His work often appears in* National Geographic, *and his books include* South Southeast, The Path to Buddha: A Tibetan Pilgrimage, Steve McCurry, *and* Looking East. *He serves on the board of ImagineAsia (www.imagine-asia.org), which provides fundamental education and health care to students in Afghanistan.*

CESAR MILLAN

RUNYON CANYON PARK, LOS ANGELES, CALIFORNIA

Dogs don't know whether they're in Italy or China or France—but wherever they are, they do know whether they're having a good time at the moment. And my favorite moments are when I'm walking with the pack in Runyon Canyon, a park in the mountains above Hollywood where dogs are allowed to walk off-leash.

Runyon Canyon Park is a magical place because it's natural, with mountains, rocks, chaparral, and trees. Yet, at the same time, you're right in the city, so the dogs have the benefit of both worlds.

I travel early in the morning and park at the top of the canyon, on Mulholland Drive. The pack knows they can't jump out of the van just because the door is open. I allow them to get out only when they're calm-submissive, and only one at a time. The pack then forms up, and sits and waits.

Most of the big dogs have backpacks to carry water. And if a little dog gets tired along the way, I'll put it in a backpack and let a larger dog carry it. Dogs won't do this naturally ("Hey, c'mon, I'll give you a ride!"), but they can learn, from us, to help each other.

If a little dog gets tired along the way, I'll put it in a backpack and let a larger dog carry it.

I like to walk in the canyon in the early morning, when the air is cool and the pack is frisky. You're dealing with more energy than you'll find in any human being on Earth. If I were to start our walk at the bottom of the canyon and go up, gravity would work against me, and pretty soon the dogs would be 300 feet in front of me. That's why I start at the top; I want the mountain to work for me. The pack forms a line, with me at the front, and we head downhill at high speed.

We see people as we go, but the dogs don't care about them, or about the scent of coyotes or rabbits. They just focus on migration—like when you see birds fly, all of them on one frequency, turning right or left together. I make sure the pack gets on the same frequency. And I do it right away, because if I gave them time to become curious about things around us, I'd have 30 dogs going in 30 different directions.

Runyon Canyon with view toward Los Angeles

I love the feeling of the pack following me with no question. We're all in tune to each other. We are all one. I'm happy just to be there in nature, and I'm happy to be with them. And whatever you're feeling, a dog feels, too—so your happiness gets multiplied by 30.

We make two trips up and down the canyon, which takes about four hours. Of course, we also rest. We have a special place about halfway down under what the locals call a Jesus Tree, because its seeds have a cross on them. It's nice and shady there, and the pack knows it's their resting place. They've created little holes and dens for themselves, and each picks its own spot. They're happy because they've accomplished something, and we all sit and relax and drink water. We don't say anything, just rest.

It gives me such happiness to be there, just to be in the moment and not looking at the clock. I don't have to go to any meetings. I don't have to do anything. It's just me and my pack. It's a beautiful thing.

COMPASS POINTS

Where: Runyon Canyon Park is located in the eastern Santa Monica Mountains, west of the Hollywood Freeway (U.S. 101) and two blocks from Hollywood Boulevard, extending north to Mulholland Drive.

Cesar Millan

Backdrop: In its earlier history, Runyon Canyon was a seasonal campsite for Gabrielino Indians; the hideout of legendary bandit Tiburcio Vasquez; a hunting and riding getaway for coal magnate Carman Runyon, who bought the land in 1919; the estate of world-famous Irish tenor John McCormack, who built a mansion that was rented to celebrities such as Charles Boyer and Janet Gaynor but has long since vanished; and the property of A&P grocery chain heir George Huntington Hartford II, who hired Frank Lloyd Wright to design a country club and hotel on the property but had his plans blocked by neighbors. The canyon became a park in 1984. In this natural/urban oasis live coyotes, deer, snakes (including rattlers), and hawks, while two subway tunnels on the Metro Red Line run beneath the mountains.

Visitor Information: Runyon Canyon Park: www.runyon-canyon.com. The canyon has two entrances on the south side (at the ends of Vista Street and Fuller Avenue) and one on the north side (in the 7300 block of Mulholland Drive). The park is open daily from dawn to dusk. Dogs are allowed off-leash on 90 of the park's 160 acres.

*A renowned dog behavior specialist with a gift for primal communion with nature, **Cesar Millan** is known for his uncanny ability to walk large packs of dogs at a time. He has a particular interest in rehabilitating aggressive dogs, with a special fondness for what he calls the "power breeds," such as pit bulls and rottweilers. His television series,* Dog Whisperer with Cesar Millan, *airs on the National Geographic Channel; it is one of the network's top-rated shows and has been nominated for two Primetime Emmy Awards. Both of his books,* Cesar's Way *and* Be the Pack Leader, *are best-sellers. Millan has received a special commendation from the National Humane Society, and he and his wife founded the Cesar and Ilusion Millan Foundation* (www.millanfoundation.org), *which supports the rescue, rehabilitation, and placement of abused and abandoned dogs.*

ISAAC MIZRAHI

OUR GARAGE, BROOKLYN, NEW YORK

*W*hen my parents bought a house in the Midwood area of Brooklyn, they built an addition that blocked the use of the garage. The garage was just empty space — and when I was ten years old, it became mine!

It was my puppet theater, and I used to focus all my creative energy there. My mother said she always knew where I was, because there would be an extension cord snaking out the window of the house into the garage when I was working in there — which was just about always.

My puppet show was this kind of amorphous revue called *Follies*. I didn't know anything about Stephen Sondheim's *Follies* or the Folies Bergère. But the puppet theater threw together every imaginable creative discipline for me. It was theater, so there was the content of the show and the writing of the different sketches. There was music, which I'd compose on the piano and tape-record. And I guess you could say that I learned how to sew by making clothes for the puppets.

It was a marionette theater. I used the frame of an old rusted swing set and built a very flashy stage on it. It actually had a lot of substance and took a great deal of weight. I would stand at stage level behind the back curtain, hunched over the aperture where the puppets slid down.

I had scenery that was covered with glitter — a *lot* of glitter! And I was very into lighting and knew a lot about it very early on. For makeshift lighting, I would collect old lamps that people were throwing away. At one point, someone gave me a Lite-Brite, which was a sort of toy light box with some Peg-Board and black paper underneath. You'd push colored pegs into the board to make signs or pictures. I figured out how to build the Lite-Brite into one of the sets for the climax of a number in the *Follies*. That was a funny thing.

I also made all the puppets in the show. I'd carve the heads out of balsa wood and paint them with model paint. I had dancing girls that would kick their legs. The marionettes were remarkable.

The costumes were really glittery and feathery. I used to swipe change from my father's dresser in the morning and go to the fabric store almost every day after school to

And then, when the garage door opened, that meant there was a puppet show to be watched. All sorts of people would come ...

Brooklyn Bridge from Old Fulton Street

buy remnants. I was mad over prints and lamé and sequined fabrics. It was my version of being a drag queen—but instead of dressing myself up, I dressed the puppets.

The show was a revue, so there were songs and dance numbers. For the big giant numbers, I used prerecorded music. I was into a whole Brazilian scene at one point, so just picture glitter, polka dots, and Sergio Mendez!

I was very pre-Basil Twist.

I would spend weeks and weeks doing this kind of stuff, preparing and rehearsing, and the garage door would stay shut. And then, when the garage door opened, that meant there was a puppet show to be watched. All sorts of people would come—my sister's friends, and the people who lived next door, down the block, and around the corner. They loved it!

The puppet theater confirmed my predisposition to polymathy and was a precursor of the work I do now. And I think it sort of accounts for this mad passion I have for so many pursuits, whether it's clothing, or television, or any of the million different things I can't stop doing.

Everything kind of came together, when you think about it, in that puppet theater in the garage.

COMPASS POINTS

Where: Brooklyn is one of the five boroughs of New York City and is located on western Long Island.

Backdrop: If Brooklyn were separated from New York, it would rank as the nation's fourth most populated city, with 2.5 million residents. Glitter is made up of tiny bits of glass, paper, or plastic that reflect light, having been coated with metallic or iridescent colors. It was invented around 1934 by a cattle farmer in New Jersey. Marionettes have a greater range of movement than other puppets and take more time to learn to manipulate. Wooden figures operated by strings appeared in Egypt as early as 2000 B.C. By the 18th century, such musical giants as Haydn and Respighi were composing adult operas for marionettes.

Visitor Information: www.visitbrooklyn.org

Isaac Mizrahi produced clothing under his first label (IS New York) by age 15, and while still a student at Parsons School of Design, he was hired by Perry Ellis. After stints with Jeffrey Banks and Calvin Klein, Mizrahi opened his own womenswear company in 1987, followed by menswear three years later. A documentary about his work, Unzipped, *won the Audience Award at the 1995 Sundance Film Festival and sparked a rapid expansion of his label to Asia and other markets. Mizrahi has also designed costumes for Broadway shows and the Metropolitan Opera, winning the Drama Desk Award for Outstanding Costume Design. He introduced chic clothing at low prices at Target stores and is now the creative director for the Liz Claiborne brand. His designs have been described as "classics, with a twist" and "a blend of ease and elegance." Mizrahi has received multiple awards from the Council of Fashion Designers of America. He supports the ASPCA* (www.aspca.org) *and Good Shepherd Services* (www.goodshepherds.org).

ROBERT MONDAVI

REPUBLIC OF GEORGIA

*W*ine is a wonderful medium of foreign exchange. I've traveled all over the world, and whenever I meet someone who enjoys the good life—a glass of wine, good food, music—I generally also find a warm and generous friend.

Once, for instance, my wife and I traveled to Georgia—not the Peach State but the then-Soviet republic. The region was a breadbasket, a cornucopia of farm products, and possibly the one place in the country where you saw lots of vegetables and meat on the market shelves and nobody standing in line.

In the capital city, Tbilisi, we went into a little wine shop. When the owner found out that I was in the same business, he insisted on giving me an entire case of Georgian wine. Such generosity was typical of everyone we met.

Naturally, I wanted to return his kindness in some way. I had a little pin that depicted the American and Soviet flags joined together, so I presented it to the

View of Tbilisi

shop owner as a token. He took it—and then started bending it back and forth, trying his best to break off the Soviet part. As the world now knows, Georgians wanted nothing more than to pull away from the Soviet Union, and my new friend showed me his feelings in a way more eloquent than words. Between us, the doors of international understanding had opened, smoothly lubricated with wine.

COMPASS POINTS

Where: Georgia is located at the crossroads of Europe and Asia, between the Black and Caspian Seas.

Backdrop: Once part of the U.S.S.R., Georgia is a democratic country about the size of Switzerland. Archaeologists have found evidence of winemaking here from 5000 B.C., and Georgia is often cited as the birthplace of wine. Today the country produces 500 different kinds.

Visitor Information: www.tourism.gov.ge

*The late vintner **Robert Mondavi** brought Napa Valley wines to worldwide prominence through his Robert Mondavi Winery by combining technical advances with marketing savvy—in particular, labeling wines according to their grape variety, rather than generically. He was inducted to the Vintners Hall of Fame and the California Hall of Fame. Mondavi was a founder and major benefactor of Copia: The American Center for Wine, Food and the Arts in Napa, California.*

CRAIG NEWMARK

GREENWICH VILLAGE, NEW YORK CITY

*M*y recurring fantasy is to have an apartment in Greenwich Village. I like the intellectually exciting life I see there, and it has a bohemian feeling that goes back to the Beat Generation. (I also have time-machine fantasies about traveling back and seeing what the Beats were really like.)

I love cafés and hanging out, and one of my favorite places in the Village is Caffe Reggio on MacDougal Street. I've been there a bunch of times, and I remember seeing a movie called *Next Stop, Greenwich Village*, about a young guy who moves to the Village with dreams of being an actor. One big scene happens in Caffe Reggio, and that was really cool.

Another of my favorite cafés is Joe: The Art of Coffee on Waverly Place. I like its neighborhood sense, and the coffee is pretty good, too. A while ago, I went into the café and the face behind the counter was familiar. She had been a barista at my favorite local hangout, the Reverie Café, in the Cole Valley area of San Francisco, where I live. That's pretty funny: You walk into a coffee place clear across the country and the person behind the counter knows your regular drink!

COMPASS POINTS

Where: Greenwich Village is a neighborhood in New York City, bounded by the Hudson River on the west, Broadway on the east, 14th Street on the north, and Houston Street on the south.
Backdrop: Among the notable residents of Greenwich Village have been Allen Ginsberg, Madonna, and sculptor Claes Oldenburg. Its well-known music venues have included the Electric Circus, Fillmore East, and CBGB, the birthplace of punk. Cappuccino was introduced to the United States by the first owner of Caffe Reggio; the café still has its 1902 espresso machine, the first of its kind.
Visitor Information: www.iloveny.com

Craig Newmark founded craigslist, a network of websites listing classified ads in 450 cities in 50 countries, with 9 billion page views per month—the leader in classified advertising in all media. Based on the ideal of community and service, craigslist does not run banner ads and charges only for commercial listings in certain cities. It has a reported annual revenue of $150 million.

Café in Greenwich Village

Craig Newmark

SANDRA DAY O'CONNOR

ARIZONA

I grew up on a cattle ranch in eastern Arizona and still have a clear picture of a way of life that you're hard-pressed to find these days. The cowboys were colorful characters with names like Jim Brister and Bug Quinn—real-life cowboys in the 20th century.

In that part of the Southwest, any place that had water was thrilling. The ranch went down to the Gila River, where there was a canyon filled with cottonwood trees. The river ran underground most of the year, but you could dig in the sand about a foot, and the hole would fill with water. As a little girl in that arid part of the state, I thought water was magical.

On the canyon walls were Indian pictographs and, farther along, little caves where Indians once stored food; you could climb up on ladders. The Indians were from very old tribes that moved with the seasons, making temporary camps, hunting game, and moving on. We used to find arrowheads—the correct term is *projectile points*, but we called them "arrowheads"—tiny ones for birds, bigger ones for rabbits. And we found lots of potsherds. Those places meant a lot to me as a child, and as an adult I found others all over Arizona.

One of the really spectacular sights in the world is a ceremonial dance up on the Hopi mesas in northeastern Arizona. Second Mesa is small and stark, with walls that go straight down to the valley floor. On top are the ancient dwellings of the pueblo. The Hopi have the oldest continuously inhabited community in North America. To be there and see one of their ceremonial dances—it made the hair stand up on the back of my neck. I felt like this was not Earth, this was some extraterrestrial place. It's like nothing you've ever seen or experienced. It's just out of this world.

They won't always tell you when the dances are going to be held, but sometimes they will. Many of them start at daybreak, and you have to be sitting out there—in the dark!—wherever they'll let you, like up on top of one of the old dwellings. Drums beat. And then the Kachina figures appear—Kachinas are Hopi ancestral spirits that act as intermediaries between humans and the gods. These are Indians dressed in Kachina costumes, with feathered masks painted red, yellow, black, and turquoise. They shake rattles made of gourds, and the dances begin. It's just pure magic.

Havasu Falls, on the Havasupai Reservation

Other places are more personal. My family had a cabin at Iron Springs, west of Prescott at an elevation of about 7,000 feet. It was the first place along the old railroad line from Phoenix up to Ash Fork that was high enough to have pine trees, so it was cool. Prosperous business people in Phoenix had built little cabins for their families. In summer, they'd stay there for a couple of months, because Phoenix didn't have air-conditioning until much later.

The railroad eventually stopped running, but the community stayed. Some cabins were a hundred years old, and my family had a little one at the top of a hill. Our deck looked west, and you could see a hundred miles across the mountains. The sunsets were not to be believed.

It was such a special, funky little place. My husband and I and our two boys went to Iron Springs every summer. Dear friends had cabins there, too, and we would entertain ourselves by having card games, hiking, exploring, and hunting for arrowheads.

Kachinas are Hopi ancestral spirits that act as intermediaries between humans and the gods.

Then in 1988 I got breast cancer. I had to be on chemotherapy and go through all the worries you have with cancer. As part of my healing, I was advised to do mental visualizations, to envision a place that meant a lot to me, a place I wanted to be. My picture of complete peace was a circle walk around the mountain at Iron Springs. On my way I'd see Thumb Butte (which looks like its name) and then Skull Valley, which was quite dramatic. I would go to sleep at night and picture myself on that walk, with the different vistas along the way. Visualizing this restful, peaceful place was a way to help my body heal itself. And it did.

For something quite different, for pure natural beauty, I love Havasu Canyon. It joins the Grand Canyon on the southwestern side, entering through the Havasupai Indian reservation. The only ways to get there are by foot or on horseback. We used to arrange with the tribe to have some horses there to meet us, because we were camping and wanted to take our food and gear.

You ride about eight miles down the canyon to the tribal center, then go another two miles—and all of a sudden, there's this magnificent 120-foot-high waterfall. It is rimmed by red rock, and the water is the color of Indian turquoise (the water picks up minerals as it flows through there). The waterfall forms a big pool where you can swim—right in the middle of a hot, dry, barren desert. It takes your breath away. In the desert, water is magic.

COMPASS POINTS

Where: Southwestern U.S.

Backdrop: The oldest Hopi village (Walpi, on First Mesa) was settled in 1690. The tribal name Havasupai means "People of the Blue-Green Waters."

Visitor Information: Arizona Office of Tourism: www.arizonaguide.com; Hopi mesas: www.hopi.nsn.us.

The first woman to be appointed a justice of the U.S. Supreme Court (1981–2006), **Sandra Day O'Connor** *was a centrist who often provided the decisive swing vote on important cases. A graduate of Stanford Law School, she served in the Arizona State Senate and the Arizona Court of Appeals. Her books include* Lazy B: Growing Up on a Cattle Ranch in the American Southwest, *and in 2002 she was inducted into the National Cowgirl Hall of Fame.*

SUZE ORMAN

A BENCH AT CRISSY FIELD, SAN FRANCISCO, CALIFORNIA

By the water near the Golden Gate Bridge, a 1920s airfield has become a park where I love to go and sit on a certain rickety bench. I take a walk, make my way to the bench, and sit for hours watching people walk, jog, and bicycle past. At the same time, there are fishermen trying their luck on the pier, sea lions barking in the water, and ships passing under the bridge.

The world goes by at a pace that money can't touch. It's wonderful for somebody like me, whose life really revolves around money—not my money, but expertise about money in general.

The people who pass my bench may be walking or running, fat or thin, well-dressed or barely dressed. On the bay, ships steam in from Asia and the Pacific bringing goods to San Francisco, and other ships leave. People sail yachts, and surfers ride waves. During marathons, runners pass the bench and wave. I see the whole world pass in front of me. It's fascinating to just watch it happen, with me not moving but just sitting on that rickety bench.

I love how that feels, because in that moment I know that life is real.

Life is real, not measured by what you have but by who you are. It's all there if you just walk, if you just sit and look—at what money cannot buy. Money can't buy the blue water of the San Francisco Bay, the sea lions and crabs, the sand and rocks, the sky and sunshine.

My rickety bench has given me an incredible entrée into life. When I walk to it and just sit, I feel like I've accomplished something in life. I've made it.

COMPASS POINTS

Where: Crissy Field faces the San Francisco Bay, just east of the Golden Gate Bridge, and is part of the Presidio.

Backdrop: Once a salt marsh where the Ohlone Indians gathered food, the area that is now Crissy Field provided a place to land for Spanish explorers and later for traders from Russia, England, and the East Coast of the United States. It was landfilled in 1915 in order to build the Panama-Pacific Exposition, a world's fair whose crowning, 435-foot-high Tower

The closing colors of day from Crissy Field

My Favorite Place on Earth

of jewels was hung with 100,000 pieces of colored cut glass that flashed in the sunlight and were lit by searchlights at night. The exposition showed the world that San Francisco had recovered from the 1906 earthquake and fire. The area next served as an Army air field from 1919 to 1963; aviation milestones achieved at Crissy Field included air mail service, night flying, and transcontinental air service. The National Park Service has transformed the former asphalt-and-rubble expanse into a 100-acre shoreline park with 100,000 native plants, a huge lawn, and a waterfront promenade. Windsurfers and kite surfers take advantage of the winds here, as do sailors.

Visitor Information: Visit Crissy Field *(www.crissyfield.org)* by car via Mason Street, or by foot or bicycle via the Golden Gate Promenade/San Francisco Bay Trail. Visitors can fish without a license at Torpedo Wharf, or search the beach for crab shells, jellyfish, and pebbles. The Warming Hut (Marine Drive) sells food to eat on a nearby lawn or beach with water views.

Money maven **Suze Orman** *hosts the award-winning CNBC-TV program* The Suze Orman Show *and has won two Emmy Awards and four American Women in Radio and Television Gracie Allen Awards. Her best-selling books include* The Courage to Be Rich *and* The Money Book for the Young, Fabulous and Broke. *Orman is a contributing editor to* O, the Oprah Magazine *and writes a column on Yahoo! Finance. As a motivational speaker, she has lectured to audiences as large as 50,000 people. She directed the Suze Orman Financial Group from 1987 to 1997 and earlier was a vice president of investments for Prudential Bache Securities and an account executive at Merrill Lynch. Prior to that, she worked as a waitress at the Buttercup Bakery in Berkeley, California.*

NATALIE PORTMAN

JERUSALEM, ISRAEL

erusalem is the city of my birth. I vacillate between thinking it's the most special place in the world and the most tragic. Only things you love very much can inspire that much passion and anger in you.

I was three when my family moved from Israel to Long Island. But we've been going back to Jerusalem pretty regularly since I was a kid. In 2004 I moved there for six months and took some classes at Hebrew University, where my dad studied and my grandfather taught. I wasn't a very serious student—I was there more for the experience of living in Israel.

It was really interesting, after mythologizing a place from afar, to be living in it. Jerusalem is much less chaotic, less dramatic, than you expect. When people see it for the first time, they think, *On TV, I hear about all these people fighting each other.* Then they come and see that day to day, and person to person, things are pretty okay.

You walk through the market among stalls where Arab men are selling spices and sandals. Then you walk a little farther, and it's touristy Jewish memorabilia. You turn another corner, and there are Armenian priests walking through the Armenian quarter, where the stalls sell blue tiles. The market is where you get the flavor of any place.

And there's something magical about a place that is both desert and near the sea, this crazy salt sea. There are mountains, and the land itself is so diverse within such a small range that Jerusalem does feel like a microcosm of something larger. But it's also maddening that people put so much emphasis on a physical space, a place. The territorial dispute just seems silly when you really think about it.

Still, when you're there, it's wholly understandable why Jerusalem is such an important place to so many people. The air feels thick with a sort of otherworldliness, thick with passions.

The Temple Mount is a very holy place for both Jews and Muslims. It's kind of funny—there's a sign outside that says something like: *Jews, beware! You will die on entering this holy space, and you will go to hell.* You're not supposed to enter until the Messiah comes, I guess, so there's a warning.

But the Temple Mount is so beautiful. There are gardens and a mosque, and it's this core of absolute peace and quiet in the center of the city. But obviously, at

Gathering for daybreak at the Western Wall

times it has also been an incredibly violent place. When you walk around, there are Israeli police/army in riot gear.

It's sort of wild that a place can be simultaneously both one thing and its opposite—both the most peaceful, quiet, spiritual place, and the ugliest side of humanity rearing its head.

The Wailing Wall is on one side of the Temple Mount. The first time I saw it, I was really overcome. It's amazing to think that you're part of a tradition that goes back so many centuries—and of all the burdens, and the joy, that go along with it.

But my favorite thing about Israel is the Hebrew language. In 1948 the state came together with refugees from many different countries, speaking Arabic, Russian, German, English, and other languages; there were Moroccan Jews, Indian Jews. And they just decided to speak Hebrew, a language that had been, basically, dead. In daily life people had been speaking Yiddish.

Because Hebrew was a scholarly language, and never spoken, even by the religious, reviving it was really magical. And there are poetic things hidden inside the language. My aunt taught me that the Hebrew word for "world" is etymologically

> *In 1948 the state came together with refugees from many different countries, speaking Arabic, Russian, German, English, and other languages... And they just decided to speak Hebrew.*

related to the word that means "disappeared" or "hidden." So what is *there* is also what's *hidden*. There are so many incredible things like that.

Hebrew is also like a secret language, a private one that you can use outside Israel. If I'm out with my parents somewhere, we can say things to each other that no one else can understand! I had sort of lost my Hebrew, and the best thing about my living in Jerusalem was that I got the language back.

In the past, I've said that my heart is in Jerusalem, or that I feel more Jewish when I'm there. But this changes all the time, and right now I'm sort of in an "anti" phase. I think that's one of the most intriguing things about Jerusalem and the whole country of Israel — it's almost like a person to me. It's like a friend, someone you love but who is so deeply flawed, fatally flawed, that your relationship changes and you go through phases over time.

It's the only place in the world that's like that for me, that's really like a person whom I have a relationship with. I guess Jerusalem is a silent partner in the relationship but it speaks to me, in its own way.

COMPASS POINTS

Where: Jerusalem is located in Israel's Judean Mountains, between the Mediterranean Sea and the Dead Sea.

Backdrop: Jerusalem's history dates back to the 4th millennium B.C.E. It is considered the holiest city of Judaism and third-holiest of Islam. The Hebrew University of Jerusalem, founded in 1925, is the nation's oldest university and offers the world's largest Jewish studies library. On its first board of governors were Sigmund Freud and Alfred Einstein, who left the university his personal papers, their copyright, and the right to use his image; today the Albert Einstein Archives holds 55,000 items from his life. In 2002 a Hamas terrorist detonated a bomb in the university's Frank Sinatra cafeteria, killing ten people, including several Americans. The Temple Mount is one of the world's most disputed religious sites. Jews believe that God created Adam with dust gathered here; Muslims believe that the prophet Muhammad ascended to heaven from this spot. The Israeli government assigned a Muslim council to manage the site and enforces a ban on prayer by visitors who are not Muslim. The revival of Hebrew—a movement that began in the 19th century and was integrated with the founding of Israel—offers the world's only example of a language that had no native speakers but developed into a national language with millions. In the ongoing Israeli-Palestinian conflict, the status of Jerusalem remains a central issue.

Visitor Information: www.goisrael.com

Actress **Natalie Portman** *got her degree at Harvard College and has published several scientific papers in psychology. She appeared in the* Star Wars *prequel trilogy as Padmé Amidala, and also in* Anywhere But Here, Garden State, *and* Closer *(receiving a Golden Globe and an Oscar nomination as Best Supporting Actress). Her other films include* V for Vendetta, Goya's Ghosts, *and* The Other Boleyn Girl. *A lifelong vegetarian and advocate for animal rights, Natalie Portman is also an "Ambassador of Hope" for FINCA International* (www .villagebanking.org), *a nonprofit organization that makes "micro-loans" to the severely poor in developing countries, mostly women, to enable them to sustain businesses and improve their standard of living.*

WOLFGANG PUCK

L'OUSTAU DE BAUMANIÈRE,
LES BAUX-DE-PROVENCE, FRANCE

hen I was quite young, I thought cooking was something you did with a recipe. Then as an 18-year-old I became an apprentice at a three-star restaurant in the south of France. It changed my world and what I do. The restaurant had a beautiful kitchen with blue-tiled walls. I worked next to the chef, Raymond Thuilier, who was 73 years old. The old man cooked from his heart. He changed things around and did what he felt. And I never saw dishes like that! That's where I said: *You know what? That's what I want to do. That's how I want to cook.*

We didn't use exact recipes. You could use as much or as little of anything as you wanted—as long as it tasted good. For example, I wasn't used to cooking with cream back in Austria. One day we were making a lobster bisque, and Mr. Thuilier said, "Okay, pour more cream in it…and more cream…and more cream." I tasted

The ancient village of Les-Baux-de-Provence

it and thought, *Oh my god, this is so delicious!* I also remember making a Dover sole. We cooked it with vermouth and shallots and a little fish stock. Then we removed the fish bone and replaced it with caviar!

Somehow Mr. Thuilier took a liking to me, maybe because I always contradicted him. When I made something, he always had to taste it. He'd say, "Oh, put more salt, and a little more pepper." And when he made something, he made me taste it—and I'd say, "Oh, a little more salt, more pepper, and a little lemon juice." So he thought, *This guy really knows!* I just worked like him, in a way, and tried to imitate him.

Les Baux is a beautiful medieval village. The countryside around it is typical Provence: rugged and rocky, with lots of herbs growing like wild sage and rosemary. The restaurant building is made of stone cut from the mountains near there, and it dates to the 1600s.

I spent two and a half years there and learned a lot. I went through all the seasons a couple of times. The restaurant had something like five gardeners on staff. We got the best green beans and apricots. We had olive groves. The fish came fresh from the harbor in Marseille. And we used products from nearby towns that were famous for their olive oil, goat cheese, and other things.

As I look back, that was really a turning point. Before that, I didn't know if I wanted to cook or not. A chef works every Friday and Saturday night. It's crazy. And when you're young, you like to go out with girls instead, so it wasn't fun. But once I went to Baumanière, I couldn't have cared less how much I worked. That's where I really started to like what I do.

COMPASS POINTS

Where: Les Baux-de-Provence is located in the Bouches-du-Rhône region in southern France.

Backdrop: Les Baux-de-Provence rests atop a rocky outcrop in the Alpilles mountains. The area was settled 8,000 years ago and later served as a Celtic hill fort (2nd century B.C.) and the seat of a feudal lordship (Middle Ages). Dante's evocation of Purgatory in the Inferno was said to be inspired by the region's impressive cliffs and rocks. Today the village has picturesque ruins, including those of a castle known in medieval times for its chivalrous court culture, which featured minstrels and troubadours singing songs to the court's maidens. The castle displays reproductions of large early weapons, including a trebuchet, which was a medieval siege warfare machine that could hurl huge stone projectiles to smash rock walls 200 yards away. The village of Les Baux lent its name to Bauxite, an aluminum ore discovered here by a geologist in 1821. Lunch at L'Oustau de Baumanière is priced at €120 and the tasting menu at €175; there is also an à la carte menu.

Visitor Information: For the restaurant: www.oustaudebaumaniere.com; for the village: www.lesbauxdeprovence

Chef and restaurateur **Wolfgang Puck** *was born in Austria, trained in France, and came to the United States. at age 24. He cooked for Hollywood's elite at Ma Maison and then opened Spago, becoming famous for his signature gourmet pizza topped with smoked salmon and caviar. Today his enterprises include 15 fine dining restaurants, more than 80 Wolfgang Puck Express outlets, lines of cookware and prepared foods, and catering; he is the official caterer for the Academy Awards Governors Ball. Puck has received the prestigious James Beard Award for outstanding chef (twice) and outstanding restaurant, and his Food Network program,* Cooking Class with Wolfgang Puck, *won two Daytime Emmy Awards. His six cookbooks include* Wolfgang Puck Makes It Easy. *Puck supports Meals on Wheels (www .mowaa.org) in Los Angeles, which delivers food to the homebound, elderly, and ill.*

PAIGE RENSE

MID-COAST MAINE

*B*ecause I travel so much, my favorite place to be is at home — and home is in Maine. My husband and I live there part of the year in a lobster fishing village. We have a little compound: our house, his painting studio, two guest houses, a storage building, and two exhibition buildings. Our cat and dog are there, too, and we all just love it.

Years ago, friends kept telling me that the antiquing was wonderful in Maine, with great country auctions, so I decided to try it out. I went up by myself and fell in love immediately. Maine is really *away*. It's far from any kind of pressure, anything work related. I finally lured my husband up there when I found the perfect studio for him. That did it.

We live in an old sea captain's house. There are low stone walls all over the property, and moss grows under the trees. The house is more than a hundred years old, so there aren't a great number of people left who know much about it. But I just learned that Buddhist monks lived there many years ago. They built the stone walls and a little pavilion in our forest, maybe as a place for meditation. So I'm really fascinated now. Maybe I'll write to Richard Gere and see if he could find out anything about these Buddhists. Why were they in a village in Maine?

Everything here is dominated by the water. From our house, I see the lobster boats come and go. They head out very early in the morning, but I don't hear them — I sleep well when I'm here.

I enjoy talking with the lobster fishermen. They must have good schools in Maine, because everyone up there is so well spoken. You hear about people in Maine being cold to outsiders, but they were very welcoming to us.

We ended up in the middle of Wyeth territory, which we didn't realize at first. The Wyeths are a wonderful family and have become friends. Jamie lives on his own island with his wife, Phyllis. Andrew summers in the same house where his father, N.C., lived.

At a local auction, I bought a few pieces of furniture from the house that was in Andrew Wyeth's famous painting *Christina's World*. And in our house we have a lot of other things from country auctions. I collect Native American dolls — really old ones that children played with once. We also found at auction some boats in

Lobster boat returning to dock after hauling in the traps

bottles — not rare, but charming — and a pastel by the great American artist Milton Avery. Also at a local auction, I got a down-filled boudoir chair for $75.

Like a lot of old houses, ours had tiny bedrooms upstairs and one tiny bathroom, so I had to do some remodeling. Now I have a bay window that overlooks the lobster-fishing harbor. I sit in that $75 chair and write letters to the very few people I still actually write to, as opposed to emailing. And I read there. My bookshelves are just to the left, and my desk is to the right. The room is filled with light, and one of my husband's paintings hangs above our bed on the opposite side of the room.

I love that room above all others on Earth.

COMPASS POINTS

Where: Located in New England, Maine has many small towns in its Mid-Coast region.
Backdrop: Maine is the least populated state east of the Mississippi. Among its other unique features: It is the only state that borders just one other state (New Hampshire) and whose name is only one syllable long. Heavily forested, Maine is the nation's largest toothpick manufacturer;

in fact, one factory alone produces 20 million toothpicks a day. Popular with tourists, the state's Mid-Coast region has numerous summer homes and small towns located in counties such as Lincoln, Knox, Sagadahoc, and Cumberland. The Maine lobster (actually the American lobster, *Homarus americanus*) generally grows to nine inches long and two pounds or so, but can reach more than three feet in length and weigh more than 45 pounds, taking the crown as the world's heaviest marine crustacean. Only one in 50 million lobsters is yellow; a Maine lobster fisherman caught one, however, in 2006.

Visitor Information: www.visitmaine.com

Paige Rense is editor-in-chief of Architectural Digest, *which she joined in 1970. Under her direction, the magazine has become the world's leading design publication, with nearly five million readers. She is also the founding editor of* Bon Appétit. *A frequent lecturer, Rense has led symposiums at the Smithsonian Institution and other cultural organizations. Her awards include being named* Los Angeles Times *Woman of the Year and election to the Interior Design Hall of Fame. Her husband is the well-known Color Field painter Kenneth Noland. Rense supports the Humane Society of Knox County* (www.humanesocietyofknox county.org) *in Rockland, Maine, and the Lange Foundation* (www.langefoundation.com) *in Los Angeles.*

SALLY RIDE

EARTH ORBIT

y favorite place on Earth is actually off the planet—around 150 to 250 miles up. In 1983 and 1984, I flew aboard the Space Shuttle *Challenger*, and it gave me a perspective you just can't get anywhere else.

It was my first chance to really see our planet as a planet—from the outside, looking down. The shuttle flies in an orbit close enough to Earth that you don't actually see the whole planet at once, the way the Apollo astronauts did when they went to the moon. It's not the *Whole Earth Catalog* view. But this means that you can see a lot more detail on the surface of Earth.

One night I floated to the window of the shuttle—we were weightless, which is just totally fun!—and I watched the moonlight reflecting on the Mississippi River. Another time, we were on an orbit that took us up the East Coast of the United States. You could look off in the distance and see Miami coming, then trace out the whole East Coast in almost continuous lights. It's an outline we all recognize, the shape of the United States.

The first time you look down from space, you have no idea where you are over the world. There are no tidy lines down there like on a map—it would really help, though. Then after a few days you start to recognize the types of land; you know when you're over the Sahara, or over Europe.

This global view gave me lots of memorable pictures of our planet. The mountains between Pakistan and Afghanistan, around the Khyber Pass, looked like Earth was wrinkled; it's the oddest thing. And an unexpectedly beautiful sight was the deserts of Australia—amazing colors, all bright oranges and reds.

We also looked down at islands, like the Maldives in the Indian Ocean with their crystal blue water and almost circular patches of white beach. We saw coral reefs, too. And if you look in the other direction, away from Earth, outer space is pure blackness—punctuated with tons of stars.

It takes the space shuttle about 90 minutes to travel around the planet. This means you change from day to night every 45 minutes. For a Californian like me, it's sunset heaven! And I probably saw the sunrise more times in a couple of weeks in space than in all the rest of my life combined.

Earth's weather is dramatic from 200 miles up. We saw a few hurricanes, and

Snow-covered ridges of Pakistan's Hindu Kush mountains from space

I got a perspective on how massive a storm like that can be, how much territory it covers. Over the Indian Ocean, there was one where you could see right through the hurricane's eye all the way down to the water.

Unfortunately, from space you can also see pollution on Earth. I watched a stream of polluted water from the Rhône River emptying into the Mediterranean Sea, forming a delta of milky white on the water. I also saw smog over Los Angeles.

What has stuck with me, and is of lasting meaning, is how fragile Earth really is. Our atmosphere is incredibly thin—just a narrow, fuzzy line of royal blue across the horizon. When you look at the atmosphere from ground level, it looks like it goes on forever, but when you look at it from space, you think, *Um, is that all there is?*

It made me realize how careful we have to be about anything we do to our atmosphere. For me, it was a new way of thinking, to see Earth as a planet. After all, I'm an astrophysicist, and we look *outward*, away from Earth. I had never thought how important it is to protect our home. It's the only planet we've got.

Sally Ride

COMPASS POINTS

Where: "Outer space" (as distinguished from Earth's airspace) is defined by the Fédération Aéronautique Internationale as beginning 62 miles above Earth's surface. The United States designates anyone who flies higher than 50 miles an "astronaut."

Backdrop: The space shuttle reaches an orbit around Earth and stays there, tracing a near-circle above the atmosphere. Although orbiting astronauts are said to be weightless, they are actually still under the effect of Earth's gravity. Their weightlessness is a sort of free fall balanced between gravity and centrifugal force. The Moon similarly orbits Earth in a "free fall."

Visitor Information: Space tourism is currently an enterprise for the ultrawealthy. Space Adventures, Ltd. (*www.spaceadventures.com*), launches travelers on suborbital flights (weightlessness included) for $102,000, or rockets them to the orbiting International Space Station for a week for $25 million.

In 1983 **Sally Ride** *became the first American woman in space. After earning a Ph.D. in physics from Stanford University, she helped NASA develop the space shuttle's robot arm. Flying twice aboard the* Challenger, *she spent more than two weeks (343 hours) in space. She later served on the presidential commission that investigated the* Challenger's *tragic accident. On leave as a professor of physics at the University of California, San Diego, she devotes herself to Sally Ride Science, a company whose programs and training materials encourage students (especially girls) to enjoy and pursue science and technology. Ride is a member of the National Women's Hall of Fame and the Astronaut Hall of Fame.*

RICK RIDGEWAY

CHACABUCO VALLEY, PATAGONIA, CHILE

*A*ll of my favorite areas of the world are wild lands, places on the planet that evoke the sense of wildness to which all of us—as animals ourselves, in our ancestral history—were once more closely connected. My mind goes back to the northwest corner of Tibet, to the savannas of Africa, to the icy plateaus of Antarctica, and especially to the southern cone of South America, the region of Patagonia.

Patagonia has the remarkable potential to be protected while it is still unspoiled. In many ways, it's similar to the American West 150 years ago. There are still huge sections of grasslands and prairies without fences, where you can travel unhindered on horseback for hundreds of miles. There are mountains covered with glaciers, vast swaths of forest, and huge herds of wild animals—in particular, guanacos, the llama-like creatures that predominate in the landscape. Their predators are mountain lions, still found in abundance, with groups of condors circling overhead for the leavings.

There are also incongruities in Patagonia that you won't find in any other place in the world: desert steppes with glacial mountains sweeping up in the backdrop, and in the foreground flocks of pink flamingos wading in the shadows of turquoise lakes.

Patagonia, in all its attendant wonders, is represented by perhaps no better place than the Chacabuco Valley. This valley is unique in the whole southern half of the Andes, first because it cuts transversely, east–west, across the chain of mountains and second because it's in the rain shadow of an outlying range of peaks that form the Northern Patagonian Ice Cap; this means it has only a fourth as much rainfall as the windward slopes of the Andes, so it's much drier.

In the early 20th century, the Chacabuco Valley was occupied by Lucas Bridges, a British descendant who set up a sheep ranch. Later it was ranched by a sequence of Chilean families. The valley was grazed extensively, and by the turn of the 21st century, had been severely damaged. The hillsides were eroded, and the valley was crisscrossed by fences that prevented the native animals from moving freely.

In 2000, my close friend Kris Tompkins asked me to join the board of her new land trust, Conservacion Patagonica, which is dedicated to preserving wild sections of

The future Patagonia National Park looks like the best of Wyoming, Idaho, and Montana rolled into one.

Patagonia's remote Chacabuco Valley

Patagonia. I had been to the Chacabuco Valley in the 1990s on a fishing trip with another close friend, Yvon Chouinard, who founded Patagonia clothing and also joined the land trust. I went to the valley again on a camping trip with my wife and three kids. We asked permission to camp on the ranch and celebrated Christmas Day on the Chacabuco River.

In 2004, our foundation had the opportunity to buy the Chacabuco Valley, with the idea of creating a national park. The Chilean government agreed to add adjacent land to the north and an existing wildlife reserve to the south. Altogether, the park will spread across more than 750,000 acres—an area close to the size of Yosemite National Park.

The effort we've got going in Patagonia is not unlike the way Wyoming's Grand Teton National Park was created in the early 20th century by the Rockefeller family, who purchased the land and turned it into a national park. The future Patagonia National Park looks like the best of Wyoming, Idaho, and Montana rolled into one.

I try to go to the Chacabuco Valley once or twice a year now. In the future, when I return there with my kids as they get older, and maybe someday with their kids, we'll all remember when it wasn't protected. We'll go there as visitors to a fully functioning national park—and that's going to be magic.

COMPASS POINTS

Where: Occupying the southernmost section of South America, Patagonia is divided between Chile and Argentina.

Backdrop: Patagonia got its name from the Spanish *Patagón* ("Bigfoot"), a word that Ferdinand Magellan's crew used for local native people they described as giants. Guanacos can run 35 miles per hour; in the open areas where they live, without hiding places, speed is a necessary survival skill.

Visitor Information: www.visit-chile.org

Climber and adventurer **Rick Ridgeway** *was on the first American team to reach the summit of K2 and the first ever to do it without bottled oxygen. He made the first transverse of Borneo at its widest point, walked 300 miles from the summit of Mount Kilimanjaro to the Indian Ocean, and made the first big wall climb in Antarctica. Producer of some 30 adventure shows for television (one of which won an Emmy), he is also the author of six books, including* Seven Summits *and* The Big Open, *published by National Geographic.*

Discoveries VI

JERRY SEINFELD

HECKSCHER FIELDS, CENTRAL PARK, NEW YORK CITY

*W*hen I first moved to Manhattan from Long Island as a young man, I used to go to comedy clubs every night. I was learning, and I worked mostly at the Comic Strip. The club had a softball team in the Broadway-show league—each Broadway cast had a team, and we somehow got in.

We played in Central Park at Heckscher fields, only a few hundred feet from the south border of the park. It's a spectacular place to be playing softball. You're in the park, but there are skyscrapers all around you.

It was such a fantasy! First, to be a comedian, and to be part of this nightclub; I was a regular at the Comic Strip and performed there every night. Second, we were playing in Central Park; my whole life, I had wanted to move into the city, and Central Park is an epicenter of Manhattan. It hit me that all these things in my life had kind of collided together—this dream of living in Manhattan, this dream of being a comedian.

And still we were doing this childlike thing in the middle of this most grown-up of places. On a Tuesday afternoon, you'd be in jeans and sneakers, running around playing ball, and you'd see the skyscrapers with all the *real* people working for a living. You couldn't escape the fact that you had just dodged this *huge* bullet in life: *I'm not up there working!*

> We were doing this childlike thing in the middle of this most grown-up of places.

I remember in the late '70s we played a game with the Broadway cast of *The Basic Training of Pavlo Hummel*, which starred Al Pacino. That day Larry David, who played for the Improv club's team, wondered: What if you injured one of these huge stars during this silly game and really affected an important Broadway show? Later, on *Seinfeld* we did an episode like that, with Bette Midler playing the part of the Broadway legend.

These days I walk by Heckscher fields every day on the way to my office on 57th Street. It's still an extraordinarily beautiful place. There are five grass fields that all intersect, so it's a giant greensward in the middle of the urban smelt-works.

The ball fields of Central Park

It was just a perfect *How did I manage to end up here?* kind of place. I think it's the greatest spot to play softball in the whole world.

COMPASS POINTS

Where: New York City's Central Park is bounded on the south and north by West 59th and 110th streets, and on the east and west by Fifth and Eighth avenues.

Backdrop: With 843 acres, Central Park is nearly twice as large as Monaco, and its annual 25 million visitors make it the most popular park in the United States. It offers 26 ball fields, theaters, a billion-gallon reservoir circled by a running track, playgrounds, a zoo, birding (more than 25 percent of the nation's bird species have been sighted in the park), and many other attractions and activities.

Visitor Information: www.centralpark.com

*Comedian **Jerry Seinfeld** cocreated, cowrote, and starred in the series* Seinfeld, *which ran from 1989 through 1998 and was one of the most successful shows in television history,* *winning Emmy, Golden Globe, and Screen Actors Guild awards; some 76 million people watched the final episode. His book* Seinlanguage *was a best-seller, and he documented his classic stand-up comedy material in a 1998 HBO special and album,* I'm Telling You for the Last Time, *which included this exchange:*

Jerry: I'm a single guy, by the way. There are no other guys attached to me. [cheering]
Jerry: Thank you very much.
Woman from audience: Jerry, I love you!
Jerry [turns to the woman]**:** Thank you. I love you, too. But I do feel the need to see other people.

Seinfeld's return to comedy clubs was documented in the 2002 film Comedian. *He also coproduced, cowrote, and voiced the lead role in the computer-animated* Bee Movie. *He supports Baby Buggy (www.babybuggy.org), which refurbishes and delivers used baby equipment to New York families in need.*

RAVI SHANKAR

VARANASI, INDIA

The magical and holy city of Benares—or Varanasi, as it's called now—is the place where I was born. One of the oldest cities in the world, it has somehow managed to retain its charm, even today.

The city is a feeling in your bones; it is beyond comprehension. In Varanasi, you find a stream of colors and sounds that challenges human brainpower to register everything at once. And the mind sees beyond the mundane and feels the spiritual beauty of this holy city—a most important pilgrimage place for Hindus, attracting people from all over India and the world.

To ride on a boat on the River Ganges during sunrise or sunset can be a spiritual experience. I remember sitting on a boat at sunrise and watching the ravishing beauty of Varanasi unravel itself with the golden rays of the dawn. Temple bells and the chanting of ancient mantras float in the air, immersing you in tranquility. Varanasi still has the aura of the ancient world.

It is an experience beyond comparison to walk down the city's many *gallis*, narrow lanes filled with shops strewn with colorful silk saris (for which the city is famous), glass bangles, and beautiful hand-woven shawls. And wow!—all the eating places, offering milk products, savories, snacks and sweets, along with the scents of jasmine, sandalwood, and mangoes, can drive you crazy.

In this city, which has been inhabited for more than 5,000 years, you can witness the complete cycle of life, from birth to death. On the *ghats*—flights of steps leading down to the Ganges—the birth of babies is celebrated by dipping them in the water. And it is every Hindu's desire to come here to die and be cremated according to the old Hindu rites, for they believe that this will indeed release them from the cycle of reincarnation. Everyone, young and old, takes a holy dip in the Ganges.

My joy was to visit the ghats with my mother and brothers, because there was so much natural entertainment and sound everywhere: *bhajans* (devotional songs), *kirtans* (sacred hymns), and in the early morning the wondrous *shahnai* (a double-reed instrument, something like an oboe). I grew up in this supremely spiritual and musical atmosphere. But today, it is probably more a cacophony, with the commercialized music of Raga, pop, and Bollywood mixed together.

Colorful main ghat in Varanasi

Along the banks of the Ganges, you also find some highly enlightened saints, as well as many semi-naked showmen with matted long hair and beards who are high on drugs; they attract naïve tourists and young hippies.

It is the old Varanasi of my early life that I remember and love. Some of the memories I will never forget are of my mother, with her beautiful face, cradling me in her arms and singing lullabies to me. Sitting together on the terrace and gazing at the sky, she would tell me the names of all the stars, and the myths of gods and goddesses.

My mother was a woman who could conceal all her pain and sorrow and still radiate a smile. I remember her smell, her touch, her voice, and the delicious simple food she cooked, the aroma of which still lingers in my mind. To this day, I remember the tasty spinach she made.

I had a lot of first experiences in Varanasi that make this place very special to me. This was where I saw my father for the first time, when I was about eight years old. This was probably also where I saw white women for the first time, two friends of my father. One was portly and one very skinny, but both were very British. I must have looked so clumsy in the posh hotel where my father was staying. I had my first English breakfast of fried eggs and didn't know what to do with the yolk, which eventually found its place on my lap, as I didn't know how to use a fork and knife. The ladies and my father initiated me in the art of using cutlery and serviettes. I still don't know how I managed to get through the ordeal—it must have been a sight!

Varanasi was also where I first saw my eldest brother, Uday Shankar, who changed and shaped my life. After ten years in Europe and America, he came back as a painter and dancer. I was completely bowled over by his "Prince Charming" personality. He whisked me away, along with my family and a few musicians from Varanasi, to mind-boggling Paris. Later I met the great *sarod* player Baba Allauddin Khan there and became his disciple.

Varanasi was the place where I built my first home as well, in 1973, with so many dreams—and it was the place where all those dreams were shattered by some unscrupulous people I had to deal with.

At different times, I've had all three of my children with me in Varanasi. Shubho, my son who is no more, visited me there and performed with me, too. Norah, or "Geetali" as I call her, came when she was very young, and I carried her around to various places. A few miles from the city, I took my youngest child, Anoushka, to visit Sarnath, the deer park where the Buddha gave his first sermon. These wonderful memories stay with me.

Varanasi is the eternal abode of Lord Shiva, and one of my favorite temples is that of Lord Hanuman, the monkey god. The city is also where one of the many miracles that have happened in my life took place: I met Ma Anandamayi, a great spiritual soul. Seeing the beauty of her face and mind, I became her ardent devotee.

Sitting at home now in Encinitas, in Southern California, at the age of 88, surrounded by the beautiful greens, multicolored flowers, blue sky, clean air, and the Pacific Ocean, I often reminisce about all the wonderful places I have seen in the world. I cherish the memories of Paris, New York, and a few other places. But Varanasi seems to be etched in my heart!

COMPASS POINTS

Where: Varanasi is located on the Gangetic plains of northern India, in the state of Uttar Pradesh.

Backdrop: Varanasi is one of the oldest continually inhabited cities in the world and is considered by many Hindus to be India's holiest city. There are nearly 100 ghats along the Ganges River, which flows 1,560 miles from the Himalayas to the Bay of Bengal, draining one-quarter of the territory of India. The river is personified and worshiped by Hindus as the goddess Ganga. Hindus hope to bathe in the Ganges at least once during their lives and consider it auspicious to die in Varanasi; bodies are cremated on ghats and the ashes placed in the Ganges. More than one million pilgrims come to Varanasi each year. Many take home containers of sacred water from the river, believing that a dying person who drinks it will go to heaven. Sri Anandamayi Ma was a spiritual teacher and mystic from Bengal whose name means "Joy Permeated Mother."

Visitor Information: www.tourisminindia.com

*The sublime sitarist and composer **Ravi Shankar** is India's best-known classical musician and most esteemed musical ambassador. Called the "Godfather of World Music" by George Harrison, Shankar has written concertos for sitar and orchestra, violin-sitar compositions for Yehudi Menuhin and himself, and music for flute virtuoso Jean-Pierre Rampal, as well as influencing musicians from the Beatles to John Coltrane. Introducing his highly spiritual music to young Westerners, he performed at the Monterey Pop Festival and Woodstock. Shankar has recorded dozens of albums and composed extensively for films, including Gandhi (for which he received an Academy Award nomination) and Satyajit Ray's Apu Trilogy. He is an honorary member of the American Academy of Arts and Letters and a member of the United Nations International Rostrum of Composers and has received three Grammy Awards as well as the Bharat Ratna, India's highest civilian honor. He is the father of singer Norah Jones and sitarist Anoushka Shankar. His autobiography is My Music, My Life. He established the Ravi Shankar Foundation (www.ravishankar.org/foundation.html) to archive his work, teach students, and work for universal peace and harmony through music.*

WILLIAM SHATNER

SIERRA FOOTHILLS, CALIFORNIA

There's a spot in the foothills of the Sierras in central California that's on a wild river. I don't want to get too specific, because I own the place. Let's just say it's east of Visalia.

I found the place many years ago, a wide expanse of land between two mountains that come together in the distance. In winter, you can see the snow that feeds the river. It's too cold to get in the water then, so you wait all summer while the heat from the San Joaquin Valley melts the snow and warms the river.

I built a house by this wild river on top of a granite rock. The house reflects its environs and is the color of the surrounding manzanita — the green of the leaves, the brown of the bark.

A sculptor made some statues for me out of redwood — figures of Indians, the Native Americans who lived on that land hundreds of years ago. I put the wooden

Mountain stream in the Sierra Nevada foothills

figures lurking behind trees and kneeling at cooking sites — the remains of living trees that represent the soul of the Indians.

I had a magical spot there on the river, with no neighbors anywhere around. But at one point in my life I was in a great deal of financial trouble, and I was sitting in the river, naked, contemplating selling the land in order to raise some money. Then I glanced at a nearby rock and saw a little lizard reaching up to grab droplets of water, which the river flung in the air as it cascaded on the rocks. I watched the lizard drink, and it was like a secret revealed to me: *So that's how lizards get water!*

My next thought was *Am I crazy? Am I really going to sell this place, or am I going to be a part of the spirit of this land for the rest of my life?*

My decision was made in an instant. I still have the house by the wild river.

COMPASS POINTS

Where: The southern Sierra Nevada foothills lie east of Visalia, in central California.
Backdrop: Travelers in the southern Sierra region can visit Sequoia National Park, established in 1890 as the nation's second national park (after Yellowstone). Attractions include Mount Whitney (14,505 ft.), the highest point in the continental United States, and the General Sherman, a giant sequoia that is the world's largest tree by volume.
Visitor Information: Sequoia National Park: www.nps.gov/seki

William Shatner's varied career has included work with the Stratford Shakespeare Festival, television dramas such as Playhouse 90, *and Broadway productions. He gained fame as Capt. James T. Kirk in the* Star Trek *television series and movies, then as eccentric law firm partner Denny Crane in* The Practice *and* Boston Legal, *winning two Emmys and a Golden Globe for his portrayal. Shatner wrote the* Tek War *series of science fiction novels; in music, his albums include* Has Been. *A horse breeder, he established the William and Elizabeth Shatner/Jewish National Fund Therapeutic Riding Consortium Endowment for Israel, designed to offer Israeli, Bedouin, Palestinian, and Jordanian children healing and to bring children of that war-torn area together in hope of building a lasting peace.*

KELLY SLATER

TAVARUA, FIJI

*W*hen you fly into Fiji's main island, Viti Levu, it's not quite the beautiful tropical place you imagined. It has pine trees and red clay dirt where they grow sugarcane, and if it has been raining, the water isn't especially clear. But just half an hour's boat ride away, you find the small island of Tavarua, where the water is crisp and clean, with 100-foot visibility. If you fly in on a helicopter, you see that the island is heart-shaped, which is quite poetic.

The whole island is a resort, catering mostly to surfers. Tavarua is covered with coconut palms, and the weather is tropical—very warm like Hawaii's. The ecosystem is really healthy, so there's abundant sea life. There *are* sharks, but only because there are a lot of fish for them to feed on. The fishing is amazing, the diving second to none, and the surfing as good as it gets.

But the people are really the best part of Tavarua. They're the friendliest people I've met anywhere in the world. They're always singing, dancing, smiling, and laughing. And they're always ready to help someone out—they have literally given me their beds to sleep in.

It's remarkable the way they take care of people who have any kind of handicap. Once I was there to make a surf film. All the kids in the village were excited to see foreigners, and we brought them little gifts like chewing gum and coloring books. One boy, though, was scared of the cameras, totally freaked out. But instead of laughing and making a joke out of him—like you'd typically find in an American school, unfortunately—the other kids gathered around and hugged him. They made him feel comfortable. Later I learned that people with problems are actually elevated in the community. The islanders have an incredible amount of empathy for other people.

Fijians are also talented musicians. They sing three- and four-part harmonies, and most of them know how to strum a guitar and play the ukulele. My friends and I sometimes join in. Their music is basic three-chord blues—but we call it the "fluorescent blues," because of the island's tropical colors and because the songs are happy rather than bluesy. The music is totally relaxed.

> *It's remarkable the way they take care of people who have any kind of handicap.... people with problems are actually elevated in the community.*

The heart-shaped island of Tavarua

I almost always go to Momi village, where I've known people for nearly 20 years. Chief Druku is the welcoming committee. His family owns the island, which they lease to the resort. There are some great stories about him, like the time he was fishing on the beach and hooked a huge fish. By the time he landed it, the fish had dragged him into the water and the chief had lost all his clothes. There he was, pulling his fish up the beach naked.

Druku was the first Fijian surfer, and around 1982 surfers from the mainland started coming to Tavarua. One great break is called Restaurants, because it's just in front of the resort restaurant. It's a left—we classify waves by whether they break to the right or left as you ride. A wave breaks here for about 30 or 35 seconds from beginning to end, and the trade winds groom it perfectly.

Below the surface are shallow coral reefs—in fact, this is probably the world's most dangerous coral reef for surfers, with staghorn and fire coral right under you. Everyone I know has lost some skin on that reef. You can also get your leash stuck on the coral, and guys have come close to drowning there.

Cloudbreak is one of the other great waves at the island. On a big wave at Cloudbreak, you're going really fast. The swell is moving forward at probably 20 miles an hour, and then you're riding down the line of it, rising and falling, surfing up and down the wave. I'd guess you can get going 40 miles an hour, and in massive surf even faster than that.

The ultimate thrill is getting barreled—when you disappear into the tube and then reappear. It's like riding the eye of a hurricane. When a wave barrels, air gets trapped inside. It has to go somewhere, so it takes the path of least resistance, rushes out the open end of the barrel—and spits you out with it. It's like having a tailwind. You get some propulsion, a little free nitro! But sometimes the air blows you off your board, and you eat it.

I had a bad wipeout there on the biggest day I've ever surfed. A wave with a 30-foot face knocked me off my board, and I was underwater for a long time and starting to get a little stressed out. I finally made it to the surface—just before another wave hit me and did the same thing. But I was fine afterward; these things happen.

Another day, I was surfing in a contest. My father had recently passed away, and I was just sitting out there, imagining my dad being able to surf one of these big waves. And no sooner did I have that thought than the best wave I ever caught popped up right in front of me. I got barreled on it for about 12 seconds. That was a very special wave.

A few years ago, I won a surf contest on Tavarua—I'd never won a contest there before—and when I came into the restaurant, all the women who worked in the kitchen, cooking for the surfers every day, came and hugged me. They were screaming and crying and laughing, celebrating my win. The people there really make you part of their life. We all got pretty emotional, because I felt like I was sharing it with my family.

What I've learned from the people of Tavarua is that the important things are happiness and laughter. Life should be simple.

COMPASS POINTS

Where: Tavarua is located just west of the main Fijian island of Viti Levu and is about a 30-minute boat ride away.

Backdrop: Fiji (officially the Republic of the Fiji Islands) consists of 322 islands (only one-third of them occupied) and 522 islets. It was settled as early as 1000 B.C. The island of Tavarua has an area of about 29 acres, depending on the tide. It lies near one of the world's largest disturbance centers, in the Tasman Sea, and gets the benefit of waves that are generated there. Tavarua's most consistent surf is during winter (from May to September), although summer surf can include hurricane swells. Popular surfing spots include Cloudbreak, Restaurants, Rights, and Kiddieland. Other water sports here include fishing, scuba diving, snorkeling, and kayaking. Fijian music resembles that of Polynesia and is played with guitars, ukeleles, and indigenous instruments such as lali drums.

Visitor Information: Tavarua Island Resort: www.tavarua.com

Kelly Slater has won the world surfing championship eight times and holds the record for most career tour victories (36), making him the top surfer of all time. He won his first world title at age 20, the youngest world champion in history. In a 2005 contest in Tahiti, he became the first surfer ever to score two perfect rides. As a musician, Slater has played onstage with Ben Harper and Pearl Jam. He appeared in the movie Surf's Up *and TV's* Baywatch, *modeled for Versace, and was listed among* People's "50 Most Beautiful People." *He is the subject of the video game* Kelly Slater's Pro Surfer *and the book* Pipe Dreams: A Surfer's Journey. *Slater supports the Surfrider Foundation (www.surfrider.org); the Sea Shepherd Conservation Society (www.seashepherd.org); the L.A. Surf Bus (www .lasurfbus.org), which takes inner-city kids surfing; the Space Coast Early Intervention Center (www.sceic.com); and Surfers Healing (www.surfershealing.org), which runs surfing therapy camps for autistic children.*

JAMES TAYLOR

THE CENTER OF THE ATLANTIC OCEAN

Once I made a passage up the center of the Atlantic, from the Caribbean to Martha's Vineyard, with a good sailor on a beautiful boat. It was an old wooden sailboat made of teak, strong and seaworthy. The masts were tall, and we operated the sails by hand. I was part of the crew.

Our captain, Nat Benjamin, who is a boat builder on Martha's Vineyard, is an expert at deep ocean sailing. We didn't have satellite navigation. He simply knew when weather was coming. We would shorten sail for a storm, the storm would hit, and we were ready for it. We went through one thrilling night with seas the size of huge houses passing under us. We just ran before the storm, feeling complete trust in our captain.

We had started our trip from the island of St. Martin and after about five days got to the Sargasso Sea. The surface was a floating mat of sargasso weed, which has a unique variety of flora and fauna within it, with eels breeding and other animals living there — an ecosystem unto itself.

The Sargasso Sea is in the Bermuda Triangle. We were becalmed there, as is often the case in the Doldrums, so we let down the sails, stopped the motor, and just sat on these oily, calm swells. And to while away the time, we went swimming — in the center of the Atlantic Ocean. The depth of the water beneath us was something like three miles. To think that if you stood on the boat and flipped a quarter overboard, it would be falling and falling and falling for a day and a half before it hit bottom — that gave me an amazing feeling.

On a boat, everyone takes turn standing watches around the clock. At night, you watch the polestar and see the entire cosmos revolve around it. It's a remarkable awareness you get of being on this planet in space. I know that as astronauts look back at Earth, they get a great sense of what it is. On our boat, I could feel myself on the surface of this water planet.

In a way, it was similar to two trips I've taken down the Grand Canyon in wooden dories. It takes 19 days to get through the canyon, and it really takes you away from ordinary experience and timetables. The fact that you're drifting with the river, and not motoring down or powering through it, also has an effect on you. You're in this great geological picture book, which goes back in time as you get

Sailing hard in the Atlantic

deeper and deeper. It gives you a profound experience of the planet—to be at the bottom of this great slice through time and into the depths of Earth. You pass a layer that was once the floor of a sea and eventually get down to the Vishnu Schist, which is two billion years old, some of the oldest rock on the planet. To see this stuff, to drift past it, to live with it, changes you—just like being in the middle of the Atlantic Ocean.

I was never taught a particular religion growing up. My father was a scientist, and I think, being from the South, he had an aversion to the available organized religious forms. So I was never given a strong religious connection. But I have a very strong spiritual need. And getting into nature is going to church for me. It's my way of surrendering to the bigger picture, to the whole.

I feel the skin of life on the planet as a sort of coevolved life form. It has a type of consciousness that we humans—with individuated consciousness and an ego-based worldview—see as alien. But it's my own belief that it is alive, a single organism on this amazing, rare, and perhaps unique planet. I really need to feel that connection.

COMPASS POINTS

Where: The North Atlantic Ocean encompasses the Sargasso Sea.

Backdrop: The Atlantic Ocean covers 20 percent of Earth's surface and has an area of 41.1 million square miles, second in size only to the Pacific. Its average depth is nearly 11,000 feet. The island of St. Martin/St. Maarten is divided between France and the Netherlands Antilles. The Sargasso Sea is the world's only sea without shores; it is surrounded by ocean currents. Eels that hatch there swim to Europe or the East Coast of North America, then return to lay eggs. A vast garbage patch of plastic and other non-biodegradable waste has been collected by the currents of the Sargasso Sea. Despite the Bermuda Triangle's reputation for mysterious forces that cause ships and airplanes to disappear, it is a busy transportation route, and both the U.S. Coast Guard and the insurer Lloyd's of London judge it to be as safe as other areas of the ocean.

Visitor Information: St. Martin (French side): www.st-martin.org; St. Maarten (Dutch side) www.st-maarten.com; Martha's Vineyard: www.mvy.com; www.mvol.com

The quintessential singer-songwriter, **James Taylor** *has earned 40 gold, platinum, and multi-platinum awards, as well as five Grammy Awards. His influential songs range from "Country Road" and "Fire and Rain" to "Shower the People" and "Never Die Young." He has been elected to both the Rock and Roll Hall of Fame and the Songwriters Hall of Fame. Taylor was introduced to the sea by his grandfather, a commercial fisherman in Massachusetts, and spent summers sailing around Martha's Vineyard with his father and siblings. He serves on the board of trustees of the Natural Resources Defense Council (www.nrdc.org), which works to protect wildlife and wild places and to ensure a healthy environment. He currently lives in western Massachusetts with his wife, Caroline, and twin boys, Rufus and Henry.*

ALEX TREBEK

HAWORTH, ENGLAND

I've always been a big fan of *Wuthering Heights,* and just before my wife and I got married, we made a trip to Brontë country in Yorkshire to visit that family's parsonage and walk the moors. I wanted to see the locale where the story took place (even though the 1939 classic movie was actually filmed in Thousand Oaks, California).

Jean and I headed to Top Withens, which was possibly Emily Brontë's inspiration for the Earnshaw family farmstead, Wuthering Heights; it's not certain, of course, but there's a plaque on the ruined farmhouse.

We started out walking among great fields of purple; the heather was in full bloom. It was incredibly romantic. Then it started to rain—hard. It rained horizontally, but Jean and I wouldn't give up. We got soaking wet and loved it. We trekked and laughed all the way up to Top Withens and back, a distance of about six miles.

On the way, we stopped for shelter in an old sheep barn built of stone. To commemorate our visit, I carved our names in one of the soft limestone rocks inside. A couple of years after we got married, we went back to the barn to see our names, and by then we'd had our son Matthew, so we carved his name next to ours. On a later trip, we walked there a third time to carve our daughter Emily's name—but by then the old sheep barn had been knocked to the ground. I guess somebody wanted to clear the space or use the rocks. So, somewhere in Yorkshire, there's a stone carved with Jean's name, my name, Matthew's name…and that's all.

The Brontës' house looks almost the same way it did two hundred years ago—just a plain, but impressive, gray brick, two-story house.

The great thing about England is that you can be almost anywhere and be surrounded by history. It helps that it's an English-speaking country, and that we grew up learning about it. In Haworth, Jean and I sat in the very same pub where Emily Brontë's brother apparently drank himself to death. We stayed in a bed-and-breakfast right across the street from the Brontë parsonage. We were above an apothecary shop, and our window looked out over the hills and dales.

The Brontës' house looks almost the same way it did two hundred years ago—just a plain, but impressive, gray brick, two-story house with a center door.

Parsonage at Haworth

Alex Trebek

It's furnished as it would have been in their day. As we left the parsonage, we walked through the little church cemetery. It was all so picturesque.

Even though Haworth is a tourist town, you can easily slip away. The Brontë home is off the main street—not only geographically, but also in time. You're in another world. It's only a block from all the little tourist shops and tearooms on the main street, but all of a sudden it's quiet, and you're transported to the past.

COMPASS POINTS

Where: The village of Haworth is situated above the Worth Valley and the Pennine moors in West Yorkshire.

Backdrop: The novel *Wuthering Heights* portrays a great deal of sickness and death; during Emily Brontë's lifetime (1818–1848), Haworth was a crowded industrial town where the average age of death was 25 years old and nearly half the babies died before their sixth birthdays. Emily Brontë (pronounced *bron-tee*, not *bron-tay*) would have known of Top Withens, but the farmstead didn't resemble the Wuthering Heights of the novel. The walk there is so popular with tourists from Japan that the footpath signs are also in Japanese.

Visitor Information: www.visitbrontecountry.com; www.visitbradford.com

Answer: **Alex Trebek**

Questions: Who has been the host of television's Jeopardy! *since 1984, earning four Emmys and a star on the Hollywood Walk of Fame? Which TV personality set a record in 1991 by hosting three national daily game shows at once (the others were* Classic Concentration *and* To Tell the Truth*)? Which native of Canada earned a degree in philosophy from the University of Ottawa and later became a U.S. citizen? Who hosts the National Geographic Bee, an annual geography contest sponsored by the National Geographic Society? Which game-show host is a spokesman for World Vision International (www.wvi.org) and tours overseas with the USO?*

DONALD TRUMP

MAR-A-LAGO, PALM BEACH, FLORIDA

I've always loved the ambience and the weather of Palm Beach, and I was able to buy what is considered the great house of this part of the country, Mar-a-Lago. It was built in 1927 as a winter home by cereal heiress Marjorie Merriweather Post and her husband, broker E. F. Hutton.

Building Mar-a-Lago took four years and $2.5 million, back when $2.5 million was serious money. The scale is beyond anything most people have seen, with 148 rooms, tremendously high ceilings and huge windows, a tower, and decorations that include elaborate carvings and 36,000 Spanish tiles.

Mar-a-Lago means "Sea-to-Lake," and this is the only house in Palm Beach that fronts on both the Atlantic Ocean and Lake Worth. In Palm Beach, if you front on the lake, that's good. If you front on the ocean, that's good. Most people front on neither—but this house fronts on both. There's no other place like it, and you could never build this house again or find a piece of land like that.

To me, the living room is the most spectacular room in the house. It has a gold-leafed ceiling that's 35 feet high, a copy of one in the Galleria dell'Accademia in Venice—but a larger version, actually. Mrs. Post would always take something she liked and make it bigger and better.

A bedroom suite called Deenie's House is where actress Dina Merrill—Mrs. Post's daughter—grew up. It was also my daughter Ivanka's bedroom. I've kept it exactly as it was. In the bathroom, set at a child's height on the walls, are rows of painted tiles that illustrate nursery rhymes—and that were designed by Walt Disney.

When I bought the house in 1985, I brought it back to its original grandeur and luster. Ten years later, I opened it as the Mar-a-Lago Club, which has become the number-one club anywhere in the country. Members are people of great stature and great wealth, a mixture of the "old" and "new" Palm Beach. Originally, the membership fee was $25,000; now it costs $175,000 to join.

Mar-a-Lago's 88-foot tower is the highest point in Palm Beach. Everybody looks up at it, but most don't know that inside there's an incredible bedroom suite.

We've had everybody at the Mar-a-Lago Club; I mean essentially *everybody* stays there. Nothing can compete with it. It's a ten-star facility. I've added a spa,

Mar-a-Lago living room, east wall

tennis courts, swimming pools, and a beach club. I also turned a patio into the Tea House, with a tented roof made of fabric. You come in through an original loggia decorated with carved stone monkeys.

Mar-a-Lago's 88-foot tower is the highest point in Palm Beach. Everybody looks up at it, but most don't know that inside there's an incredible bedroom suite. I usually have young people stay there, because the guests have to have the capacity to walk up the stairs. In 1994, Michael Jackson and Lisa Marie Presley honeymooned in that suite. They were there for three days, and they never left. I don't know what took place, but I guess something did.

I also added a 25,000-square-foot ballroom to Mar-a-Lago. It has huge crystal chandeliers, and one wall is lined with floor-to-ceiling mirrors. The ballroom has really taken over Palm Beach, and we have many of the great events there, including the International Red Cross Ball, which is very popular and important. We have raised tremendous amounts of money for charity.

Employees have told me about the great parties that Mrs. Post used to have at Mar-a-Lago. I think she'd be very happy with what I've done with the house, because I continue that tradition. *All* the great parties in Palm Beach are now held at Mar-a-Lago.

COMPASS POINTS

Where: Mar-a-Lago is located at 1100 South Ocean Boulevard in Palm Beach, Florida.
Backdrop: A National Historic Landmark, Mar-a-Lago was designed in Spanish-Moorish style by architects Marion Sims Wyeth and Joseph Urban; Urban originally came to the United States from Austria to design sets for the Ziegfield Follies and the Metropolitan Opera. In creating the living room ceiling at Mar-a-Lago, Marjorie Merriweather Post used up all the gold leaf available in the United States and had to import more from Europe. The library (now a bar for club guests) has walnut paneling that she imported from an English estate. For one party, Mrs. Post had the Ringling Brothers and Barnum & Bailey Circus put up its tent in her garden; for another, she flew in the cast of a Broadway show, who after their performance were her guests for a week. During the social season in Palm Beach, Mar-a-Lago was tended by a staff of 73.
Visitor Information: www.maralagoclub.com

Donald Trump has interests in real estate developments from New York to Dubai, as well as in gaming, sports, and entertainment. Known as a peerless deal maker, he is chairman and president of the Trump Organization. Several buildings in New York City bear his name, including the Trump International Hotel & Tower, designed by Philip Johnson, and the 90-story Trump World Tower, the tallest residential tower in the world. Other eponymous enterprises include a vodka and a line of men's clothing. Trump co-owns the world's three largest beauty competitions: Miss Universe, Miss USA, and Miss Teen USA. His autobiography, The Art of the Deal, has sold more than three million copies. His reality television show, The Apprentice, has received three Emmy nominations, and he has a star on the Hollywood Walk of Fame. Trump became the world's most highly paid speaker when he gave a one-hour talk for the Learning Annex for a fee of $1 million.

MARILYN VOS SAVANT

THE LEFT BANK, PARIS, FRANCE

*A*rriving in Paris for our honeymoon back in August 1987, my husband and I climbed the steep, crooked little spiral staircase in an 18th- or 19th-century stone building, located in a quiet middle-class neighborhood on the Left Bank, with some trepidation. At the top, we found the third-floor attic apartment that would be our home for six weeks, and it looked like a scene out of *La Bohème*.

The old wooden beams were hand-hewn, and the ceiling sloped down to irregular plaster walls. Ancient tile gave way to wide-plank wood floors in most of the bedroom and living room. A sleeping loft complete with creaky wooden steps took good advantage of the open space above. Little windows peeked out here and there and everywhere, it seemed, so I opened one of them and peered outside: the famous Paris rooftops were everywhere.

The Paris Metro leads to charming neighborhoods.

It was raining, and we could hear footsteps down on the cobblestone street. Couples walked by under dark umbrellas, arm in arm. Stooped old women with canes made their way down the sidewalk, either unable to hold up their umbrellas or not caring much about the rain.

When it stopped raining, we pocketed our bulky brass key—which looked a lot like an old skeleton key—and headed out. After passing a schoolyard, we found ourselves at Rue Mouffetard, which was bursting with street market stalls. I pondered a pile of avocados for a moment too long, and the proprietor quickly appeared beside me. "For today or tomorrow? Or after?" he asked (yes, in French). I replied, "Tomorrow." He scanned the avocados and reached for one. "This is the one you want." Ah, yes.

And so we blended into the scene and soon joined the ranks of the people we saw carrying their daily baguette home after work every day. We returned the following fall and many falls after that, always to a little apartment off the beaten path.

COMPASS POINTS

Where: The Left Bank (La Rive Gauche) of the River Seine makes up the southern half of Paris. **Backdrop:** The historic haunt of romantics, artists, and writers, the Left Bank was a favorite of painters Pablo Picasso and Henri Matisse, philosopher Jean-Paul Sartre, and expatriate American authors Ernest Hemingway and F. Scott Fitzgerald. The area includes Montparnasse, an artistic district, and the Latin Quarter, for 750 years the hub of student life around the Sorbonne. **Visitor Information:** Paris Convention and Visitors Bureau: http://en.parisinfo.com

Marilyn vos Savant writes the "Ask Marilyn" column in Parade *magazine, posing quizzes and answering questions from readers. She has been listed in the* Guinness Book of World Records *under "Highest IQ"; hers was measured on the Stanford-Binet test at 228. Her books include* The Art of Spelling: The Madness and the Method, *and* Growing Up: A Classic American Childhood. *Marilyn vos Savant is also a lecturer and playwright, and is married to Robert Jarvik, M.D., inventor of the Jarvik Artificial Heart and the Jarvik 2000 Heart. She supports the American Heart Association* (www.americanheart.org).

COMMODORE
BERNARD WARNER

ST. KITTS, WEST INDIES

As dawn was breaking on April 11, 2006, the *Queen Mary 2* approached St. Kitts. The twin craters of Mount Liamuiga towered above the horizon, and the green pastures so reminiscent of the rolling fields of England spilled down to the turquoise Caribbean Sea.

Looking through my binoculars, just five miles to the west I could make out Old Road Bay and the beach where in 1623 one of my ancestors, a young Capt. Thomas Warner, together with his wife Rebecca, his son Edward, and 14 others had landed from the schooner *Marmaduke* to found the first English settlement in the West Indies.

I felt a tingle of pride. Following in the tradition of Tom Warner's early voyage, I would be berthing the world's largest ocean liner at the island home of my forebear. As coincidence would have it, I too was traveling with my wife and two young sons.

St. Kitts is a regular winter port of call for the *QM2*, which docks at the main port and capital, Basseterre. Five miles beyond, you come to Middle Island village, where St. Thomas Church has a special meaning for me. In the churchyard is a tomb carved with my family's coat of arms, the heraldic shield of the Warner family. It reminds me that I am a direct descendant of the man buried there, Sir Thomas Warner.

Sir Thomas came from a long line of farmers in Suffolk, England. He chose St. Kitts because it had fertile soil and good rainfall, so they could grow corn for their sustenance and tobacco as a valuable export to take back to England. Later, the island's agriculture revolved around sugarcane.

Today, a few old sugar plantations have been made into small inns, intimate places in natural surroundings. St. Kitts is relatively unspoiled, with rugged volcanic mountains and rain forests in the interior, and a coastline fringed with coral reefs and beaches, some of them black sand.

When I think of St. Kitts, I always picture Sir Thomas Warner as he stepped ashore nearly 400 years ago.

I like to imagine Sir Thomas approaching on his small schooner and to consider the number of miles he sailed with

View from atop Brimstone Hill Fort, on St. Kitts, across to Nevis

only the most basic navigational skills and aids. I compare all this to the ship I command today, the *Queen Mary 2*. Her technology is astonishing. She stretches 1,130 feet and yet is so maneuverable, with her rotating propellers and bow thrusters, that docking the ship at St. Kitts is almost like parallel-parking a car.

When I think of St. Kitts, I always picture Sir Thomas Warner as he stepped ashore nearly 400 years ago. That connection drew me to the island, and now I have stood in the footsteps of my seafaring ancestor.

COMPASS POINTS

Where: St. Kitts lies in the West Indies, 1,300 miles southeast of Miami, Florida.

Backdrop: The east side of St. Kitts is on the Atlantic Ocean, while the west side faces the Caribbean Sea. Its formal name is Saint Christopher Island. The official language is English, and 98 percent of residents are literate. With the island of Nevis (located two miles away), St. Kitts forms the smallest nation in the Americas in both area and population. Sir Thomas Warner, who was appointed the island's first governor general in 1625, amassed a fortune that today would be valued at nearly $200 million. The island's sugar industry, which for centuries was the economic mainstay of St. Kitts, was shut down in 2005. The *Queen Mary 2*, which sailed on her maiden voyage in 2004, has five swimming pools, the only planetarium and the largest dance floor at sea, 3,000 telephones, and more than 5,000 works of art. The wheel of the mighty ship, surprisingly, is barely six inches in diameter. Passengers annually consume 230,000 bottles of wine and enough beef to feed the city of Southampton for one year. In 2005 the *QM2* carried a locked steamer trunk containing the first U.S. autographed copy of J. K. Rowling's *Harry Potter and the Half-Blood Prince*. **Visitor Information:** www.stkittstourism.kn

The senior captain of the Cunard Line, **Commodore Bernard Warner** *has been at sea for 40 years. As a boy in England watching the original* Queen Mary *and* Queen Elizabeth *sail past his navigation college at the University of Southampton, he felt inspired to command a transatlantic Cunard liner one day. First he served aboard ships for P&O and Princess Cruises, in the 1970s sailing as first officer on the* Pacific Princess, *where television's* Love Boat *was filmed. Commodore Warner later met both Princess Diana and his future wife, Tina, aboard the* Royal Princess. *He realized his career ambition in 2005, when he was appointed to command Cunard's* Queen Mary 2.

ALICE WATERS

MY PARENTS' VICTORY GARDEN,
CHATHAM, NEW JERSEY

My life's work began with my mother's Victory Garden at the end of World War II. In springtime, when everything bloomed, she parked my carriage under the apple tree to let the white blossoms drop down around me like snow, gathering on the carriage's mosquito net. It was a pretty big garden, about a quarter of an acre. Chatham, New Jersey, is only 17 miles from Newark, but it felt rural. Trees surrounded our lot and a stream burbled across one end, and I remember my mother always out there before dinner; she knew the names of every flower and tree, and when I got older, I learned them, too. You might say this was the core curriculum of my early education.

I remember also my father in that garden, hoeing. He was always trying to get his four kids to pick weeds—the slave labor department! But we did help out, and as the seasons turned, that work taught us the cycles of the natural world and how the health of our garden contributed to our own well-being.

There was nothing abstract about it, either. We ate out of that garden all the time—asparagus and peppers, apples and rhubarb. My father told me years later that whenever he lost track of me as a little girl, he'd find me in the strawberry patch, eating berries in the sun. Once, my mother even dressed me up for a local competition as the Queen of the Garden—with an asparagus skirt and a lettuce-leaf top, and bracelets made from radishes, all of it from our own property and all of it pinned to my bathing suit. I had a crown of strawberries, too, and little anklets of peppers.

Gardens also teach us that the healthiest foods on Earth—the fresh fruits and vegetables we all know we're supposed to eat—are actually the most delicious.

My mother cared a great deal about our health, so we always had square meals with fresh vegetables and dark bread, and only fresh fruit for dessert. But she wasn't much of a cook—it didn't interest her one bit—and only our tomatoes and corn gave me an inkling of how much deliciousness depends on freshness. The corn we picked and husked and dropped right in a pot of boiling water, and the tomatoes we sliced right off the vine, and nothing ever tasted better. But the rest of the produce—the asparagus and peppers—I don't think my mother ever knew what to do with them.

Fall brings the garden's full bounty.

So I didn't wake up to the broader relationship between great flavor and "just picked" until I went to France, at age 19. I had a meal in Brittany where the chef served trout with almonds, cured ham with melon, and raspberry tart. The trout came out of the stream below the house, the family cured their own meats, and the raspberries were picked out back. And there was no mistaking what made it all so good—the very fact that it came from nearby.

By the time I opened Chez Panisse, in 1971, I knew that only local farms and gardens could give me the tastes that I wanted. I started by planting lettuce in my own backyard; every morning, someone from the restaurant would harvest the lettuce and take it over to the kitchen. Over time, my backyard garden grew and so did the community of small local farmers I could trust, until we'd built a network of people who took care of the land even as they grew gorgeous food and made a living.

To this day, the gardens in my life bring me a lot of happiness. I think gardens ought to be in everybody's life, especially children's. Gardens teach us the cycles of nature—how to enrich the soil, the natural role of bugs and worms, the importance of planting according to the seasons, how things grow and ripen, and when it's time to harvest. Gardens also teach us that the healthiest foods on Earth—the fresh fruits and vegetables we all know we're supposed to eat—are actually the most delicious, as long as they're raised right, prepared simply, and eaten while fresh. Better still, when our leftovers go back into our garden soil, further enriching it, we become a part of nature ourselves.

Every child deserves to know and experience all of this, and not just because it's beautiful: this sort of knowledge is like a key that unlocks a wholesome, nutritious, and, best of all, delicious relationship to food and to the earth.

COMPASS POINTS

Where: Chatham is in Morris County, New Jersey. Brittany occupies a peninsula in northwest France.

Backdrop: During World War II, American citizens planted Victory Gardens at home to reduce the pressure on the commercial food supply, which was needed for the troops. Some 20 million Americans, both urban and rural, took part. People learned the basics of gardening from public service booklets put out by companies such as International Harvester and Hearst (*Good Housekeeping*). Tending a Victory Garden was a family or community endeavor—not a chore, but a national duty—and a morale booster in difficult times.

Visitor Information: New Jersey: www.state.nj.us/travel; France: http://us.franceguide.com

One of America's most influential chefs, **Alice Waters** *created a revolution in 1971 when she introduced local, organic fare at her restaurant, Chez Panisse, in Berkeley, California. Credited with helping to change the food landscape in America, Chez Panisse was named best restaurant in the United States by* Gourmet *magazine in 2001. Waters has championed sustainable farms and ranches for more than three decades, and she has brought her vision to public schools through the Chez Panisse Foundation (www.chezpanissefoundation.org). The foundation operates the Edible Schoolyard at Martin Luther King Jr. Middle School in Berkeley, where students plant, harvest, and prepare fresh food as part of the academic curriculum. Waters is the founder of the Yale Sustainable Food Project and vice president of Slow Food International. She was the recipient of the Natural Resources Defense Council Force for Nature Award in 2004 and the Harvard Global Environmental Citizen Award, alongside Kofi Annan, in 2008.*

Discoveries VII

TONY WHEELER

NEPAL

*K*athmandu was the major crossroads and destination point on the Asia overland trail of the 1970s. You started out in London, and you ended up in Kathmandu. At that time, it definitely had an exotic feeling. As Kipling said, "The wildest dreams of Kew are the facts of Kathmandu."

When my wife Maureen and I arrived in 1972, we were tired and dusty. We had come up from the Indian border, a long and tedious trip on a crowded bus. Western travelers stayed on Freak Street, where there were funky hotels. Another part of the attraction was pie shops. One place was called Aunt Jane's—the story was that the original Aunt Jane was the wife of the Peace Corps director in Nepal, and the people who ran the place had learned their all-American pie-making skills by working for staffers at U.S. AID. Freak Street also had lots of little restaurants. It just had a nice feel to it. A couple of years later, the whole center of gravity shifted across town, up to an area called Thamel, which is still the backpacker's center of Kathmandu.

On that first trip, we explored only the Kathmandu Valley. We rented bicycles and rode to the other main towns, Patan and Bhaktapur. Each has a palace square. (Once I was in Bhaktapur when they were filming *Little Buddha* with Keanu Reeves. To make the palace square look like a medieval square, all they had to do was hide the telephone wires and it seemed to be a thousand years old.)

Maureen and I also walked to Dhulikhel, up on the valley rim. We waited for dawn the next day and saw the sun rise over the Himalayas. If it was nice and clear, you could even see Mount Everest. These days, the valley's major problem is that it has some similarities with L.A.—it suffers from smog.

Travelers also stay in Pokhara, about half a day's bus ride or 100 miles west of Kathmandu. And they go to the Terai region, which is the lowlands area, the jungle, down toward the border with India. They go there to see rhinoceros—and if they're really lucky, a tiger—just like you'd go on a wildlife safari in Africa, except that you ride out on an elephant to look for the animals, which is much better than in a minibus or a 4WD.

But the main attraction in Nepal is walking. People come to trek, to walk for a week or two or three in the mountains. There are basically two ways of trekking

Porters cross suspension bridge over river, Arun Valley, Nepal.

Tony Wheeler

(theoretically three—you could take your own tent and camp out, but nobody does). The first way is in a trekking group, where you've got porters and Sherpas and guides, and they put up the camp every night. It's pretty much like a 1950s mountaineering expedition on the trail—lots of people and equipment. A cook prepares food every night. It's a lot of fun.

As you're walking, you talk with the Sherpas and guides and commiserate with the porters who are carrying all the stuff. It's like a family on the move, or a tribe. It is often said that travelers go to Nepal to be thrilled by the mountains, but when they get home, it's the people they remember.

The second way of trekking in Nepal doesn't require all that stuff. You just walk from guest house to guest house. This first became popular on the Annapurna Circuit, a three-week walk that goes around the Annapurna massif, which rises to 26,538 feet. You see it first from one side, then you come around and see it from the other side. It's a spectacular walk.

All the way around, you go through little villages. Fifty years ago, they wouldn't have had any way to accommodate trekkers—not that that was a problem, because there were no trekkers coming through. But now the villages along the way have set up guest houses and cafés and restaurants. The idea has spread to other walks as well. You can go up to the Everest base camp and find a bed and a place to eat every night along the way. I walked to the base camp in 2003.

It is often said that travelers go to Nepal to be thrilled by the mountains, but when they get home, it's the people they remember.

People complain about the crowds on Nepal's trekking routes, but I've heard a comparison that goes roughly like this: All the trekkers on all the routes in Nepal for a whole year are about the same as on a busy weekend in Yosemite. It's not such a huge number.

Once I went trekking with a group of friends. We flew to the west of Nepal and then walked for a week up to the border to cross into Tibet and walk around Mount Kailash. Most of the locals we met coming in the opposite direction were leading trains of goats, and each goat carried two little bags of salt. We were following an age-old trade route that hadn't changed for millennia.

About 20 years ago, Maureen and I went on what we called the Children's Trek with a bunch of friends and a lot of kids, including my daughter, who was the oldest—she was 11 then—and my son who was 8. Stan Armington, who wrote our Lonely Planet trekking guide to Nepal and has lived in Kathmandu on and off for more than 30 years, runs a trekking agency up there. He put the trek together for us, and one of the nice things he did was to send along a bunch of Nepalese kids. The cook brought along his two young sons, who had never really been on a trek before. We ended up with about half a dozen Western kids and half a dozen Nepalese kids. They walked for eight days, even the youngest—and they all got on like a house afire. Every night, when the adults were exhausted, the children were running around playing games. They had a great time.

Like all of our walks in Nepal, it was just a lot of fun.

COMPASS POINTS

Where: Nepal is located in South Asia, between China and India.

Backdrop: The Himalayas of Nepal are home to eight of the world's ten highest mountains. Annapurna I is the tenth highest, Mount Everest the highest of all. By long tradition a Hindu kingdom, Nepal today is a secular state; the monarchy was abolished in 2008. Nepal's national flag is the only one in the world that is not a quadrilateral shape. The oldest building in the Kathmandu Valley has stood for 1,992 years, despite earthquakes, and Kathmandu has many 17th-century palaces and Hindu and Buddhist temples. A major stop on the "hippie trail" from the 1960s onward, Kathmandu was also used (minus the "h") by Bob Seger as a song title on his 1975 album, *Beautiful Loser*.

Visitor Information: www.welcomenepal.com/brand/index.asp

Tony Wheeler is the founder of Lonely Planet Publications, the world's largest independent guidebook publisher. It all began with a 1972 trip from London across Asia to Australia. After six months, he and his wife, Maureen, ended up in Sydney with 27 cents and no jobs. Other travelers were curious about their trip, so they wrote and hand-stapled 1,500 copies of a simple travel guide called Across Asia on the Cheap. *Today Lonely Planet has 500 titles in print in eight languages, covering virtually every country in the world, with sales of more than six million guidebooks annually. "Whether penniless backpackers or heads of a global company, Tony and Maureen somehow always exemplify the very best kind of travelers' enthusiasm and curiosity," says author Pico Iyer. The Wheelers recount their adventures in travel and business in* Unlikely Destinations: The Lonely Planet Story, *and they still travel for about six months a year.*

JACK WHITE

CLARKSDALE, MISSISSIPPI

*I*t's almost as if every town down in Mississippi fostered a great blues singer—Charlie Patton, or Son House, or Howlin' Wolf. And a lot of them either were from Clarksdale or came and played there.

I didn't expect to feel the way I do about Clarksdale. I thought maybe I'd find that it's all Wal-Marts and commercialized chain stores, like a lot of the Western world now.

When you're driving around the country, you think it would be nice to pull off the road and eat at a mom-and-pop diner or café, but you can't do that anymore. They're gone, and it's really sad. Now it's "take your pick of which corporation you want to have lunch at." So I was worried that my idea of Mississippi wasn't going to be there anymore. But that wasn't the case. Clarksdale was the Mississippi I had in my head.

The culture there hadn't been chopped up and homogenized and made into something plastic. It was still alive, like a field of grass. It was breathing. Walking around Clarksdale made me feel like I was living in the real United States of America.

Clarksdale is called the "crossroads of the blues," and one night I went to a blues club owned by Morgan Freeman, who's a local. Nowadays a lot of the blues has turned into a creamy thing, but his place had the real grit, a real earthiness to it. I sat on the porch for a while and felt really comfortable there.

My hero is Son House, who was born near Clarksdale around 1902. He was the first to speak to me in the blues, and he shattered every notion I had about music. Before that I was into everything from *The Music Man* to the Beatles. When I heard Son House, on vinyl records, it was an explosion. All of a sudden, all these roads were open to me, nothing was off limits, and all my emotions and feelings about music and social interaction and environment were intertwined at the same time. I saw that there is an America to be proud of, and there's a thread that keeps everyone together, whether we know it or not. I didn't know it, either, until Son House told me with his music.

There's a myth about blues singer Robert Johnson going down to a crossroads in Mississippi and meeting the Devil; he trades his soul in exchange for becoming

Bluesman Frank Frost blows his harp in Clarksdale, Mississippi.

the greatest blues guitarist anyone has ever heard. When I drove into Clarksdale, I was with some friends, and they dropped me off at a crossroads at nighttime. I got out of the car—and they just drove away. They thought that would be funny.

I had about five minutes by myself before they came back. At first, I thought it was a good joke they played, because of the myth about the crossroads. For a few minutes, I was laughing. And then it turned to fear. Maybe I was finally going to come to terms with everything. Maybe I was going to be faced with—not the Devil, but God. It's funny how certain things, such as silence, or a place, can really inflict a lot of self-reflection on you. I could imagine someone in that situation back in the 1930s, and the impact of being out there in complete darkness.

When I think of Clarksdale now, I picture dirt—whether it's dirt roads or a plowed field. That's how it felt to me—real. A lot of towns in America make the mistake of knocking down their historical areas, and then they recreate them in a Hollywood style. But it's a shame to see a replica of something. This is a generation when "replica" and "retro" and "relic"—all those words that start with "re-"—are okay with everybody. It's acceptable to have a place in Vegas that looks exactly like Manhattan, and you take your photo in front of it, and that's good enough.

Jack White

But that's never been good enough for me. I despise it and cringe at all that. I'm trying to find something to grab hold of that makes sense. And when I'm down South in a place like Clarksdale, it feels as if the culture—whatever it is, white or black or Latin—has this horse sense, and I totally relate to it. People's sense of humor, and their politeness and generosity, are so compelling that I've ended up living in the South. I just had to move down there!

COMPASS POINTS

Where: Clarksdale is in the Mississippi Delta, in the northwest part of the state.

Backdrop: In the early 1900s, Clarksdale was known as the "Golden Buckle on the Cotton Belt." The town stands at the legendary crossroads where Highway 49 meets Highway 61 and has been home to blues singers Robert Johnson, Charlie Patton, and John Lee Hooker. In 1937, Bessie Smith died at the Riverside Hotel (then a hospital) after a car accident on Highway 61; Ike Turner wrote "Rocket 88" at the hotel. Reflecting a sad legacy of racism, when the Delta Blues Museum was looking for permanent quarters in 1995, the chairman of the county tourism commission shouted during a meeting: "Nobody is gonna come to Clarksdale, Mississippi, to hear a black man play the git-tar!" Now going strong, the Clarksdale museum displays B. B. King's "Lucille" guitar, the one-room cabin where Muddy Waters lived on a nearby plantation as a child, and other blues artifacts. Morgan Freeman's Ground Zero Blues Club showcases Delta performers such as Super Chikan, who built his homemade guitar from a cigar box, an axe handle, and various wires. Son House recorded in the 1930s, making records that are full of surface noise and scratches, but his emotional singing and slide guitar, said one reviewer, "cut through the hisses and pops like a brick through a stained glass window."

Visitor Information: www.clarksdaletourism.com

*A resident of Nashville, **Jack White** is the guitarist, multi-instrumentalist, songwriter, and lead vocalist of the White Stripes, a duo that has won five Grammy Awards. He also sings and plays guitar and keyboards with the Raconteurs, a rock group that has headlined at festivals and earned three Grammy nominations. Born in Detroit as the seventh son in a family of ten, and playing instruments since he was five, White was ranked number 17 on Rolling Stone's list of the "100 Greatest Guitarists of All Time." As an actor, he was in* Cold Mountain *(also performing songs on the sound track) and* Coffee and Cigarettes. *The album he produced and played on for Loretta Lynn,* Van Lear Rose, *won two Grammys. He has also performed live with Bob Dylan and the Rolling Stones. White supports the American Red Cross (www.redcross.org).*

ROBIN WILLIAMS

SAN FRANCISCO, CALIFORNIA

*M*y vision of San Francisco has always been, *This is it! This is the place!* I was 16 years old when my father retired from the auto industry in Detroit and we moved to the Bay Area. There was the Golden Gate Bridge, like a big "Welcome!" To me, it's kind of a *Wizard of Oz* feeling:

Step into the sun, step into the light
Keep straight ahead
For the most glorious place
On the face of the Earth

San Francisco does almost look like the city of Oz. And the one spire that everyone hated at first—the Transamerica Pyramid—is now the main distinguishing feature in the cityscape. It adds a quality that's somewhere between mystical and magical.

As my parents and I drove in, the fog was coming in over the hills, and I didn't know what it was. I thought, *Let's see, it's not a fire, it's not poison gas . . .* My dad explained that it was fog, and that it happens a lot in San Francisco. I think the fog is quite beautiful. It comes in and just cools off the whole city.

As I grew up, I discovered that San Francisco is a city of neighborhoods: Chinatown, Nob Hill, the Mission, Japantown, Pacific Heights. I love North Beach and Broadway. The titty bars are still there, but so is City Lights, a bookshop that's like a pilgrimage spot, one of the great places of poetry. It was a home for the Beats. The founder, poet Lawrence Ferlinghetti, is still alive, the place looks the same as always, and they still publish a lot of new poets.

Writers and artists go to a bar across the street called Tosca's. It serves cappuccino "corrected" with brandy and chocolate, and it's famous for Irish Coffee. Around the corner on Broadway, the hungry i has started to have comedy again. The original club dated back to the days of Jonathan Winters, Mort Sahl, and Bill Cosby. It was run by a character named Enrico Banducci—the only guy who could own a club and steal from himself.

Another famous neighborhood is Haight-Ashbury. It's like a Civil War reenactment done by Timothy Leary. The sidewalks are packed, and there are still shops from the Sixties. There are also upscale new places geared more toward young people. But it's still the Haight.

The Castro is literally Boys Town, but I lived there for a while and it's a true neighborhood, and a wonderful one. The Victorian houses have been renovated. People wander around shopping at places like All American Boy, and you can have brunch at Moby Dick. San Francisco was a pioneer in allowing same-sex marriages, which seemed like a no-brainer for this city.

Nearby, Noe Valley is a bit of Berkeley in the middle of San Francisco. It's got everything—unusual shops, restaurants—almost like a tasting menu for the whole city.

There's an old joke that "the coldest winter I ever spent was a summer in San Francisco," and they must have been talking about the Sunset district, out toward the ocean. But when it's beautiful there, it's totally beautiful. When the sun comes out, it's like, *Ah! Dear God!* And then you see the great collection of Irish tanning heroes.

The Pacific Ocean and the bay make San Francisco one of the world's great cities located on water. But I don't think a lot of people actually go *in* the water—except for your occasional members of the Polar Bear Club who take pride in having nipples. There are surfers at Ocean Beach, but I don't surf; it doesn't help that great white sharks breed in the Farallon Islands just offshore.

Another famous neighborhood is Haight-Ashbury. It's like a Civil War reenactment done by Timothy Leary.

Water is a big part of San Francisco, and it's also the lungs of the city, making the air feel fresh. People are always saying, "Oh, it's so cold!" Well, get over it. Even gray days when it's foggy are kind of beautiful, I think. And San Francisco still has foghorns, even though they're electronic now: *VOOOOOOH-ooohhhhhh.* They remind me of *The Maltese Falcon* and Sam Spade: *Yeah, I saw her. She walked through the mist. I waited for her by the bridge....*

On days when the wind is up, you can go to the Marina and the bay will be full of sailboats—they look like they've come to mate. It's incredible, one of the most beautiful things you'll ever see.

Europeans love San Francisco, too, because I think it's the closest thing to Europe they'll find—the water, the hills, the neighborhoods. Another European aspect is that people enjoy food and being alive. They're not so driven; they're living slightly slower. When my father retired here, I saw him all of a sudden start to appreciate life.

View from Alamo square of the Painted Ladies and San Francisco skyline

Robin Williams

Food and wine are part of the culture in San Francisco. The old Ferry Building has been renovated and is full of restaurants and little shops that sell cheese, bread, olive oil, chocolate, and lots more. The food people, they go nuts there. Sampling day is like the Running of the Bulls.

San Francisco has great energy, and that includes financial energy, with the dot-com—and then the dot-bomb—eras, and now the biotech industry. The city thinks of itself as big. It's actually like a little dog that barks a lot—it's a handsome dog, even an alpha dog, but a Pekapoo alpha. *Rowf! We're huge!* No, you're not really, but it's okay.

Take the new ballpark; it's just small enough that it's got a great feel, like smaller ballparks do. It's in a perfect spot by the water, and the weather is 90 percent great. The ballpark's name has been changed a few times. What is it now? "Your-Name-Here Park"? "X-Box 360 Park"? "I've Got $5 Million Park"?

San Franciscans are proud people but are willing to make fun of themselves pretty quickly. You develop a certain amount of humility because earthquakes shake things up every once in a while. Carpe diem is literal when you live on a fault line. You think, *All this could go!* But it gives you a sense that today is a really good day. It's a very San Francisco feeling.

This is a city with a lot of character, but also something more. There's a distinct feeling that you come here because you want to be kind of free-range. I don't think this part of San Francisco has really been captured in a film scene yet. Maybe it would be a midget transvestite nun…having brunch.

I'm proud that San Francisco is this amazing collection of people, that we have a city council that's like the Tower of Babel, that we have so many things going on and existing in harmony—not necessarily quiet harmony, but we try to allow for all types and needs.

Glide Memorial Church is a great example. It has a wonderful outreach program for everyone, from after-school programs to free legal care for the homeless. And you really get a sense that it's open to all. No matter what your beliefs, creed, sexuality, anything—*come on in!* This is sort of like San Francisco itself. I mean, we have a mayor in rehab, which is great, and even the folks who live on Nob Hill, basically your wealthy people, have a certain eclectic quality to them.

Sometimes it's easy to think, well, everyone's like this. And then you drive about 30 miles and go—*Mmm, not really. Quick, back to the city! Flee!*

San Francisco has big art and literary communities, as well as a film community.

A lot of people call it "Hollywood North"—but *shhh!* Don't even say that. We don't want *them* coming here.

For me, it's perfect being 400 miles away from Hollywood. It's kind of like being in Switzerland. If there's ever an atomic explosion—you can go, "What was that noise?" I can travel to Hollywood, enjoy visiting, do my business, and get out before I start worrying about my career.

It's great to know that I'm going home to San Francisco, back to a life that isn't involved with "How am I doing?" I really do love this place.

COMPASS POINTS

Where: San Francisco is located in Northern California, at the tip of a peninsula between the Pacific Ocean and the San Francisco Bay.

Backdrop: Summer fog pours through the Golden Gate at speeds up to 20 miles an hour. The shape of the Transamerica Pyramid allows more light to reach the street than a standard box design; its 3,678 windows pivot for easy cleaning from inside—a one-month job. A champion of lesser-known literary writers and poets, City Lights bookstore was named after a Charlie Chaplin film, a symbol of the little fellow fighting the big, impersonal world. Behind its stage, the hungry i nightclub had a bare brick wall, a feature that later became standard in comedy clubs. During Haight-Ashbury's heyday around the "Summer of Love" in 1967, it was known as the "Hashbury" for the clouds of suspicious-smelling smoke in the air, and the neighborhood was home to bands that created psychedelic rock, including the Grateful Dead and Jefferson Airplane. The San Francisco Giants play at AT&T Park, located on the waterfront with views of the Bay Bridge. *The Pursuit of Happyness*, a movie starring Will Smith, told the true story of a homeless man and his son who were helped by the outreach services at Glide Memorial Church. The city's character as a liberal, do-your-own thing bastion began early, as people from many cultures and countries poured into the city during the California Gold Rush. Everyday life became a wild pageant, and San Franciscans embraced their eccentric characters. All this created a uniquely diverse and tolerant society, later amplified by the 1950s Beat Generation and the flower children of the Sixties.

Visitor Information: San Francisco Convention & Visitors Bureau: www.onlyinsanfran cisco.com

Academy Award– and Grammy-winner **Robin Williams** *began his career as a stand-up comedian and has created a repertoire of indelible characters, first in the hit series* Mork & Mindy *and then in numerous film roles. In 1997, he received Academy and Screen Actors*

Guild Awards for his performance in Good Will Hunting, *having been previously nominated by the Academy for performances in* The Fisher King, Dead Poets Society, *and* Good Morning, Vietnam. *Williams's many films include blockbuster comedies like* Mrs. Doubtfire, The Birdcage, Jumanji, Hook, *and* Night at the Museum; *darker roles in* Insomnia *and* One Hour Photo; *and the animated films* Aladdin, Robots, *and* Happy Feet. *His stage credits include* Waiting for Godot, *directed by Mike Nichols and costarring Steve Martin. When he returned to stand-up after a 16-year absence, the resulting 2002 HBO special,* Live on Broadway, *was nominated for five Emmy Awards. Offstage, Williams has made four trips to the Middle East with the USO to entertain the troops. He has also been affiliated with Comic Relief since its inception in 1986; to date, the efforts of that organization have raised more than $50 million.*

BRIAN WILSON

LONDON, ENGLAND

The first time I went to London was in 1964, and I've been there quite a few times over the years. The best experience I had there was at the Royal Festival Hall. The hall has really great acoustics. That's where we premiered *Brian Wilson Presents SMiLE* in 2004. And in 2007, I premiered my newest album there: *That Lucky Old Sun*. (If you know the song "That Lucky Old Sun," I based the album on the first and third verses.) Then in the summer of 2008 I went back to the Royal Festival Hall and performed my greatest hits.

The people in London are very friendly. At my concerts there, I met Eric Clapton and Elton John and Paul McCartney. They all played on one of my albums—*Gettin' In over My Head.*

I like the layout of London. It has a very beautiful street plan. Taking a taxicab somewhere is an exciting way to travel around the city. The streets twist and turn a lot—I love those turns! I always stay at the InterContinental Hotel, and when I'm

Harrods department store at dusk

not playing, I go to restaurants, go shopping at Harrods and buy some shirts, and take walks in Hyde Park—*fun* stuff!

COMPASS POINTS

Where: London is located in southeast England, on the River Thames.

Backdrop: London is one of the world's great cities for culture, finance, fashion, and music. Paul McCartney has said that his favorite song of all time is Brian Wilson's "God Only Knows." A London taxicab has a turning circle of just 25 feet, allowing it to make U-turns on narrow streets. The InterContinental London Park Lane hotel is located between Mayfair and Knightsbridge, in view of Buckingham Palace. Harrods has 330 sales departments, filling more than a million square feet.

Visitor Information: www.visitlondon.com

*One of rock's most revered figures, **Brian Wilson** is a songwriter, producer, arranger, and performer. He cofounded the Beach Boys in 1961, blending Chuck Berry–style rock 'n' roll with the sophisticated pop vocal harmonies of the Four Freshman. Wilson made a musical leap in creating the richly textured* Pet Sounds, *which influenced the Beatles'* Sgt. Pepper *album and ranks #2 behind it on* Rolling Stone's *list of the greatest albums of all time. His solo albums include* Brian Wilson, Imagination, Gettin' In over My Head, Brian Wilson Presents SMiLE, *and* That Lucky Old Sun. *Wilson has received a Grammy Award and was recognized at the Kennedy Center Honors. The Beach Boys were inducted into the Rock and Roll Hall of Fame in 1988.*

JONATHAN WINTERS

ENGLAND

*T*raveling is a great education, and I see every trip as a classroom. You're fortunate enough to be able to step in, take the course, and benefit by it—or flunk it, I suppose, like I flunked medieval history in college.

Fortunately, history is one of the "makeup classes" available in Europe. I'm a history buff, and the wonderful thing about visiting England, for instance, is that the British have held on to their traditions: the castles, the queen in her carriage, the house where Dickens wrote. History and art are there for everyone. It doesn't matter what faith you are when you step into Westminster Abbey on a Sunday, with the choir singing and the light streaming through the windows.

I learned that the English like to put Yanks on their toes right away: *We're going to joust with you and have some fun verbally and find out what you're all about.* The first time I went to Portobello Road, which is the flea market section in London, this Cockney guy says: "Let me ask you, guv'nor—I hope I'm not out of line—do all

Picturesque cottages in Sandsend

you chaps over there in America live on a farm? Or why is it you're wearing Levi's, those bloody jeans, to Portobello Road?"

"I'm here to antique," I told him. "I'd hardly wear a tweed jacket. I'm not going off to shoot grouse at Coventry."

The English teach you to defend yourself, so when you go back to Poughkeepsie or wherever, you're in shape.

Back home later, I was at a party, and a Frenchman said, "Forgive me. *Pardon*. But how is that all these people know you? Your name, please?"

I said, "I'm Jonathan Winters, and they know me because I used to be a star, I guess. But I became a meteor and ended up in some meadow in Illinois." See, I threw a little shot at him—it all goes back to the English.

Another part of English tradition through history is that they've always loved their eccentrics. In this country, we see someone like that and say, "Oh, he's not playing with a full deck—he ought to be in the asylum," whereas the English approach such a person differently: "Who did he say he was? Winston Churchill? How sweet. Of course, Churchill's been dead for some time, but if he's brought him back to life, that's marvelous. Let's have him over this evening and simply address him as the prime minister."

Since I'm pretty sure that *I'm* Winston Churchill, I like the English!

COMPASS POINTS

Where: England, the largest country of Great Britain, is the largest of the British Isles.
Backdrop: English monarchs are traditionally crowned at Westminster Abbey. Luminaries buried there include Geoffrey Chaucer, Charles Darwin, and Laurence Olivier. Winston Churchill (1874–1965) was prime minister of the United Kingdom during World War II and once said: "History will be kind to me, for I intend to write it."
Visitor Information: www.visitbritain.com

Madcap comedian and pioneer of improvised humor, **Jonathan Winters** *is known for his comedy albums (which introduced characters like the not-so-sweet old lady Maudie Frickert), films including* It's a Mad, Mad, Mad, Mad World, *many TV appearances, and the book* Winter's Tales. *He has received an Emmy, a Grammy, and the Mark Twain Prize for American Humor.*

JAMIE WYETH

SOUTHERN ISLAND, MAINE

I live in a lighthouse on an island in Maine. The island covers only 22 acres, and when I stand on top of it, I can see the perimeters of my world.

Most of the time I'm the only person on the island. Once a week, I bring out supplies from the mainland, which is about a mile away. I paint all day, and as a painter I don't need a support group. I don't need an orchestra; I don't need a publisher. If anything, I need focus—and an island sure as hell gives you that.

I live in the lightkeeper's house, a white New England clapboard structure built in the 1850s. To go into the lighthouse, you have to walk through my living room. The lighthouse is all brick and heavy granite—they built it like a fortress, because they didn't want it to blow away in a storm. Lighthouses were vital for shipping, and in the days before foghorns they also used bells. Down on the water I have a bell tower with a sort of clock mechanism inside to ring the bell—so if you were going by in a ship, you'd know where you were.

The lighthouse and the island create a real mood. But it isn't all romantic. Island life has a lot of edge to it, too. You're always aware of the weather. Wind and heavy seas keep you from going ashore. To communicate, all I have is a radio telephone, which generally doesn't work. It's tough living out here—but I like that.

I stay on the island in winter, too. When storms come ripping through and the sea crashes over the island, I go up to the top of the lighthouse, and from there it's fantastic to see.

As a child I always wanted to live on a ship, but a boat gets pretty cramped after a few weeks. An island has all the elements of a ship, but also the elements of land. It couldn't suit me better.

My wife comes out here, of course, but she prefers the wide world of the mainland and just visits off and on. After all, island life is not for everybody. There are people who come to this island and say: "Good God! What do you *do* here? Aren't you running out of things to paint?" Actually, I feel I could live here for three lifetimes and still not scratch the surface.

I painted a whole series on seagulls—the one thing I do have plenty of. I've lived among seagulls for so long that they now look at me as another seagull.

Jamie Wyeth's lighthouse home, Southern Island, Maine

I painted a whole series on seagulls—the one thing I do have plenty of. I've lived among seagulls for so long that they now look at me as another seagull. I sit there and they fall asleep next to me.

Another bird I'd always been intrigued by was the raven, so I asked various ornithologists how to attract ravens to my island. They told me to wear the same clothing every day and feed the birds at the same time. Soon I had 200 crows crawling all over me. I had crows standing on my head! But no ravens.

Finally I asked a raven expert named Bernd Heinrich to come to the island and tell me how to attract them. He's German and looks rather like a raven himself, a wonderful man. He said, "Well, what you need here is a cow." And I thought, *What the hell is he talking about?* What he meant was a cow *carcass.* I contacted farmers on the mainland and said, "If you turn up with a dead cow, let me know." Finally, at five o'clock one morning, I got a call on my radio telephone saying, "We've got one here for you."

Of course, a difficulty with islands is getting things out to them, even little things—and a cow weighs about 2,000 pounds. I had to take a front-end loader to the farm, lift the cow onto a truck, drive it to the dock, off-load it onto my barge, and bring it out to the island. It was a huge effort.

It was early spring when I did this, and it turned out to be a very warm spring. The cow started to decompose, and the wind blew the smell southwest to the mainland and into Tenants Harbor. Everybody in the village was saying, *What in hell is he doing on that island?* The smell of this thing was unbelievable.

But it worked. I now have a pair of ravens living on the island. I've been painting them for four years, although I still can't get any closer than 20 feet. Ravens are kind of sketchy birds; they do *not* welcome human contact.

For company, I also have dogs—Jack Russells. Once the island had a huge infestation of voles, and they were eating everything, so somebody suggested getting a feral cat. I brought two of them out here. Of course, they beat up the dogs, and the dogs spend all their time chasing the cats around. So far, it's Cats: 10, Dogs: 0.

Somebody said that living in a lighthouse is kind of like running away with the circus. I guess he was right.

COMPASS POINTS

Where: Southern Island lies just off Tenants Harbor on Maine's St. George Peninsula and is about 90 miles northeast of Portland.

Backdrop: The light in a lighthouse is called the "lamp" whether electric or oil-burning. Varying intervals between flashes help mariners to identify individual lighthouses. The lighthouse on Southern Island, completed in 1858, was decommissioned in 1933. Jamie Wyeth's parents bought the island in 1978. The lighthouse appears in his paintings Iris at Sea and Pumpkinhead Visits the Lighthouse. The Common Raven displays high intelligence (shown in its problem-solving ability) and playfulness (young ravens play "catch me if you can" with dogs and wolves, and even slide down snow banks). Pairs mate for life. In world mythology, the raven is a powerful symbol and may represent anything from a trickster to a ghost to a god.

Visitor Information: www.visitmaine.com

Jamie Wyeth *had his first one-man show in New York at age 19 and was soon painting portraits of John F. Kennedy, Andy Warhol, and Arnold Schwarzenegger—but his perennial subjects are the people, creatures, and landscapes of rural Maine. He lived and worked on Monhegan Island before moving to Southern Island in the early 1990s. Wyeth paints primarily in oil but is also accomplished in watercolor, tempera, lithography, etching, drawing, and mixed media. Widely collected and exhibited, his work is on view at the Farnsworth*

Art Museum and Wyeth Center, the Brandywine River Museum, the National Gallery of Art, the National Portrait Gallery, and the Museum of Modern Art. As a boy, he studied art with his aunt, Carolyn Wyeth, and painted alongside his father, Andrew Wyeth. His grandfather was artist N. C. Wyeth. Jamie Wyeth supports his wife's nonprofit school, Herring Gut Learning Center (www.herringgut.org), which teaches marine science and aquaculture to students of all ages to help sustain fishing as a way of life on the coast of Maine.

RODNEY YEE

BALI, INDONESIA

I've led many yoga retreats in Bali, and I feel as if the spiritual teachings I've studied are actually *lived* there. The connection to the spiritual world is not only believed in, it's a part of everyday life. Take Bali's shadow puppet theater. A lot of people think it's a performance or a form of entertainment, but really the story being told is based on the *Mahabharata* from ancient India, the world's longest epic poem, which is all about Hindu religion and philosophy and has many stories within it.

Shadow plays are performed on auspicious occasions in open-air pavilions. They can go on all night. A silk cloth backdrop hangs from the roof, and the puppeteer has a coconut filled with oil that he lights and places where the flame casts the shadows on the cloth. The puppeteer I saw had made all his own leather puppets. They were flat, with joints at the elbows, hips, and shoulders, and he manipulated them with sticks. He had about 150 characters from the *Mahabharata* and played all the parts himself. He could do as many as a hundred different voices. Meanwhile, a gamelan orchestra played, and the puppeteer used his heel to strike a drum and keep a beat. You could see that the puppeteer went into sort of a trance.

A shadow play tells familiar stories, but at the same time, the puppeteer is a channel and spiritual lessons come through him. He bridges the gap between the spirit world and the manifested world. The silk onto which the shadows are projected is like a thin layer between the two worlds, visible and invisible. You experience that connection everywhere in Bali.

Once I led a yoga retreat in a little village called Munduk. A yogi came down from the mountains to talk with the group, and he told me a lot of things that still come back to me. Particularly, he said I should start meditating at nighttime instead of in the morning.

For the Balinese, religious devotion isn't separate from everyday life. Along the roads and paths, you see altars and temples.

Late that night, the shutters of the small cabin where I was staying suddenly blew open, and it sounded like someone was doing fast cartwheels around the camp. It was just the wind—but, whatever it was, it definitely woke me up. I thought: *I'm not going to meditate now. I have to get up early in the morning and teach.* The shutters had closed again; it was almost like I'd had a dream.

Indonesia's Wayang Puppet Theater is a UNESCO cultural treasure.

Finally, I decided, *Okay, there's no harm in getting up and meditating*—and as soon as I did, the shutters blew open again and I got an illuminating vision of this man. I climbed to the top of a little peak nearby, where I sat and meditated for a couple of hours, and then went back and got in bed. It was one of those strange, incredible experiences, with someone I'll probably never see again giving me bits and pieces of helpful information.

The funny thing is, the wind I heard—a sound like someone doing cartwheels—I've heard many times since then. It doesn't matter where I am. It happens both when I return to Bali and in other places. It's wonderful, and it reminds me every so often that I really am limited in my understanding of what's possible, of what amazing phenomena take place in the universe.

I know a yoga teacher in Tennessee who is 75 years old, and every time I see her, she says, "You know, I think the yoga's working, because I feel just a little bit more grateful."

For the Balinese, religious devotion isn't separate from everyday life. Along the roads and paths, you see altars and temples. Every home has a special corner with altars for prayer and religious activity. The women make offerings, weaving little baskets of palm leaves and filling them with bright, colorful flower petals, then burning incense. In the realm of the senses, Bali is overwhelming, yet it's also a completely spiritual place.

As a yoga practitioner, I feel that the human body is a vehicle for our spiritual growth. Everything we experience passes through our five senses, so the body is our contact point with both the outer world and the inner one. It's like the sheet of silk in a shadow play. The body joins the two worlds, visible and invisible. And so does Bali.

COMPASS POINTS

Where: Bali is one of Indonesia's Lesser Sunda Islands, just east of Java.

Backdrop: Almost entirely Hindu, Bali's people produce vibrant art, music, and dance. The *Mahabharata* contains 1.8 million words and 74,000 verses—making it ten times longer than the *Iliad* and *Odyssey* put together—and it portrays Hindu religion, philosophy, and human life through mythological tales of princes, demons, gods, and battles. According to legend, the mountain village of Munduk was settled by people escaping an invasion of ants.

Visitor Information: Ministry of Tourism: http://bali.my-indonesia.info

One of America's most recognized and popular yoga instructors, **Rodney Yee** *leads workshops and retreats worldwide. His blend of Iyengar Yoga and his own invented style is taught in books such as* Moving Toward Balance *and more than 25 DVDs. He has been featured on* The Oprah Winfrey Show *and CNN.*

JERRY CAMARILLO DUNN, JR.

RAJ KAPOOR FILM STUDIOS, MUMBAI, INDIA

*I*n 1970 I arrived in India as a young vagabond with a backpack. Wandering without a plan, I stayed at temples with meditating holy men, and I slept in jungles where tigers growled in the moonlight.

In Bombay (as Mumbai was called then) I also discovered the glamorous side of India—Bollywood, the Hindi-language film industry, one of the world's largest purveyors of movie fantasy. I had found a cheap room (sixty cents a night, bring your own bedroll) at the Hotel Stiffles, which turned out to be an unofficial recruiting center where movie studios rounded up young foreign travelers to work as extras.

This ramshackle rathole was located only a block from the luxurious Taj Mahal Hotel, but it was a world away. The Stiffles' guests—rock-bottom budget travelers who came to this hippie Hilton from Europe, the United States, and Australia—spent their days lounging on rickety balconies, watching the street scene, and sipping Fanta sodas. In late afternoon the sun would hit the palm trees out front, turning them to gold. The Hotel Stiffles had its own crumbling tropical charm, something out of a Somerset Maugham story.

Ready for celluloid adventures, I signed on as a movie extra. Early the next morning I waited outside the hotel, where sidewalk vendors poured tea into stained cups and peddled flyspecked fruit. Soon an assistant from the movie studio appeared, wearing a red turban, and ushered me into a taxi. We barreled down the street, scattering women in bright saris as if they were party balloons.

Half an hour later we passed through the ornate gates of R.K. Films, a studio founded by movie megastar and director Raj Kapoor. He had begun his career as a clapper boy and by age 11 had made his first film. His namesake studio was a fantasyland, with movie sets ranging from palaces to nightclubs.

First stop: the costume department. A couple of European girls, hired as extras like me, were issued harem outfits that looked like castoffs from a high school production of Kismet. I was a band leader and got a yellow caftan and a prop mandolin.

We walked to the soundstage, where the courtyard of a maharaja's palace had been fashioned of lumber and plaster. It reminded me of a birthday cake, with confectionary pink rosettes and swirls of plaster icing. Lavender chiffon festooned the papier-mâché pillars, which vanished above camera range into a raw wooden framework. To a first-world Westerner, the set was almost laughably low-rent, but I soon found out that a hit movie in India can gross $30 million. The producers laugh all the way to the bank.

A production assistant told me that Bollywood movies are almost always musicals. Often based on Hindu mythology or classical theater, they emphasize traditional Indian values. I'd seen a few Bollywood movies but hadn't realized that these values took in nightclub dancing, fist fighting, and driving sports cars at high speed. I was new to the country, though, and there was much that I didn't understand.

Suddenly an expectant mood swept the set. The star was approaching, the famous dancer Helen. Of Anglo-Indian-Burmese heritage, light-skinned and lovely, she was trained in Indian Kathak dance and appeared in movie after movie, usually playing a vamp or cabaret dancer. She looked beautiful, with spangled ribbons cascading from her waist and a skimpy sequined top.

An assistant director briefed the extras on our roles. We weren't exactly treated like "cattle," as Alfred Hitchcock once referred to actors—after all, in India cows are sacred. We were more like flies. The other band members and I were told to buzz over to an oriental carpet, which I noticed was acrylic, and sit cross-legged.

India gave me my first view of the exotic—a world of storybook adventures and far-off wonders.

"Big smiles, now!" The assistant director coached us in lively facial expressions and rhythmic nods. The upcoming scene would use a prerecorded sound track—in Bollywood movies, musical numbers are sung by "playback singers," while the on-screen actors merely lip-synch. The lyrics I'd be mouthing had just two syllables: "Vay-lah, vay-LAH!" (Oh well, at least it was a speaking part.)

The music crackled through a loudspeaker and spiked to deafening volume. "Action!" the director yelled. Helen whirled onto the scene in her strategically fringed costume. We boys in the band pretended to play our instruments as Helen swooped and shimmied, twirling a long scarf with one hand. Her eyes shone with sultry

The author at age 22, center, in Bollywood

promise. Excitement mounted. Then, suddenly, Helen stopped in her tracks. The camera dollied in for a close-up shot of one bare foot as it gyrated, teasing. Slowly—oh, so slowly—the camera panned up her calf, to her knee.

Then, as the camera followed the shapely curve of her leg upward, the lens suddenly shifted focus to the middle distance—just before the big payoff, with every man in the movie audience gritting his teeth!—and settled on…my face. With a sprightly tilt of my head, I sang out the chorus: "VAY-LAH!" My wide-eyed facial expression was so animated, I looked like a cartoon character.

For this performance I got paid 40 rupees. That was about $4.

But even this pittance sounded good to a nearly broke vagabond who was halfway through a yearlong trip around the world. And anyway, my true reward had been discovering a slice of life I had no idea even existed—over-the-top yet oddly artistic Bollywood. Through its lens, I saw a new side of India. For me it was a great adventure. At the same time, I realized that every week, in darkened movie houses all over India, Bollywood movies provided a few hours of precious escape from heat and poverty for hundreds of millions of people.

I have come to believe that such discoveries come to you when you travel without a plan, staying open to each unfolding moment. In exploring India, I also got to ride a horse along a flower-strewn lake in Kashmir, visit a maharaja's palace whose marble walls were set with colored gems, cool off in a river with elephants as companions, and see other marvels without number.

I was only 22 years old, and India gave me my first view of the exotic—a world of storybook adventures and far-off wonders that I'd only dreamed about. My time in India played out like a Bollywood movie, bigger than everyday life and filled with color. Forty years later, I'm still profoundly grateful for the lesson I learned on that trip: Sometimes you should just take a leap, shout *Action!*, and see what happens.

COMPASS POINTS

Where: Mumbai (Bombay) is located on India's west coast.

Backdrop: Mumbai is the world's most populous city (13.6 million). In a typical year Bollywood produces more than 1,000 films and sells more than 3.5 billion movie tickets. Audiences expect plenty of entertainment for their rupees—a good actor or dancer is referred to as *paisa vasool* ("money's worth")—and a movie may fill three hours with songs, dance numbers, romance, and action. Now retired, Helen (Jairag Richardson Khan) performed countless tantalizing dance numbers, often wearing a skin-colored body stocking beneath her skimpy outfits. Playback singer Lata Mangeshkar was listed in the *Guinness World Records* for recording more songs than any artist in the world—about 30,000 between 1948 and 1987.

Visitor Information: www.tourisminindia.com

Jerry Camarillo Dunn, Jr., is the author of this book, see bio p. 272.

ACKNOWLEDGMENTS

The most common question I'm asked about this book is, "How *did* you get in touch with all those famous people?" The simple answer is: 1) Try to sidestep publicists and their assistants' assistants, and 2) find a direct human connection. Many people helped me.

Big thanks go to John and Marion Anderson, Sergio Aragonés, Perla Batalla, Rinaldo Brutoco, Barnaby Conrad, Bill Couturié, Kim Deisler, Marie Laure Frere and Sean Donovan, Edie Frere, Olivia Frere, Marty Fujita, Sarah Hadeler, David Hinckle, Jim Lenfestey, Ted Levine, Marcia Meier of the Santa Barbara Writers Conference, Judy Munzig, Eleanor Najjar, Susan Nelson, Stephanie O'Neill, Cecilia Ortiz, Tucky Pogue, Monte Schulz, Leone Webster, J. B. White, and Larry Yee.

Thanks to Ted Danson for being the first celebrated person to take part.

Of course, many requests didn't work out. I sent hundreds of them, even to people I didn't expect to hear back from. One kind refusal came on heavy stationery engraved with "Buckingham Palace," and it began, "The Queen has asked me to thank you for your letter...."

People who work with the book's participants helped things such as interviews and correspondence go smoothly. I'm indebted to Wayne Bernath, Maggie Boone, Jennifer Braxmeyer, Joyce Cellars, Mary Beth Dolan, Kathy Dukes, Mike Dunn, Rhonda Grant, Lynne Hale, Anne Hillerman, Christin Jones, Talin Kalfayan, Ellyn Kusmin, Mia Malm, Beverly Montgomery, Gudren Noonan, Jennifer Olsen, Carolyn Rangel, Veronica Romero, Patsy Lynn Russell, Danielle Shang, Jean Sievers, Karen Sligh, Judi Smith, Rebecca Erwin Spencer, Sandra Squires, and Tenzin Taklha.

Wei-Ying Lin kindly translated Chinese into English for Jiang Zhi's chapter. Robert Evans shared helpful information.

At National Geographic, it was a pleasure to work with editors Elizabeth Newhouse and Caroline Hickey. Agnès Tabah did a seamless job of ironing out legal wrinkles. Penny Dackis worked on publicity.

Merry, "my beautiful and talented wife" (she makes me say that—or face the consequences), offered insightful suggestions, looked over every chapter with her superb editorial skills, and encouraged me, especially in those early moments when I wondered whether anyone would come to the party. My love, I fall at your feet (and not only because I tripped over the dog).

CREDITS & PERMISSIONS

Illustration Credits

Cover, Selahattin Bayram/iStockphoto.com; 16, Jason Lee Pack/iStockphoto.com; 19, NASA/Neil A. Armstrong; 22, Christophe Testi/Shutterstock; 25, © Richard Gunion/Dreamstime.com; 29, Christian Wheatley/Shutterstock; 32, Kenneth Sponsler/Shutterstock; 36, Theo Westenberger/NGS; 39, Virgin Limited Ed.; 43, Marc van Vuren/Shutterstock; 46, Michael Westhoff/iStockphoto.com; 50, © Feije Riemersma/ Dreamstime.com; 54, S. Greg Panosian/iStockphoto.com; 58, © Pavel Bernshtam/Dreamstime.com; 61, Latham Jenkins/iStockphoto.com; 64, Valery Shanin/123RF; 67, Douglas Peebles Photography/Alamy; 70, Sarah Folsom © 2008/ShutterPoint; 74, Janet Cussler; 77, Terraxplorer/iStockphoto.com; 80, Denis Tangney, Jr./ iStockphoto.com; 84, © Matt Fowler/Dreamstime.com; 89, Francisco Javier Alcerreca Gomez/Shutterstock; 93, Geanina Bechea/Shutterstock; 96, Ronnie Edlund/iStockphoto.com; 99, alandj/iStockphoto.com; 102, Lawrence P. Bestmann, courtesy of the Eastern Shore Chamber of Commerce; 105, Photo by Tom England, courtesy of Camp Sunshine; 108, David Broberg/iStockphoto.com; 111, Simon Gurney/iStockphoto.com; 116, Michael Nichols/NGS; 120, Samantha Reinders/NGS; 124, Noel Powell, Schaumburg/Shutterstock; 127, fritzkocher/Shutterstock; 133, Mike Norton/Shutterstock; 137, Kevin Smith/iStockphoto.com; 141, Courtesy of the artist and DF2 Gallery, Los Angeles; 144, Chris Johns/NGS; 147, © Nalukai/Dreamstime.com; 150, Brian Morgan; 152, Vera Bogaerts/Shutterstock; 155, Mikhail Nekrasov/Shutterstock; 158, iofoto/iStockphoto.com; 160, Tennessee Department of Tourist Development; 165, Joe McDaniel/ iStockphoto.com; 168, Larry Eiring; 172, Steve McCurry; 175, Folkert Gorter; 178, Bob Coyle/iStockphoto.com; 180, Alena Yakusheva/iStockphoto.com; 183, Carlos Sanchez Pereyra/Shutterstock; 185, Mike Norton/Shutterstock; 188, © Can Balcioglu/Dreamstime.com; 191, James L. Stanfield/NGS; 194, Alison Cornford-Matheson/iStockphoto.com; 198, © David Kay/Dreamstime.com; 201, NASA, #STS047-88-20; 204, Antonio Vizcaino/AmericaNatural; 209, Nicole K. Cioe/iStockphoto.com; 212, Regien Paassen/ Shutterstock; 215, Rick Hyman/iStockphoto.com; 218, Jeff Divine/Getty Images; 222, Cay-Uwe Kulzer/ iStockphoto.com; 225, Paula Connelly/iStockphoto.com; 228, Courtesy of The Mar-a-Lago Club; 230, Dan Moore/iStockphoto.com; 233, Travel Ink/Getty Images; 236, Robert Gubbins/Shutterstock; 241, © Steve Estvanik/Dreamstime.com; 245, William Albert Allard/NGS; 249, Alexandre Quillet/iStockphoto.com; 253, James D. Hay/Shutterstock; 255, ronfromyork/Shutterstock; 258, © Jeremy D'Entremont/Shutter-Point; 262, A. S. Zain/Shutterstock; 266, Courtesy of the author. 272, Author photo: Graham Dunn..

Text Permissions

pp. 16–17, Reprinted from *National Geographic Traveler,* July/Aug. 1992, "Travels With…Kareem Abdul-Jabbar" written by Jerry Dunn.

pp. 28–30, Reprinted from Dave Barry column on U.S. Virgin Islands © Dave Barry.

pp. 53, Song lyrics from "The Little Church," recorded by Donovan on "Brother Sun, Sister Moon" © 1972, 2004.

pp. 76–78, Text excerpted from *My Land and My People: The Original Autobiography of His Holiness the Dalai Lama of Tibet,* © 1962/1990 by His Holiness the Dalai Lama of Tibet pp. 31–34, 196; with permission from the Office of His Holiness the Dalai Lama.

pp. 104–106. © Jeff Foxworthy, 2008.

pp. 180–181, Reprinted from *National Geographic Traveler,* March/April 1992, "Travels With…Robert Mondavi" written by Jerry Dunn.

pp. 255–256, Reprinted from *National Geographic Traveler,* Jan./Feb. 1990, "Travels With…Jonathan Winters" written by Jerry Dunn.

The author of this book, **Jerry Camarillo Dunn, Jr.**, *appeared in two Bollywood films (see pp. 264-265), one of them impressively titled* International Crook. *His books include* National Geographic Traveler: San Francisco *and* Idiom Savant: Slang As It Is Slung. *Dunn's work has been honored with three Lowell Thomas Awards from the Society of American Travel Writers. He lives in a small Southern California valley with his wife, Merry, and two sons, Graham and Locke. None of them is properly awestruck by his film career in Bollywood, though he has told them that his autograph is available.*